TOO MUCH
OF A GOOD THING

TOO MUCH OF A GOOD THING

RAISING CHILDREN OF CHARACTER IN AN INDULGENT AGE

DAN KINDLON, PH.D.

For Ethan and
Sean —

Dan Kindlon

miramax books

HYPERION

NEW YORK

Library of Congress Cataloging-in-Publication Data

ISBN: 0-7868-8624-2

FIRST EDITION

10 9 8 7 6 5 4

ACKNOWLEDGMENTS

There have been many people who accompanied me on the long car ride that has been the writing of this book. Some sat in the backseat and let me know when I had missed a turn, and others took the wheel when I needed to rest or when I was incapable of successfully navigating a rough stretch of road by myself.

Susan Mercandetti and Jonathan Burnham of Talk Miramax have been with me from the start of the ride. I want to thank them for their inspiration, encouragement, and wisdom, without which this book would never have been written. Gail Ross, my agent extraordinaire, has been a delightful traveling companion and navigator.

I want to also thank Eleni Spartos, my research associate, for all that she contributed to this book project including conducting interviews, helping to design the PPM survey, doing data analysis and coordinating the logistics of the PPM project. The energy, intelligence, and knowledge about adolescents she brought to the project have been invaluable.

My deepest gratitude goes to Kenneth Wapner, my personal editor. He is a fine wordsmith, collaborator, and friend. He helped me turn my academic prose into something readable, forced me to continue to work on the flow, structure, and organization of the text beyond the point at which I normally would have thrown in the towel, and continually challenged me to clarify my thinking.

There were many people who crammed into the car during the drive. Through their skill, hard work, and dedication they were able to help me turn raw data into solid research findings in a fraction of the time that would take in most institutional settings. I'd especially like to thank Dr. Mary Beth O'Hagan for help with the design of the PPM survey, Keri Frisch for library research, data entry, interviewing, and being a level-headed sounding board, and Kai Orton for library research. Adam Kraus and Ryan Moore, two remarkable high school students, were fabulous data entry assistants for me at my home office. They also provided me with frontline feedback on some of my ideas as well as conducting interviews on people's recollections of their "best" and "favorite" teachers. Stacy Klickstein and Emily Nichols worked with Eleni in the Boston data entry office. They have my thanks for their thorough and careful attention to this often tedious task. Carole Flynn was largely responsible for transcribing the interview tapes. I thank her for her extraordinary work.

I would also like to thank several people who rode with me for only a short while, yet still made significant contributions to the book. Ginny Faber, my former editor, was an immense help in the proposal phase of this project. Bob Miller, of Hyperion, came up with a great title, after I had struggled to do so unsuccessfully. Paul Smart was an enthusiastic collaborator during the conceptualization of the Seven Deadly Syndromes and Inner Parent parts of the book.

My heartfelt thanks goes to my wife, Catalina Arboleda, for making it easy for me to write this book. Her insights, especially those concerning the Inner Parent, were an enormous contribution. My daughter Diana discussed many of these ideas with me and provided some valuable insight. I'd also like to thank her for graciously giving me permission to write about some of her personal experiences and allowing me to suspend work on her tree house in order to take on this book project.

My other daughter, Julia, showed a remarkable ability to delay gratification while I wrote this book. There were too many times when I had to spend time with the "stupid book" rather than with her. I thank her for her patience.

Finally, I humbly thank all of the anonymous parents, teachers, school administrators, counselors, and students who participated in the PPM research. I appreciate their time, their honesty, and their desire to make a difference in the lives of children. I have done my best to deserve their efforts on behalf of this book.

CONTENTS

INTRODUCTION

I was sent a survey for my twenty-fifth high school reunion. On it they asked where life had taken us. What was our biggest accomplishment? Our most memorable experience? When they asked about my family life, I surprised myself. "I'm avoiding the mistakes my parents made, but I'm making others," I wrote. This was the first inkling I had of the subject of this book.

As parents, we do a great job in some areas but not others. Compared to earlier generations, we are emotionally closer to our kids, they confide in us more, we have more fun with them, and we know more about the science of child development. But we are too indulgent. We give our kids too much and demand too little of them. I see it in the homes I visit, at the schools where I speak, in the family counseling I've done, and in the exchanges between parents and children I encounter in shopping malls, supermarkets, and video stores.

I find myself at the center of this problem as I try, with my wife, to balance the two major tasks of parenting: showing our kids that we love them and raising them with the skills and values they'll need to be emotionally healthy adults, which often requires that we act in ways that can anger and upset them.

Our generation of Baby Boomers too often blurs the line between friend and parent. By our disinclination to set appropriate limits for our kids, we undermine their character development. Character is hard to define, but it's easy to tell when someone has it, or doesn't. People who have character know who they are; they are centered and have the courage to be honest with themselves and others. Having character means being honest, charitable, compassionate, and emotionally intelligent. When we stop blurring the line between friend and parent, we can help our kids develop the healthy attitudes and good habits that are character's foundation.

We indulge our children at least partially because we can afford to. Ours is an affluent society, perhaps the most affluent the world has ever known. We want to share the good things in life with our kids; and we know that money can protect us from at least some of life's problems. As parents, we naturally want to extend this protection, and the advantages that money can buy, to our kids. But by protecting them from failure, adversity, and pain we deprive them of the opportunity to learn important coping skills; a realistic sense of their strengths and limitations.

Through writing this book, my perception of myself has changed. I have seen my own indulgent parenting more clearly, and, as a result, I have changed many aspects of how I interact with my children. As a family we are happier for it. My primary goal in writing this book is that you, the reader, will also come to see yourself more clearly, because one of the most striking aspects of indulgent parenting is that it's often easy to see in others but hard to see it in ourselves.

In order to clarify what *indulgence* is, how it relates to current social conditions, and the way it can erode character, I draw on stories from the children, parents, teachers, princpals, and counselors that I have worked with in my nearly twenty years of clinical psychology practice and as a consulting psychologist in schools.

In writing this book, however, I felt case studies were not enough. I was trained first as a scientist, and my respect for hard, numerical data runs deep. So before I could write on indulgence, affluence, and character, I wanted to get the lay of the land. Does every teenager in America have a cell phone and a TV in his room, or only the rich ones? How many kids help with the dinner dishes? How often do families today eat together? What percentage of parents think their kids are spoiled? What percentage of kids consider themselves spoiled? Are our kids anxious and depressed, or do they have an "I don't give a damn" attitude? How many are taking drugs and having sex, and at what age? And, most important, what kinds of parenting practices are associated with our kids' emotional and behavioral problems?

My research assistants and I undertook The Parenting Practices at the Millennium study (PPM) to try to gather data on these questions. We designed questionnaires that were distributed in nine schools in the United States, with locations in the South, Midwest, Northeast, and Mid-Atlantic, and far West to 654 teenaged children. We mailed another questionnaire to 1078 parents of kids between the ages of four and nineteen (for a fuller discussion of our survey methods, see the Technical Appendix).

A second component of the PPM study consisted of approximately fifty in-depth interviews with parents, teachers, teenagers, counselors, therapists, and school administrators. These were transcribed. Verbatim excerpts from them are included in the text. Many of the chapters contain case narratives, but the individuals portrayed in them, while based on fact, are disguised composites.

In addition to the data gathered in the PPM survey and interviews, I also reviewed studies on families and children done by other scientists and examined some previously unanalyzed data. My findings are presented here for the first time.

By combining this research with the findings of the PPM survey and interviews, I felt that I had a secure empirical grounding, informed by clinical experience, from which to draw conclusions and make recommendations to parents about how they might better instill the habits of character that will help insure that their kids will grow up happy and psychologically healthy.

The vast majority of the parents and children I studied were middle income and above, and many were wealthy. This is unusual in this kind of research. The bulk of my scientific career, and the careers of nearly all my colleagues who study health and social issues, has been spent studying the poor. There are good reasons for this: health problems, including mental health problems, are more prevalent among the disadvantaged.

But we miss something when we only study the poor. Fifteen years ago when I was teaching a psychology course at Harvard on human motivation, I came across a remarkable book by Robert Coles, *Privileged Ones*. In the Introduction, Coles recounts a conversation he had had with Ruby Bridges, a young African-American girl who had helped integrate an all-white school in Mississippi in the 1960s, which had spurred him to write *Privileged Ones*. Bridges had asked Coles how his book on rich people was coming along. Coles was surprised since he wasn't actually working on such a book. He asked her why she thought he was.

"If you want to know about the people who will be running the country in ten or twenty years," she had said, "then you'd better go and visit the big-deal important people—the well-off and rich. The rich folks are the ones who decide how the poor folks live. Like my daddy says, 'They cough and we feel the house shake.' "[1]

As you'll see in Part One of *Too Much of a Good Thing*, there are other reasons that I wanted to focus on the well-to-do. Foremost among these is that upper middle-class and upper-class adolescents have their share of behavioral problems—drug abuse being the most common. Too often, middle-class and affluent parents—who live in safe neighborhoods, whose kids go to good schools and get the best medical care—are lulled into a dangerous sense of complacency.

Due to our hectic lives, these advantaged kids are often neglected in ways that we as parents are unwilling or unable to see. We need to take a hard look at how our often work-obsessed lives affect our ability to be effective parents. On one hand, our children are the center of our lives, but, on the other, how often are we fully present when we're with them?

While most of the survey data and many of the interviews and anecdotes in the pages that follow focus on teenage children, it's important for parents of younger children to realize that indulged toddlers can, unless checked, become indulged teenagers who are at risk for becoming adults prone to many of the syndromes—excessive self-absorption, depression, a lack of self-control—that I discuss in the second part of this book.

My recommendations for dealing with indulgence are not based on moral outrage, and I don't advocate a regression to the harsh discipline and an emotionally distant style of parenting that has been common in the past. Instead, I give advice that tries to keep the best of both worlds—the emotional closeness and informality with our children that characterize parents today, as well as the ability to clearly comprehend and set limits entailed in building character. As a generation of parents, I think we must ask ourselves what kind of adults we want our kids to be—what we think is most important to teach them. I hope this book will give you a clearer view, as it has me, of why we parent the way we do, and I offer it as a guide into the hearts and minds of our children.

———

PART ONE

THE AGE OF INDULGENCE

CHAPTER 1

Giving Too Much and Expecting Too Little:

PARENTING AT THE MILLENNIUM

Come mothers and fathers throughout the land,
And don't criticize what you can't understand;
Your sons and your daughters are beyond your command . . .
Your old road is rapidly agin'.
Please get out of the new one if you can't lend your hand
Because the times they are a-changin'.

—BOB DYLAN

The Case of Connor

"What do you want for your child?"

In my twenty years as a therapist, I've asked that question hundreds of times to parents like Bob and Annie, who sit across from me now looking annoyed. We are talking about their sixteen-year-old son, Connor, who has been suspended from school for three days because his history teacher has accused him of plagiarism. Connor's parents are unhappy with the school's disciplinary measures and have asked for a conference with the headmaster and the teacher who made the accusation.

Because I know Connor, I have requested that I meet with his parents first, before they bring their complaint to the school.

Bob, an attorney, points out that the case against Connor isn't airtight. The boy's teacher strongly suspects that Connor used a paper-writing service he found on the Internet to help him prepare a term paper on the Vietnam War. Connor admits he bought material on-line, but insists that he only used it for information. This assertion is hard to substantiate because Connor claims that he threw out the "informational" paper and didn't save it on his computer.

"If this was a criminal case it would never come to trial," says Bob. "Whatever happened to due process or burden of proof? Don't they teach about those kinds of things in that history course?"

Bob is a tall man in his mid-forties, a successful corporate lawyer in a downtown Boston firm. Wearing an expensive charcoal suit, a Hermès tie knotted neatly at his throat, he's come to meet the tweedy headmaster. Annie is tall and blond; her slacks and cashmere sweater advertise her aerobically toned body. She defers to her husband. He's not hostile, in your face, but he radiates authority. He knows what he wants and he's going to get it.

The worst part of this whole business for Bob and Annie is that Connor has not only received an F on the paper in question, but will also get a zero on a chemistry quiz that he'll miss because of the suspension. His grades so far this school year have been pretty good—As and Bs—but he now stands to get a C minus in history and his low B in chemistry is in jeopardy.

"It's not fair to penalize him so much," says Annie. "This could hurt him on his college applications. Even if he did use material from that paper, what's the difference between that and downloading something from an on-line encyclopedia like Encarta? Everybody in the class probably did that."

I explain that, thankfully, my role is not to determine disciplinary penalties or rule on the exact definition of "plagiarism." I just wanted to talk to them about Connor because I'm worried about him. "Can we put a hold on the details for a moment," I say, "take a step back, and look at the big picture? Let me ask you a more general question. What do you want for Connor?"

I can almost read Bob and Annie's minds. They're thinking: What do you mean "what do we want for him?" It's obvious isn't it?

Then Annie says, "We just want him to be happy."

This is the answer most parents give. Of course we want our children to be happy.

"And what do you think will make him happy?" I ask them.

This follow-up question presents a greater challenge. It tends to take parents by surprise. Their answer is often vague: "If he can feel good about himself and what he does," or "If he can have a fulfilling life." Many parents of high school students will say, as Annie does, "We'd like him to be able to get into a good college so he'll have the opportunity to do what he wants with his life." She cannot resist the opportunity to mention that that is one of the primary reasons they decided to send him to the expensive private school, adding, "Isn't it ironic that our decision is going to backfire on us? I mean you people could be ruining his life with this decision."

I try to bring the conversation back to my worries about Connor. What I cannot explicitly tell them, because of my profession's code of confidentiality, is that Connor smokes a lot of pot. At weekend parties he frequently gets drunk and has oral sex with a series of partners whom he talks about in disparaging terms to me and his circle of male friends. He also has a reputation as a wild driver; other kids won't ride in his Jeep, a present from his parents on his sixteenth birthday.

I first started seeing Connor several months prior to my meeting with his parents. His teachers in the prestigious New England prep school he attended, and where I spent one day a week as a consulting psychologist, had asked me to talk to him. They said he was often negative and contrary. He made fun of other students when they struggled with their work, when he thought they weren't cool in their behavior or attire, or when they expressed opinions with which he disagreed. He was a smart kid and his comments not only cut to the quick: they often seemed gratuitously cruel.

I had first flagged Connor down in the hall of the school's computer center, stocked with row upon row of gleaming IMaCs. "Do you mind if we talk? Some of your teachers are worried about you."

"Who?" he had asked, a little defiant, wanting to know who had ratted him out.

We walked out of the ivied building into a crisp, autumn day. I noticed that Connor didn't mind being seen with me. Fifteen years ago, when I started visiting schools, my offices had tended to be in dark, remote corners. But there's almost no stigma around a kid seeing a shrink these days.

Through the fall and into the winter I established a rapport with Connor. He was tall and blond like his mother. His longish hair flopped and floated as he walked. He was a skateboarder and snowboarder par excellence, a cocky kid who, like so many kids I see, had fearful eyes that belied his swagger.

Connor had eventually confided in me. He had given me permission to tell his parents that he occasionally smoked pot, and he also said I could tell them I was worried about him. The conversation when this occurred was instructive in itself.

"Can I tell them you smoke pot?" I had asked.

"Fine. They probably already know."

"How?"

"They found rolling papers in my room. I said they weren't mine, but I don't think they believed me."

"What did they do?"

Connor did a dead-on imitation of his father's sonorous

voice: "You're too young to be smoking pot. We're going to take these, if you don't mind."

"And that was the end of it?"

"Yes."

I had laughed at Connor's clever imitation of his dad, but I was also concerned. His parent's response had seemed lax, to say the least. Connor didn't want me to mention sex to them.

"That's my business. I need my privacy," he had said.

Drinking: ditto. He was worried they might not let him go out on weekends if they knew the full extent of his activities.

Now, face-to-face with Bob and Annie, I mentioned that Connor might be a bit depressed, and, given that, I worried that he might be using drugs to make himself feel better. I didn't expect fireworks, but I was startled when they skimmed over my concern. "He's a teenager," said Annie. "He's supposed to be moody and experiment with drugs. He has probably tried pot, but so did we at his age. I don't think it's something we have to worry about; at least not yet. He's not a drug addict. It's hasn't taken over his life."

Bob noted that we were running out of time. Appealing their case to the headmaster was foremost on their minds. I told Annie and Bob that I would like to continue meeting with Connor periodically.

"Sure, that's probably a good idea," Bob judiciously replied. "Let us know if you think he's in trouble."

I rose and showed them to the door of the office. We shook hands and they walked down the hall, an elegant couple, chins held high.

I respect Bob and Annie's instinct to try to protect Connor. They truly want what's best for their son and are willing to make enormous sacrifices for his happiness. But I found myself thinking that they should be more concerned about what this incident could mean for the kind of person Connor was in the process of becoming.

As adolescents we think we have an endless series of chances, that we can remake our lives indefinitely. To a degree this is true. On the other hand, as adults we know that the choices we make when we're young form us. A kid that lies to get out of a tough situation is more likely to lie again. Eventually he finds it is easier to lie than to tell the truth. Lying becomes a habit. As a psychologist I have seen how these seemingly small events incline children down one path rather than another, shape their predispositions, and, to use an older term, mold their characters. The word *character* has been usurped by the Christian right to become synonymous with conservative political ideas, but it was originally used by psychologists like William James in the beginning of the twentieth century to mean the habits of behavior that shape our lives and define who we are.

In their wish for their son's happiness, Annie and Bob are like almost every parent. We all want our kids to be happy, or at least to avoid too much pain. I know from my own experience with two daughters that our children's happiness is the one thing in life about which I always feel unequivocal. I would do anything for my girls, and I feel intensively protective toward them, so I can empathize with Bob and Annie.

It's relatively easy to know how to care for our children when they're infants. We give them food, a clean diaper, and lots of physical affection. Sleepless nights are balanced by the bliss that comes from caring for an infant. Is there a better feeling than having your baby sleep with his head on your chest?

When infants become toddlers, their needs change. To do a good job of parenting, we have to protect them from hurting themselves. The toddler's world is full of danger. They seem to gravitate toward steep stairs, electrical outlets, and household poisons. Sometimes what we have to do to protect them makes them cry (when we remove a sharp object that they've been using for a toy, for example).

When our children are older, a parent's job becomes more complex. We need to prepare our kids for the time when they will be responsible for themselves. We need to help them develop habits of character to equip them to face adult challenges. On some level, we can't believe that our kids will ever have to face divorce, illness, financial setbacks, death—but they will.

What we want for our children is a perfect life devoid of hardship and pain. We want them to live in the cocoon of safety we were able to provide for them when they were infants. We don't want to let them go. But their happiness as adults is largely dependent on the tools we give them; tools that will allow them to develop emotional maturity—to be honest with themselves, to be empathetic, to take initiative, to delay gratification, to learn from failure and move on, to accept their flaws, and to face the consequences when they've done something wrong. We'll explore this psychological toolbox in Part Two, but for now let's observe that Bob and Annie are like many of us today who think that we can protect our kids from the pain of growing up.

Although it is wonderful, like Bob and Annie, to have the kinds of advantages money can buy, a comfortable life can lull us into complacent child rearing. Money does help protect us—we can live in safe neighborhoods, get high quality medical care, go to good schools, drive in crash-resistant SUVs. But money can't protect our kids from the discomforts of maturation, and it can't buy them character.

My clinical experience and the interviews I did for this book have shown me what many parents can't see: the pain, confusion, worry, and depression that lurks just under the surface of their kids' comfortable lives. It may sound trite, but Connor's behavior is really a cry for help. He wants his parents to take a more active role in helping him make the right decisions, because he doesn't yet have the maturity to make them on his own. He wants them to set firmer rules, to monitor his behavior more closely, to become more involved in his life. But Connor doesn't know how to express his needs. He may not even be aware of them, for reasons we'll discuss.

Most of the children you will meet in this book were not chosen from the ranks standing outside the detention hall or school psychologist's office. They were representative of kids who attend private schools or good, suburban, public high schools.

Despite all the advantages they have, I found disturbingly high incidences of anxiety and depression in these children.[1] To illustrate how common these problems are, the PPM (Parenting Practices at the Millennium) study showed us that in a typical suburban high school ninth grade class, out of three hundred students, one hundred would say that it is "very true" that they "worry a lot"; an additional one hundred would say that frequent worrying was "somewhat true" of them. Almost two hundred would feel the pressure "to be perfect." One hundred sixty will say that they are "unhappy, sad or depressed." And, remarkably, eighty would say that during the past two months there was at least one time when they felt so sad or hopeless that almost every day for at least two weeks they had stopped doing some of their usual activities. To summarize: whether we asked about worry, depression, sadness, or the feeling that they needed to be perfect, the majority of students indicated that they were suffering.

These findings were consistent across the country in suburban high schools and private schools, and they both confirmed and quantified what I had been seeing in the field as a growing trend. I had observed that the more affluent and success oriented we've become, the harder in some ways the pressures are on our kids.

Keeping kitchen cleansers out of a child's reach is a breeze compared to knowing how to protect them from becoming anxious and depressed, or developing related problems such as obsessive perfectionism, pathological dissatisfaction with one's body, or chronic irritability. It's difficult to know what to do, how to act, how to do the right thing at the right time in the right way.

This is especially true today. Our society is focused on achievement and success in place of the development of an inner life. Too often I see kids who lack an inner compass; kids like Connor, who fail to take responsibility for their actions and have difficulty developing meaningful, fulfilling relationships. Annie and Bob are like many of us: well-intentioned parents who give their children too much and expect too little from them.

The bracelet on Annie's wrist jingles as she opens the door to the headmaster's office. I don't envy him. Connor's parents are formidable, to say the least. I walk out of the office I use the one day a week I'm here, past the well-equipped science laboratories, to the phys ed building with its new hockey rink. I sit watching the kids do drills, skating back and forth at top speed, stopping on a dime.

I wonder if Bob and Annie will get Connor off. I'm in a quandary. One thing I haven't been able to tell his parents, history teacher, or the school's headmaster is that I know that Connor did, in fact, commit the crime of which he is accused. He plagiarized his paper, and the most worrisome part about it for me is that he doesn't recognize that he's done anything wrong.

"I'm not the only one in class who did it," he told me. "So why should I take the rap? It was a stupid assignment. The paper I bought taught me more than the teacher."

I watch the skaters. Ice shoots out from under their sharp, metal blades. At some level Connor believes his rationalizations. After all, he didn't really hurt anyone, did he? He doesn't think about all the kids who didn't cheat. He doesn't worry that he may be forming a pattern that will get him into real trouble later in life. He's myopic and self-centered. I'm angry with his parents for not pushing him to grow and take responsibility for himself, and I'm also angry at myself for not doing a good job of communicating my concern to them. Connor's teachers and headmaster have a vague sense of what's going on, but they really have no idea of the full extent of Connor's problems. The skaters practice their shots. Pucks slam off the boards, the sharp sounds echoing through the empty arena.

Why We Indulge Our Kids

In other times and places, children have been viewed as economic assets, unlikely to survive into adulthood; youngsters better seen than heard, offspring best left to nurses or nannies until they were old enough to dine properly with adults. But for my generation, the Baby Boomers, our children are at the core of what gives meaning to our lives.

We are the generation who didn't have to get married to have sex. Many of us waited to have children. We saw how many of our parents married young, had kids right away, and seemed yanked straight from adolescence into adulthood. Many of us chose to defer "settling down"—that 1950s term that seemed like the kiss of death to those of us raised in a youth culture that exulted in its freedom and sense of limitless possibility. Many of us wanted to prolong our youth and establish our careers before becoming saddled with a family.

We were the first generation to worry about a biological clock. When it finally did kick in, sometime in our thirties, the intensity and wonder of the parenting experience often took us by surprise. As one thirty-eight-year-old first-time mother put it, "You just fall in love, completely, head over heels in love. The other things in your life that had given you satisfaction pale in comparison."

Our generation came up with the bumper sticker "Question Authority." The debacles of the Vietnam War, Kent State shootings, and Watergate break-in made us lose faith in our leaders. When we became parents, this attitude meant that we were often uncomfortable exerting authority over our children. We felt uneasy about setting strict limits.

Families tend to be smaller now than they were in the past, making each child all the more precious to us. We tend to hover, trying to make everything right for our kids. One outspoken high school principal I talked with said, "This hovering causes a situation similar to one in which a mother bird with only one or two precious eggs to protect works very hard to protect and manage each egg. And it's the overmanagement which, I think, causes the most difficulty. Some tough things are going to happen to the kid. Parents both embarrass themselves and embarrass and hurt their children by being overprotective. Too many parents are unable to assume that a little pain is not only manageable but is actually desirable; that their child may actually grow from the experience."

Connor in a nutshell. As it turned out, his parents did not get the headmaster to reverse his decision. Afterward, Connor said the suspension had been a wake-up call. "I realized I needed to learn how to play by the rules," he told me the following fall. "I needed to know what I'm capable of without cheating."

A social worker at a small private elementary school in New Hampshire tells a similar tale. "For the typical parent I see— and it's true for me, too—money is not a problem. We can cover our external needs. We've turned our attention to making sure that every part of their [our children's] lives are taken care of. Do they have the right friends? Are they caring, considerate people? Are they being bullied? We want to control everything and make their lives perfect. An example: The third and fourth grades at my school go skiing Thursday afternoon at Killington. A bus comes to get them. One cold day last week, a mother came in with a hand warmer (one of those packs you rip open that make heat) and warmed her son's mittens. She hung them in his cubby so when he went to ski his hands would be warm. At first, it seemed absurd, but I can imagine my husband doing the same thing for our daughter. And do you know what? The kid forgot his mittens."

Being overindulged also extends to children's sports activities. According to the National Association of Sports Officials, over the past five to eight years there has been an increasing number of physical assaults on officials when parents feel their kids have been penalized unfairly. A National Public Radio report dubbed the phenomenon "youth sports rage."[2] You'd think it refers to kids having tantrums over striking out, missing a goal, or losing a game. But it refers to adults, not kids. Recently, a Massachusetts father and volunteer hockey coach died after being attacked by a parent during his kids' hockey practice. While the tragic death in Massachusetts may be an extreme example, these incidents of violence are increasing. Last year the National Association of Sports Officials started offering assault insurance to referees and umpires of youth leagues. With many parents placing more and more emphasis on winning, playing just for the love of the game is in danger of becoming a thing of the past.

This aggressive approach on the part of parents is also seen by school administrators in regard to discipline. Bashing the umpire on a bad call is a physical manifestation of what Bob, Connor's dad, is doing when he argues for "due process."

Ken is a principal at a prep school in Silicon Valley. He's in his fifties with kids of his own, and he taught history for many years. I told Ken that in disciplinary situations in schools in which I've been involved it seemed that parents inevitably tried to get their kids off the hook instead of understanding the school's position. I asked him if that had been his experience.

KEN: Avoiding discipline is endemic to affluent parents. As soon as I hear that there is a disciplinary situation that we will have to act on, I assume that's the end of any good relationship with that family. I've even come to the point where I say the best thing for both school and family would be, in many situations, for me to kick the kid out. Because even if it's a minor offense, the school is going to be so trashed by the parents that any beneficial aspect of punishment will be lost. Academic dishonesty, social problems, sexual flaunting—in the main those are *not* disciplinary issues here. Usually we try to deal with them on a counseling level, but every once in a while, you get an incident that is so flagrant it flaunts the idea of respect for others and so I've disciplined some kids. If sex is involved, the parents pull back because acknowledging their children as sexual beings is so painful that though they will hate the school, they won't attack us. But if it's something besides sex, the school is usually in for a battle.

DAN: How does it affect the kid when the parent steps in and says, "Oh, he cheated, but he doesn't deserve three days suspension" or "he doesn't deserve zero as a grade. . . ."

KEN: Every kid responds differently. I've had kids who have said, "Don't listen to my father—he's crazy." Then I had one case very recently when the parent came in and lied. We didn't charge the parent with lying, but it was obvious from what the kid and mother said later that the father was lying. He told us that his son couldn't have sent the anonymous and inflammatory email comments that were posted on our school web page because the two of them were watching a football game when the email was sent. The kid and the mother said the father had been out of town. I mean it was completely outrageous! You see the desperation in parents' eyes. They don't want their kid kicked out of here because they feel that somehow that is going to translate into something disastrous.

DAN: Like he won't get into Harvard.

KEN: Right. And the other part is a little less practical, but in some ways even more significant—the feeling that my son has failed, therefore, I've failed. Most of these parents can't accept their kids as they are. I don't blame them—it's painful. Some parents are wonderfully objective about things—but, you know, they're usually not the ones whose kids get into trouble for some reason. . . .

DAN: That's the point, isn't it? In every disciplinary situation where or in which you see the parents try to cover it up, it's clear that they're part of the cause.

A headmaster at a Manhattan private school had disciplined a kid for sexual harassment. The kid had been touching girls in the hall who didn't want to be touched, and making comments in public on their proficiency in fellatio. He had also been suspected of date rape with freshman girls. The headmaster, a guy in his sixties who thought he had seen everything, got a call from the boy's father, a partner at a major investment banking firm, who said, "Before you proceed any further, can you come over to the house?"

"I come over to the house," the headmaster said, "I go up this private elevator in their Park Avenue building into a lobby the size of Grand Central. A maid in uniform takes me into the father's home office, which looks out over the city. He barely says hello and flips on the speaker phone. He introduces me to the man on the other end who was a very high-profile defense attorney. He cuts to the chase. 'You go another step with this sexual harassment bullshit and we'll get six lawyers and shut your school down,' he tells me. Bam! That's it! End of story. Don't play tough with me! As it turned out, I didn't have enough evidence to throw the book at the kid. But at the recommendation of the disciplinary committee, which is made up of faculty and students, the kid was given thirty hours of community service at the school. But because of what his father had done, and because he continued to harass me about the treatment of his son, we didn't invite the family back. We have a clause in our guidelines that states that if we can't establish a harmonious relationship with the parents, we can decide to dismiss their child. This was clearly a case in point."

The overprotective, overidentified attitude of parents is pervasive today. We are driven. And our kids feel driven—driven to get good grades, get into the right college, get a good job. We are indulgent. And our kids also feel indulged; adrift in a world where the lines between childhood and adulthood are blurred. We are consumers. And the highly sophisticated and manipulative marketing apparatus of big corporations and advertising agencies targets our kids as consumers with their own discretionary incomes. We try to set standards of morality for our children while the media sexualizes them for profit. Rather than looking to a common culture of shared values to help us raise our children, we all feel challenged and a little alone. We don't necessarily agree with censorship, but we are at a loss as to how to protect our kids from the miniadulthood conferred by the world around them.

Amid this confusion we often want to be friends with our

kids, abnegating our authority. We are less strict than we were a generation ago because we have chosen to be that way. Infused with sophistication, we have set out to be different kinds of parents from the ones we had. In the PPM survey, we asked parents whether they saw themselves as less strict than their own parents had been. A lot of them do. It didn't matter whether they were millionaires or middle class or if their children were in high school, middle school, or elementary school. It didn't even matter what part of the country they came from; in every instance a near majority of parents—usually around 45 percent—said that they are less strict than their parents were. Over of a third of these said that they are "much less strict." [3]

Friend or Parent? Stephanie and Craig

Let's take a look at how kids respond to the ways in which parents are indulging them. This is a scene from the life of Stephanie, a teenage girl in an Atlanta, Georgia, suburb.

"Shit, my parents are home! I thought they were going to stay in the city," yelps Stephanie, a pretty, blond, seventeen-year-old, to Thatcher, the boy who has given her a ride home. She crushes her half-smoked cigarette in the ashtray of his Saab convertible. Then, with a softer, more vulnerable voice, she groans, "They're gonna kill me!"

It's two in the morning, way past her curfew. She's been having a great time at a friend's party, luxuriating in a bath of loud hip hop music, frozen daiquiris, and Thatcher's attentions, but the unexpected sight of her parents' car is a complete buzz-kill. She gives Thatcher a quick kiss, tugs her J. Crew cord miniskirt down closer to her knees, and slips on her high, wedge sandals. Popping a small handful of peppermint Tic Tacs into her mouth, she hops out of the car and readies herself for the coming inquisition. The floodlights on the roof of her home assault her bleary eyes as she hustles up her curved driveway, covering her face to hide from the glare like Monica Lewinsky walking past an obtrusive TV crew. When she gets to the door, Stephanie thinks, At least I'm not that drunk anymore.

Inside, her parents are getting ready for bed. Her mother calls down the stairs, "Stephanie? It's late, honey, where were you?"

"Sorry, Mom!" Stephanie lies in her best matter-of-fact voice. "I couldn't get a ride until now."

"Sweetie," her mom pleads, "you should have left a message."

Stephanie switches to a more helpless, girlish voice, "I know, Mom. I tried to call but my cell phone died." Then, the adult again, Stephanie asks, "How was the play?"

Her mom replies in a louder voice, which is directed more to her husband than to Stephanie, "Well, your father thought it was boring, but I rather liked it." Then, happy to have her daughter home safely, her mom adjourns the meeting with: "Now get to bed, Stephanie! It's late!"

Once inside the safety of her room, Stephanie relaxes. She closes her door and flips off the light switch, leaving only the pulsating glow of her screen saver. Before she crawls under her quilt, she dashes off a quick email to Thatcher: "I thought they were going to go postal, but they didn't do anything. I'm not even grounded."

This incident is typical and illustrates the trend that most of us sense: kids get away with a lot more than they used to. Or in the words of another seventeen-year-old girl at another school, "About half the kids are really spoiled and they know it. They can get away with anything. It doesn't matter what they do, their parents are like, 'Oh, it's okay, honey.' "

Being less strict can mean that parents set fewer rules, or that they are more tolerant than their parents were when the rules they set are broken. We saw this clearly in the responses parents gave about questions of discipline in our PPM survey. We asked parents what they would do if they caught their kids drinking or smoking pot. We also asked teenagers what they thought their parents would do in both instances.[4]

About one out of every four parents said that they would not punish their teenage son or daughter if they caught them drinking or smoking pot. Instead, they would "calmly" discuss the issue and perhaps seek counseling. The teens' perspective was also that their parents would most likely talk to them and perhaps try to make them feel guilty about what they had done. Only about half of them thought they would be grounded.

We want to talk things out with our kids, reason with them, rather than impose authoritarian punishments such as taking away privileges; we want open and honest communication, not dictatorial rule. This philosophy has both benefits and risks. We want to be emotionally close to our kids, to have fun with them, to be, to some extent, their friends. This blurring of the line between being a friend and being a parent is one of the most significant trends in parenting today, and it often results in confusion for us and our kids.

We blur the line, in part, because so many of us had extended childhoods. Although many of us had part-time jobs as adolescents, we didn't contribute to the family in any real material way. Many of us were financially dependent on our parents well into our twenties and sometimes thirties. It makes sense that since we were dependent for so much of our lives we should identify with our children and their emotions. There is often no defining line for us between who we were as children and who we are as adults. And we have created a culture that perpetuates this confusion. The culture we grew up in worshiped youth, and it still does; we want to remain young, and we identify with our kids in a way that our parents did not identify with us.

I don't mean to imply that identifying and wanting to be emotionally close to our kids hurts them. As I said in the Introduction, I am not urging a return to the stereotypical family of the 1950s in which the father's word was law and physical punishment the remedy of choice for misbehavior. But the desire to form a close bond with our children should not come at the expense of not being able to set an unyielding limit or rule when a child needs it. At the extreme are parents who smoke pot with their adolescents, or buy beer for them. Some of us swear or are unguarded in our speech around our fourteen-year-olds. Others blur the distinction between friend and parent and feel rejected if their child prefers to be with their friends rather than with us, as most kids eleven and older do.

The case of Craig and his dad illustrates how a friendship between father and son can go awry. Craig, an eighteen-year-old, attends the same well-to-do suburban high school as Stephanie. He describes himself as a "techno"—into computers, video, and other electronic toys. His dress is goth: black pants, black shirt, and big, black Doc Martens. His hair also seems unnaturally black. I don't see any tattoos, but his eyebrows and ears are pierced. Craig is likable and talks easily. He does not appear to be a kid in major trouble or with an obvious psychological disorder. He tells me that he does smoke pot, but mostly on weekends. He recently started smoking cigarettes. He seems a bit aimless; he doesn't express clear goals or look forward to his future. Like everyone else at his school, the main blip on his radar screen is getting into a good college, but he is not sure what he'll study when he gets there. "Maybe computers," he tells me. What intrigues me the most is his relationship with his dad. He says of his mom, "I don't like her much. She and I argue a lot. But me and my dad are pals. We do things together a lot. Lately we've been bowling and playing pool. My dad likes doing that so he and I go out and do that on weekends, grab dinner and stuff like that. He sort of knows a lot about jazz and classical music, and I know a lot about electronic, heavy metal, and all that stuff, so music is a big part of his life and it's a big part of my life, too. And we sort of exchange ideas and he—at any given moment—he'll have about ten of my CDs and I'll have about ten of his."

But as we go on further, it's clear that the closeness sometimes blurs the line between his dad-as-friend and dad-as-parent. And it makes Craig uncomfortable in the sense that he feels the need for his dad to set limits when he doesn't. An example he gives me is when he wanted a CD burner for his birthday and his dad, in an effort to build character, told him he would have to work in order to pay for half of it. "I told him I'd be happy to work for the other half," Craig said. "But then I didn't do anything. Come my birthday, he just went out and bought it for me. Pretty expensive piece of equipment. He kind of tried to put the idea in my head that it's important to work for things so that you'll value them, but, you know, in practice, he's not showing me that. He's just sort of telling me."

I feel for Craig's father. I can imagine doing the same thing myself. But Craig's father is trading the lessons he's trying to teach his son about the value of money and working for something you want for the quick fix of making his son happy and sustaining their good relationship. Craig's father relishes their closeness. He enjoys their shared interest in music. He imagines that when Craig gets a CD burner, they'll burn a compilation of some of his favorite jazz—Miles Davis, Charlie Parker, Thelonious Monk. He imagines Craig taking the burned compilation CD with him to college and beginning to fall in love with jazz the way he did in his twenties. At some level he wants, perhaps unconsciously, for his son to see how cool these jazz greats are and, in turn, see what a cool father he is for turning Craig on to them.

*   *   *

Friendship with one's child can be a bright spot in an otherwise unhappy life. Our divorce rate is high—about 50 percent. When our marriages or jobs are frustrating, when we are depressed, time with a happy child can be uplifting. Enjoying a child's company is one of the main reasons that we have kids in the first place. But if we spoil our children with material goods in order to get a hug, or fail to set appropriate limits out of fear that they will withdraw their love or be upset, we have burdened them with protecting *us* from unhappiness.

We are more psychologically savvy than our parents were. We took psychology courses in college, many of us have been in psychotherapy, and we read books like this one offering psychological insight into how to be a more effective parent—books that didn't exist for our parents. Professionals who work with children and their parents often comment to me on how psychologically sophisticated parents today are. One Colorado psychologist put it this way: "There is a high level of understanding of child development issues among these people [parents at her school]. Maybe too much so, with everybody overanalyzing and overunderstanding and overcompensating for every move their child makes."

As a psychologist, I think it's great that we think about children as emotional beings and worry about their inner lives. But we worry that we will scar our children, causing them to spend their adulthood complaining about us to their therapists. Too often, we fear that our children will be traumatized or their spirits crushed if we're not perfect parents.

A psychologist friend of mine met a group of fifth grade parents at his school because a war was brewing. One set of parents allowed coed parties at their homes, tacitly encouraging sexual experimentation by allowing the kids to be unsupervised for extended periods in a darkened room. In the opposing camp were parents who thought the parties were completely inappropriate, but didn't want to prohibit their children from attending because they were afraid that they might be seen as "uncool." And the antikissing clique were worried that their children would be traumatized if they couldn't attend these parties. My friend had to convince them that their kids would not be scarred for life.

What happens when we can't be perfect parents? We feel guilty. We think that we owe our children everything and we feel bad when we can't provide it. Almost all parents have at one time given into a child or bent a household rule because they felt guilty about something they had done. Often this guilt relates to our hectic lives. We acquiesce because we haven't spent enough time with our kids. In our survey, parents, most of them moms, listed work obligations as the number one obstacle to being a better parent. Kids sense this guilt and use it to their advantage. Toy stores in airports help business travelers assuage guilt by bringing home a Beanie Baby or model plane.

Intense competition is another cultural trend that has affected our parenting. In order for us to consider that we have done a good job, our child must be an achiever. For many of the adolescents in our survey group, this means not only stratospheric GPAs in honors courses, but also athletic and/or artistic accomplishments. In the short term, achievement means getting good grades, then big numbers on the SATs, and, finally, acceptance at prestigious colleges. Beyond that, it means the right graduate schools and jobs that are both lucrative and fulfilling.

A college counselor in the Boston area addressed how students feel when they don't get into a top-ranked college: "They feel they've failed everybody. Their school, family, friends, grandparents! A kid last year had grandparents hounding her because they wanted to know which college sticker they should affix to their windshield. I had some kids this year whose parents won't visit Colby College or the University of Vermont because their kids didn't get into Harvard. They won't even talk about it, so now this kid can't feel good about getting into some great college because it's not Harvard. They need the ego gratification of being able to say it because these children are so tied to their parents that there's no divorcing from them. The child is a physical extension of the parent."

New Challenges

We face new challenges today as parents. How do we balance the emotional closeness to our children we all want with setting limits? How do we keep the line from blurring between parent and friend? How do we protect our kids as they grow, but not become overprotective? How do we maintain our authority without becoming authoritarian? And, finally, how can we temper the message of our increasingly materialistic, success-driven age? How should we handle kids like Connor—and there is a little bit of Connor in most children today—who have had every advantage and flaunt their sense of entitlement? Kids who seem to want all of the benefits and none of the responsibilities? How do we help them grow and mature? And how do we help them fill what all too often seems to be a hollowness at the center of their being—a hollowness that makes them anxious and depressed?

It's not just a little ironic that our success and newfound prosperity—the very accomplishments and good fortune that we so desperately desire to share with our children—put them at risk. Not for drug abuse and sexually transmitted disease, but for insidious ills. Connor may be at the upper end of the spectrum of wealth and privilege, but our culture is now so steeped in its celebration of money and privilege that kids in the middle and lower-middle classes aspire to his self-indulgent way of life.

Let's look in the next chapter at the impact that America's growing affluence has had on us and our kids.

_____

CHAPTER 2

We're in the Money:

GROWING UP IN THE NEW GILDED AGE

Being rich ain't what it's cracked up to be. It's just worry and worry, sweat and sweat, and a-wishing you was dead all the time.

—MARK TWAIN
Adventures of Tom Sawyer

The New Gilded Age

In a recent series of articles the *Washington Post* christened our era the "New Gilded Age."[1] The "Old Gilded Age" ran from about 1890 to the beginning of World War I. Like today, it was a period of booming economic expansion and the emergence of a class of entrepreneurial men with mind-boggling wealth. We associate vast fortunes with software billionaires Bill Gates and Paul Allen, or communications magnates Ted Turner and Sumner Redstone. In the nineteenth century, the super-rich—men such as Andrew Carnegie, John D. Rockefeller, Leland Stanford and Cornelius Vanderbilt—made their fortunes in steel, oil, railroads, and steamships. It was an era of magnificent opulence. Although the fortunes amassed by the wealthy few during the Old Gilded Age were greater (there was, after all, no pesky income tax to contend with), there are many more people today who are rich. The current economic boom affects tens of millions of Americans.[2]

As I wrote this, at the height of the economic boom, jaw-dropping statistics about wealth and money were everywhere:

- Sixty people became millionaires in America each day.[3]
- Ten thousand dollars invested in Dow Jones Industrials in the mid-1980s would be worth nearly $100,000 today.[4]
- Among the richest 20 percent of Americans (about 56 million), the average after-tax income was $102,300, a 43 percent increase since 1977. Average after-tax income averaged $515,600, up 115 percent since 1977, among the top one percent of households.[5]
- The average starting salary and bonus for a new law school graduate in a big city law firm was $155,000 per year. The average CEO of a large corporation made $2.8 million a year.[6]
- The average home price in affluent zip codes reflected the wealth of their inhabitants: Sudbury, Massachusetts—$387,000; McClean, Virginia—$410,000; Chappaqua, New York—$453,000; Hinsdale, Illinois—$469,000; Highland Park, Texas—$735,750; Montecito, California—$900,000; Greenwich, Connecticut—$1,130,000; Aspen, Colorado—$1,750,000; and Manhattan's Central Park West—$2,297,500.[7]

With new millionaires having sprung up like dandelions along with their seven-thousand-square-foot homes, the stock market on a fifteen-year drunken joyride, and top CEOs making more in salary, bonuses, and stock options than the gross national product of many developing nations,[8] we live in interesting times. Money talk is thick in the air. We inhale it with each breath. Although the stock market has begun to sober up, there is still money everywhere; we are all affected, whether rich, poor, or in-between; whether we think the quest for big money is our best shot at achieving happiness or the root of all evil—and whether we are a parent or a child.

Like characters in a Harry Potter novel, Connor, Stephanie, and Craig are all under a spell cast by the sorcerers of Wall Street, Silicon Valley, Hollywood, and Madison Avenue. The spell causes them to see much of their experience through a purple haze of acquisitiveness, opulence, and comfort. The spell lulls them into a belief that the good times are here to stay—an endless summer where the livin' is always easy. My children are under this same spell. Their school recently had a $5 million facelift and added a new gym, library, and computer lab. My children, their classmates, and our neighbors all live the good life. We take exciting, exotic vacations *and* have weekend vacation homes. We buy lots of fun toys. We hire people to cut the grass, rake the leaves, and clean the kitchen floor. Don't get me wrong; I'm happy as a clam to be living this way. Some of my happiest moments as a parent have come from playing cards with my wife and children next to the wood stove in our little New Hampshire house after a day of skiing together. I feel very fortunate to have a field on our property big enough for family games of soccer and softball. And holding hands with my daughters inside the Great Pyramid was an indescribably wonderful experience. But like many of my privileged friends, I worry that the New Gilded Age may have a dark side. Can our children grow up in this affluent environment and still be caring and kind, or will they become materialistic hedonists?

When so many people can afford all the expensive symbols of the lush life—fast cars, exotic vacations, and personal indulgences once available only to royalty—it raises the bar for everyone. Luxury fever is in the air. Keeping up with the Joneses has taken on a new meaning.

Luxury Fever

I experienced luxury fever when I lived briefly at Lismore Castle—the ancestral home of the dukes of Devonshire in County

Waterford, Ireland. My parents had gathered their sons and our families together for a week of extravagant diversion. The current duke lets out a wing of Lismore to well-heeled groups for family reunions, executive getaways, or whatever else people might want to do in a castle when he is at his far grander estate in England. The wing has ten bedrooms, a banqueting hall, billiard room, and assorted drawing rooms.

I didn't grow up rich. My father made his money in the paper industry when I was in my late teens. As a child, I had a paper route, my father worked nine-to-five, climbing the corporate ladder at the Continental Can Company, my mother kept house, and we inhabited a modest neighborhood in Wheaton, Illinois. Then my father quit his job, borrowed some money, and started his own highly successful business manufacturing corrugated boxes. Now he enjoys being able to play at being the duke of Devonshire for a couple of weeks.

A duke in training was not something I ever pictured for myself, but I soon felt the seduction of peerage. I fell into a comfortable routine at Lismore. Up early, I worked on this book, situating myself in the largest of the castle's drawing rooms, notebook computer on my lap. The surroundings distracted me. Huge tapestries depicted scenes from *Don Quixote*. An exquisite pair of oriental vases flanked the black marble fireplace. Dennis, *our* butler (as I quickly came to call him), or perhaps James, his assistant, would appear, throw a log on the fire, and pour coffee into my elegant bone china cup from the silver service.

Shifting my gaze from the room itself out the big bay window, I became absorbed by the stunning panorama of dawn breaking over the tranquil Blackwater River as it meandered under an ancient, arched bridge into the surrealistically green valley of the Knockmealdown Mountains. I soon found myself wondering what it would be like to inherit Lismore and its one thousand acres of grounds. I pictured myself ambling through the castle's lavish gardens, seeking inspiration for my next book! My life would be enriched by the pleasure of having my meals served to me in the chandeliered dining room surrounded by its breathtakingly beautiful Van Dyck paintings. My comfortable house in Massachusetts no longer felt good enough. I had luxury fever.

Robert Frank, an economist at Cornell, introduced this term into the American lexicon in his recent book *Luxury Fever: Why Money Fails to Satisfy in an Era of Excess.*[9] Frank documents recent changes in the spending habits of Americans, fueled by the booming economy. Houses are, on average, twice as big today as they were in the 1950s. The average car now costs $22,000, almost double what it cost just a decade ago. The New Gilded Age has expanded the market for luxury goods. Even if you are lucky enough to be able to afford an above-average $30,000 Jeep Grand Cherokee, it might not seem like enough when compared to the $50,000 Mercedes SUV driven by the other mom in your daughter's carpool or the $100,000 Porsche 911 your son's friend just got for a high school graduation present.

Go, for example, to the *Dupont Registry: A Buyer's Gallery of Fine Homes.* Leaf through the pages that describe the digs that would be available to you if you had sufficient means. Perhaps you'd like this $800,000 home in Alpharetta, Georgia:

> Street of Dreams home with quality and detail throughout. Located on a cul-de-sac street with running creek in backyard, this brick home is landscaped to perfection and features 6 bedrooms. A gourmet kitchen, vaulted sunroom with Palladian windows and formal living and dining rooms, first floor library, elegant master suite with sitting room and fireplace, 10-foot ceilings on the main level, three car side-entry garage, plus finished terrace level with sauna.

But after living awhile on the "Street of Dreams," it might not seem quite good enough. Why settle for a creek running through the backyard? Soon you'd find yourself eyeing this new beachfront home in Swampscott, Massachusetts:

> Currently being built on one of the North Shore's most magnificent sites. This 6800-square-foot shingle style 6 bedroom, 6 bath home will feature the highest quality materials and spectacular views. Plus 325 feet of ocean frontage and deeded private beach rights. $3,200,000.

This too might soon fail to satisfy. There would, after all, be neighbors close by. And where would you house your in-laws when they came to spend a week? Where would you keep your stable of antique cars? Despite having the sound of the ocean to lull you to sleep, you might toss and turn thinking about how nice it would be to own this $10 million estate in Bedford, New York:

> Designed for grand living and entertaining, glorious gardens and four sparkling ponds provide the ideal backdrop for enchanting 1928 French country Manor. Exquisitely detailed interiors with sweeping views. Pool, pool house, tennis, guest house, caretaker's apartment, 2 greenhouses and 9-car garage.

This, too, might eventually not seem enough and soon, like me, you would be longing to own your own castle.

What is it in our psychology that sabotages our feelings of adequacy; our satisfaction with what we have, with what's enough? What is the acquisitive urge in us that seems to have taken over our lives? Our drives for dominance, supremacy, hierarchical ascendance, and a threshold for pleasure that seems boundless, have all been exacerbated by a media that bombards us with tantalizing images of the good life—a good life that revolves around things. But, say the sages, attitude is everything. The Talmud and the Dalai Lama are on the same page here: "You are rich if you are satisfied with what you have"[10] proclaim these receptacles of ancient wisdom. Unfortunately, what we have all too often becomes who we think we are. And if this is true for us, it's doubly true for our children.

There has been a sort of backlash against all this acquisitiveness and opulence in our culture. Books like the bestseller *Simple Abundance* tells us to take pleasure in the ordinary things of life that are all around us, free of charge. But how many of us have *Simple Abundance* on the pleasingly rustic windowsills in the reading nooks of our second homes? Or on the marble countertops of our newly renovated kitchens?

Children Are Running a Temperature, Too

Young children and adolescents have no built-in immunity to luxury fever. In fact, they may even be more susceptible than adults, especially if their parents have spared no expense in making them happy. They don't have a perspective on life. Images of wealth are spun in a posh cocoon around them. Like the young Siddhartha, they're protected by us from seeing the harsh side of the world.

But how many of them are spoiled in the material sense? One of the goals of our survey was to describe what possessions children own. Specifically, we asked whether they had a computer, television, or telephone in their room, and if they owned their own car, cell phone, horse, or had a credit card for which their parents paid. We also asked about vacations, travel, and allowance. We chose kids and parents who were not poor. We wanted to know how our new affluence was affecting the lifestyle and attitudes of parents and kids. The one thousand parents in our sample all had at least one child who attended a private or suburban public school. Over one-third had yearly incomes under $100,000, two-thirds under $200,000. Five percent had incomes of over $1 million a year and another nine percent over $500,000.[11]

In many cases, there was a close relationship between how much money parents had and what they bought for their kids. In others, there was no direct correlation between parents' income and kids' possessions. We often found there was a "critical mass" or "tipping point": what kids owned was constant until parents made more than $500,000 a year. Then things changed dramatically.[12]

- Computer in child's bedroom—Among parents of preteens, there were only small differences between the wealthy and not-so-wealthy in whether their child had a computer in their room: at all income levels, between one-third and one-half of these children had computers in their rooms. For teenagers, the majority (sixty-five percent) of the most wealthy—those whose parents made more than $500,000 a year—had their own computers. This was true for only about a half to a third of teens at lower income levels.

- Television in room—A TV in a child's bedroom was not a sign of affluence; rather the reverse. More children at lower income levels owned TVs; at income levels below $100,000, it was more likely that a child had a television in his or her room than a computer.

- Telephone—For both preteens and teenagers, income mattered little in whether a child had a phone. About 30 percent of preteens and 55 percent of teenagers at all income levels had a phone in their room.

- Cell phone—The cell phone is still a status symbol among teenagers. Almost two-thirds of millionaires' (using a

definition of millionaire common among investment bro-
kers: earning one million dollars a year) children had cell
phones; this was true for only about one-fourth to one-
third of children at lower income levels.

- Credit card—A parent-financed credit card is a privilege
  enjoyed by only 18 percent of teenagers. One out of four
  teenagers in the two hundred thousand-plus income
  bracket and one out of three of millionaires' children have
  their own cards.

- Car or motorcycle—The more money a family has the
  more likely it is that the kids aren't taking the bus to
  school. Two-thirds of the wealthiest adolescents (family
  income greater than $500,000) own cars compared to
  around one-half of everybody else.

- Horse—Nelson W. Aldrich, Jr., in his book *Old Money,*
  calls upper-class Brahmins the equestrian set because of
  the importance they placed on horseback riding (polo in
  particular).[13] In our sample, millionaires' children were
  far more likely to own a horse than anyone less fortunate,
  although only 16 percent of our most affluent group had
  a trusty steed close at hand.

- Allowance—Teenagers say that their median allowance is
  $20 to $25 per week. Parents report slightly lower allow-
  ances, with younger teens (under 17) receiving a median
  of $10 to $15 weekly and older teens $20 to $25 a week.
  The allowance rises with parents' income, but not dramatically. After adjusting for the adolescent's age (older teens
  get more money), a millionaire's child only gets $10 a
  week more than a kid whose parents make less than
  $50,000 per year.[14]

- Travel—Almost no one (less than 1 percent) went on a
  trip to Asia with their kids unless they earned over
  $200,000 per year; at income levels up to a million dollars
  per year, only 3 percent made the trip last year. More

millionaires' children (8 percent) went last year than any other group. Europe is a much more popular destination. Of kids and adolescents in the survey group, 20 percent went in the year 2000. The more the family had, the more likely it was that the kids listened to Big Ben chime, took a cruise down the Seine, or fed the pigeons in St. Mark's. One of three families with incomes between $200,000 and $500,000 made the trip across the pond, as did nearly half of those with incomes over $1 million.

Buying a child a horse, a cell phone, or giving him a charge card could be viewed as an extravagance. On the other hand, isn't a computer or a trip to a foreign country educational, and, as such, worth the money? Studies show that students who have access to computers at home as eighth graders are more than twice as likely to attend tier 1 universities (e.g. Harvard, Yale, Stanford) than those who don't.[15]

Most parents will spare no expense to help their child get ahead, and when affluence and the drive to achieve converge, the result is parents who have given their kids a head start in the race for academic honors, high test scores, and admission to the best schools.

The game starts early. It's become a cliché that admission into the right preschool has become as selective as admission into a top college—and that it is just as important for future success. Our little ones deserve a preschool designed to "stimulate their minds, strengthen their bodies, and nurture their hearts," which is what the aptly named Crème de la Crème in Atlanta sets out to do.[16] Crème's state-of-the-art environment includes a "Wee TV studio that builds self-confidence and self-esteem, enhances communication skills, and teaches important values." All for a mere $10,000 a year! But it's worth it, according to Candace Stone, mother, nurse, consultant/law student, who says, "Crème's curriculum gave our children the educational advantages to attend the private school of *our* choice." (Italics mine.)

Private school will typically cost about $15,000 per year plus another $1,000 or more in contributions to the annual fund drive and perhaps another $1,000 or more at the annual auction fund-raiser.

Then there is the crucial choice of college. Start thinking about this early! Admission to a top college gets tougher each year. Applicants are not only expected to have high grades and SAT scores: they should be well rounded. Your kid better excel at some activity, be it playing the cello, designing software, or scoring goals on the soccer field.

As you cart your kids to and from their extracurricular activities, you might ask yourself: how in God's name did this happen to me? You'll probably feel guilty (I do) when you miss your kid's soccer game because you're away on business or chained to your desk due to a deadline. And, as every parent knows, the lessons that contribute to developing your well-rounded child are expensive; but, hey, nothing's too good for your child, right?

It also won't hurt on your child's college application if she has some fascinating life experiences to write about— community service in Africa, an archaeological dig in England, perhaps a summer studying El Greco at the Prado while brushing up on her Castilian accent.

Who wouldn't want to give their child the opportunity to travel and experience the world, or the best education that money can buy? Who wouldn't want to shower them with gifts like computers and cars, which make them feel loved, valued, and give them a sense of autonomy and independence (while sparing us the necessity of running what can often seem like a full-time taxi service). But there are dangers to what begins as a laudable impulse, as we're finding out. Unfortunately, as we will discuss in Part II, children have become increasingly scheduled and feel increasing pressure to achieve. This can lead to pathological perfectionism and anxiety.

In our book *Raising Cain,* my coauthor, Michael Thompson, and I talked about the root of the word *discipline,* which comes from *disciple.* If our children are driven on the one hand, and indulged on the other, we can only look at the lessons we've taught them and what we will teach them in the years to come. We might also ask ourselves what kind of parents they will be. Compared to much of the rest of the world, we are all living in Lismore Castle. Many of our children have been free from want all their lives. They have grown up in a society where, it seems to me, we often exalt celebrity and wealth, denigrate poverty, and tend to view ordinary lives as dismal and boring.

We have been getting richer and richer. We rule the roost. For our children it must seem that the good times will stretch on forever. Childhood is a time of invulnerability anyway, and for our children this is particularly true—they are new caesars. Finally, for them, this country has fulfilled the promise of "every man a king." There will be more and better things to buy, new movies to see, new television shows produced, better and faster computers, slicker cars, cooler gadgets, better drugs, and diverting kaleidoscopes of hip music and fashion. Why, then, do they often seem so bored, depressed, and filled with ennui?

The great French existentialist Jean-Paul Sartre said, on numerous occasions, that the time he felt most free was when he was fighting the Nazis in occupied France. His actions as part of the Resistance gave his life meaning. He chose to face danger and discomfort. He was acting in accord with his desires. Enervating existential questions were subsumed by the need to *act* moment by moment.

Unfortunately, more college students today dream of becoming dot.com billionaires at age twenty-six than contemplate the purpose of life or the nature of good and evil. According to yearly surveys that ask about the value of higher education, today's freshmen list "becoming very well-off financially" as the number one objective. The proportion of college freshmen that consider this "very important" or "essential" has risen from 39 percent in 1970 to 74 percent in 1998. In 1970, the year when many of their parents were college-aged, the most important reason stated for going to college was to "develop a meaningful philosophy of life."[17]

Our children have nothing left to fight for or against. By indulging them we have taken away the first—and final—barrier for them to push against. In the New Gilded Age, it is almost impossible for them to connect with life outside their computer and television screens; a velvet rope circumscribes their enclaves of privilege. The dragons they have to slay are all internal. Perhaps that's the way it should be. But they are naive about the way the world works.

Caroline and Denise

In the student interviews that were conducted as part of the research for this book, the theme of "not living in the real world" repeatedly surfaced. Here is an interview with Denise, an earnest, bright, athletic girl of seventeen who attends private school outside of Washington, D.C. Blond and fast-witted, she's the child of well-educated government employees and has traveled with her family a great deal. As a result, Denise is prone to discussing her world with a more objective, nuanced tone than many of her peers. In the midst of a longer conversation, she comments on her friend Rachel, who is "clueless" about money.

DAN: You were telling me that you have a friend who seems clueless about the way the world works.

DENISE: Yeah, Rachel. It's unfortunate, because she's a very smart person, but there are lots of things—and I'm not trying to say like I know these things and no one else does—but there are lots of just commonsense kinds of things that she doesn't understand. She's wanted me to do stuff with her, and I've had to say, "No, I can't." "Why not?" she'd ask. And I had to spell it out to her slowly: "Rachel, my family can't afford to send me to Aspen for spring break. I just can't go!" And she still doesn't get it. She's almost like the little kids I baby-sit. They can't understand that even if they want something really badly, there are times when it's just impossible.

DAN: How does she respond?

DENISE: She'll say, "Den, it'll be a blast! Just go ask your dad." It's hard to explain to her that that's not the way things work.

DAN: Her family is wealthy?

DENISE: Very wealthy.

DAN: Is she preoccupied with money?

DENISE: She's not concerned about money. I don't think she understands the value of money because she gets a brand-new car for her birthday. She has no concept of how money works or how you earn it.

DAN: Because it's always there?

DENISE: Yeah. Just like water. You turn on the faucet and out it comes.

Caroline, an eighteen-year-old, tells a similar story. I interviewed her at her class-conscious prep school in Connecticut.

She suggests that by not talking about their net worth, cash flow, or buying power, her parents have helped her evade the focus on money that overwhelms so many of her peers.

DAN: You said your parents have helped you not to be so focused on money because, even though they're well off, they never talk about it. How has this helped you?

CAROLINE: It's kept my focus away from, like, shopping on the weekends. I hate malls; I'd much rather spend my time outside. And I think it's kept me away from the scene of kids who are too interested in the new things they bought this weekend, and who are, like, "look at the new Mercedes my parents bought for me"—that kind of thing.

DAN: That goes on a lot here?

CAROLINE: It goes on a *ton* here.

DAN: What do you think, not so much with you but with the people you see around here—what does all the focus on things do to them, or what is it going to do to them as they get older?

CAROLINE: I don't know. I think money can sort of give people immediate friends. They have huge houses so they throw the parties. It's a security net. But after high school and college, people are going to have to rely on more than money and what they own to be successful in their lives.

DAN: You can buy friends here? Is that what you're saying?

CAROLINE: Buying friends is a little steep. But if you're not one of the more affluent kids, you stand out. Maybe you're not ostracized or kept out of cliques, but not having money definitely makes a difference.

DAN: Could you rank people in this school by how much money they have?

CAROLINE: Yeah, it's sad, but it's definitely true. I could.

Caroline recognizes the role wealth plays in her school's social dynamic. Not having money (relatively speaking anyway, since there is virtually no one at the school who lives below the poverty line) can be an obstacle to fitting in. In her milieu, it makes people uncomfortable to mix with people less fortunate than themselves. Perhaps they feel guilty. Perhaps the kids with less money can't keep up. Perhaps the wealthy just like being with their own. They have their own language, their own codes. Fitzgerald recognized this when he wrote, "Let me tell you about the very rich. They are different from you and me. They possess and enjoy early, and it does something to them, makes them soft where we are hard, and cynical where we are trustful."

Is this what we want for our children?

Social Consciousness, Now and Then

For many of us Baby Boomer parents, social activism (protesting against the war in Vietnam, fighting for civil rights, or trying to raise social consciousness about women's issues) was a defining piece of our adolescence and young adulthood. A majority of us have moved from protest to prosperity, into the fullness and flow of middle age, where what is important to us are the responsibilities we have to the lives we've created, to our families, friends, and communities. The intractable problems of the wider world don't touch us personally, and we feel the shortness of life. We want to savor what we have. Perhaps we have lost our nerve. In any event, we still intuitively feel that adolescence should be a time of idealism—that there's something wrong with our kids if they're not burning, as we were, to change the world and make it a better place.

For whatever reason—too much homework, no galvanizing social issues, apathy—students seem less interested in changing the world than they once were. Laura, a thirty-eight-year-old English teacher at a private school in a Los Angeles suburb, put it this way:

LAURA: I mean, I know this sounds like a cliché, but it's true. Kids don't appreciate what they have. They have great clothes, houses, vacations, gadgets. You name it, they've got it. And they want more! They all own great cars, a big thing on campuses in California. Now their parents are paying for the school to be redone. In the process of rebuilding, they've done away with student parking here—only the teachers were allocated space. This is what finally moved the kids to protest! In my six years I was excited that they finally protested about something. But I thought, How awful; teachers here don't even live in this community—we can't afford it! We *have* to drive. But there are kids who live a half a block away. They want to drive to school and they're protesting! I mean, they just don't get how lucky they are. Maybe they're not supposed to get it, but I like to think that when I went to school we weren't as selfish. I don't think we were. These kids are selfish. Being kind isn't natural to them.

The mind-set of the affluent is affected by the times. Even though the gap between the wealthy and the rest of society is larger now than it has been since records on this have been kept,[18] many teenagers today seem blind to these differences.

Jill, a sophomore in a school outside San Francisco, bemoaned the sense of entitlement she sees in her peers. She wished they would develop a sense of compassion for people less fortunate than themselves and an appreciation of what they have.

DAN: Tell me about the kids at your school.

JILL: Just, sometimes I feel like people here don't know how lucky they are and that bothers me a lot. But I probably don't know how lucky I am, either. I mean, I know a little, but I've been to private school my entire life. I have no idea what public school is like or what my life would be like or my education. But I definitely, you know, feel like there are kids here who are really spoiled.

DAN: What do you mean?

JILL: Like someone worked it out in the beginning of the year to see how much it cost per class to go to school here and it's something like $26 for each student every period of the day. Then I look at these kids who skip class all the time. And I sit there and I get mad. They'll just sit in the student center and talk to their friends and not do anything productive. I just feel like that's such a waste of money. And like they won't do their work or they won't study for tests. It bothers me that there is some poor kid out there who would die for the opportunity to go to school at a place like this, and then here are these kids whose parents can easily afford the tuition, and their kids don't know how lucky they are so they just blow off school.

DAN: Why do you think you have a different perspective on this than a lot of the other kids at your school? Why are they spoiled and you're not?

JILL: (laughs) Um, well, I'm definitely spoiled, too. I know that. But is that to say I'm unappreciative? Definitely not. Especially this year because this past summer I went to South Africa on a community-service trip. That's just given me such a greater perspective on the world and seeing how much I do have compared to how little other people have. I mean, I know I'm spoiled; look where I go to school, look at the car I drive, my house, and the things in my room. I know I'm spoiled, but I think my parents have done a good job in making sure I appreciate how spoiled I am! That's why they sent me to Africa, to make me realize how other people in the world live. Most of the kids at school haven't had that chance.

I'll say! Most kids, period, don't get sent away to develop social consciousness. It's telling that the parents feel they have to send their kids to South Africa to learn about the world (when South Central L.A. might make for an equally effective lesson), or on wilderness survival courses like Outward Bound to help make them tough and self-reliant, and strip the cluttered opulence of their lives down to the bare bones. We know that for our kids there is a missing dimension.

I do think in this new era of prosperity, as Jill recognizes, we need to address the sense of entitlement and the unrealistic perception of the world that our new affluence has wrought. In Part III, I'll suggest ways of tempering, mitigating, and even channeling in positive directions our kids' attitudes and kinds of behavior in the New Gilded Age.

It should be clear from the high rates of anxiety and depression in our kids that money does not buy happiness, although it does, without a doubt, act as a shield against life's infelicities. So what does lead to happiness? What is the answer to the question I posed to Connor's parents at the beginning of Chapter 1?

CHAPTER 3

God Bless the Child
That's Got His Own:

GIVING OUR CHILDREN LIFE SKILLS
THEY'LL NEED AS ADULTS

The most important thing that parents can teach their children
is how to get along without them.

—FRANK A. CLARK

I started this book with the question: "What do you want for your child?" "I want him or her to be happy," is the inevitable response. But how often do we stop and think about what it is that actually makes people happy? The origins of happiness were once investigated by John Locke, Rousseau, Plato, and Aristotle, among other philosophers. Then, in the early twentieth century, psychology came to dominate the study of human behavior, and happiness was deemed too unscientific a topic for serious thinkers. Only lately have psychologists turned their attention back to the fundamental questions, including—what is it that truly leads to happiness? And what can parents do to help their children lead happy lives?

A recent issue of *American Psychologist*, the official journal of the American Psychological Association, was devoted to the topic of happiness.[1] Recent research shows that happiness does come more naturally to some than to others; some of us seem to have a genetic advantage. Parents find this out when they have two temperamentally dissimilar children; children who almost from the moment of birth seem to react differently to the world. One child smiles easily and takes everything in stride, the other is somber, frustrated, and hurt by every slight. Or as one child put it in a college essay, "I was the Mercedes Benz of babies, whereas my sister was more like our old MG sports car—exciting, but prone to break down."

We cannot control our children's genetic predispositions (at least not yet). But we can control at least parts of their environment, and many of us believe that giving them things and providing them with comfort and security will make them happier people. It's clear, however, that the old adage is true—money does not buy happiness, for us or our kids. As a nation we are twice as rich as we were in 1957. We own twice as many cars per person and eat out twice as often. We also have more conveniences: dishwashers, microwaves, air conditioners, and personal computers. Yet despite increased wealth and comfort, despite the fact that we live in a New Gilded Age, since 1957 the rates of suicide, depression, and divorce are all up. These trends also hold true for Europe and Japan.

If money could purchase happiness, big money lottery winners should live on cloud nine. While it is true that these instant millionaires are initially ecstatic, the euphoria quickly fades.[2] In many cases, they become paranoid, develop health problems, have difficulty with jealous family or friends, and end up with unlisted phone numbers. They often stop working. The incentives that motivated them are gone. They often become idle, and idleness—a lack of purpose—becomes a curse. One of the most consistent findings about happiness—and this is a very important area where parents can have some influence over their kids—is that people report being happiest when they are absorbed in a challenging activity.

This state of absorption goes by many names: being in the zone, engagement, flow. It doesn't matter what the activity is as long as it takes skill and concentration—tennis, composing music, reading to a child. People in the zone say that they lose themselves completely in what they're doing. I know personally that some of my most satisfying and ecstatic moments have come when I was playing music with a group and we were all cooking along in the zone together. I have had similar joyfully absorbed moments while writing, playing sports, teaching, and even doing psychotherapy.

It is especially important for affluent parents to help their kids develop the ability to become absorbed by an activity. Studies reported in the *American Psychologist* issue devoted to happiness suggested that children from more affluent families are more likely to be bored, less enthusiastic, and less likely to be able to derive pleasure from their activities.

I have seen parents who were immersed in the world and they communicated through their actions that this kind of engagement was exciting and worthwhile. Friends of mine in a nearby town are involved in a sister-city project in El Salvador, helping a small village build a school. Their kids have stayed in the village and the kids from the village have come to their suburban neighborhood. The kids have seen the pleasure and fulfillment their parents have derived from the sister project. The greatest truism of parenting is that children learn what they see us *do,* rather than what we tell them to do.

Engagement doesn't have to be socially conscious. We teach our kids through example, whether it's practicing the guitar or honing our fly-fishing technique, that doing something well, and sticking to it, is important and will pay off in the long run. I have seen too many affluent children who are unable to engage in this way because no activity is ever quite good enough for them. They flit from one career path to another, never fully investing themselves. Sometimes this occurs because parents never push their children hard enough or give them the skills that will enable them to fully immerse themselves in an activity. They don't make them practice the piano or stick with their skating lessons.

But the attitude in our kids of not wanting to try also comes from our culture. We fear that unless we are very good at something, and look like winners, we will be marginalized, left behind. This can make it hard for kids to become absorbed in an activity. Failure is defined as not being the best, and we tend to define all activities on a continuum of winning and losing.

Our kids might feel okay if they could learn a few chords, practice the piano twenty minutes a day, and be on a team, even if they aren't a star. But too often we send them the message that this isn't good enough. It's no wonder our kids often fail to fall in love with something. Why invest themselves when they will never be Eric Clapton, Lance Armstrong, or Britney Spears? They'd rather not risk failure.

An acquaintance, Diane, was complaining that her fourteen-year-old son showed little interest in any activity. She was concerned about helping him "find his passion." After she and her husband had talked to him repeatedly about finding something he liked to do, he finally said he wanted to play the electric guitar. They leapt at the opportunity and went out and bought him a $300 electric guitar and arranged private guitar lessons once a week at $50 an hour. A friend in the music business brought Michael backstage after a Clapton concert, and he actually met Eric Clapton. And for the boy's birthday Diane rented out a recording studio so that Michael and his friends could "jam."

I saw Diane six months later and asked how Michael's guitar playing was coming along. She said Michael rarely practiced the guitar. During lessons, it was mostly the sounds of the guitar teacher playing she heard through the door. Eventually she put her foot down, threatening to cancel the lessons unless Michael practiced at least twenty minutes a day. A year later, Michael was apparently really playing the guitar. Diane said she understood how she had loaded the situation by introducing him to Clapton and giving him the studio time as a gift too soon. She had helped set him up for failure when all she really wanted was for him to be happy.

As we shall see in a later chapter, when children can't derive pleasure from engagement, they will sometimes take drugs to stimulate the same brain centers as those that are stimulated during active engagement. The set of brain structures involved in these feelings of pleasure is known as the behavioral activation system (BAS). The BAS, buried below the cerebral cortex in an ancient part of the brain,[3] is responsible for activating us toward something in the environment that we associate with pleasure or relief of pain. Think of a man plodding through a desert without water, then suddenly seeing an oasis ahead. His whole posture changes; his eyes widen and he moves forward toward the water. Like a lab rat who spies the cheese at the end of a psychologist's maze, when this thirsty man sees water, his behavior is energized and he feels pleasure as he moves forward toward the goal. Psychologists sometimes link the word "incentive" with the activity of the BAS. As any good manager, animal trainer, or parent knows, when an animal or a person has an incentive that he desires, he will work hard to achieve it. And more important, he will derive pleasure in being absorbed in this goal-directed activity. For parents of affluent children, incentives do not have to be material. Money and toys often hold little incentive value for them. They are like the lab rat who has just finished a large chunk of cheddar—a run in the maze is no longer that exciting a prospect. Affluent parents must be able to give their children the ability to derive pleasure from the pursuit of nonmaterial incentives.

Dopamine is the brain chemical or neurotransmitter that gets released when the BAS is activated. But dopamine is also released in large quantities in the brain when many different types of drugs are taken, including marijuana, cocaine, nicotine, and alcohol.[4] There are several theories as to why drugs such as these become habit-forming, or why people are drawn to take drugs in the first place, but at a basic level, when a person cannot achieve dopamine-mediated pleasure through engagement in an activity, drugs can be an artificial substitute.

This is one of the reasons I was concerned about Connor: his pot-smoking seemed not so much adolescent experimentation to me, as Annie liked to think, but a way in which the boy was trying to ameliorate underlying feelings of aimlessness and a lack of engagement in the world.

I Think I Can, I Think I Can—the Development of Feelings of Self-Efficacy

So how do we teach our children engagement? How do we help them enter the zone? In some cases it requires commitment, nagging, and close supervision in helping them become competent at a sport or skill such as music or dancing. At other times, it requires just getting out of their way to let them master a task on their own and develop self-efficacy. Because parents do so much for their children today, many are robbed of the chance.

I think of Karen, an accomplished, happily married lawyer and her husband, Peter, a filmmaker, who have two children, Andrea and Beau. Karen spends at least an hour each evening helping her kids with their homework and checking to see that they haven't made any mistakes. When Andrea was busy on a recent weekend with a soccer game and a friend's birthday party, Karen spent several hours in the library doing research for Andrea's paper on the history of the Agora in ancient

Greece. Andrea is in fourth grade. Peter recently hired a college student to practice basketball with Beau twice a week after school so that Beau will be able to make friends with the other boys in his class more easily. Beau is in second grade. These are good people, and they mean well. They want only the best for their children. But, like so many of us, they occasionally allow their fear to overwhelm their good sense.

Most mothers have lived through the following scene. Mom is in a hurry to get somewhere but can't leave until her two-year-old is dressed. The child insists that she must accomplish this task "by myself!" This declaration of independence is stated so emphatically that the mother wonders whether her daughter believes that her survival depends on whether or not she can master this task. Perhaps it does.

Modern psychology uses the terms "effectance motivation," or a more recent variant, "self-efficacy,"[5] to describe the human drive to master the environment. This motive is seen in the prone two-month-old struggling to turn himself over, the intensely focused six-year-old trying to "sound-out" an unfamiliar word, and the lanky sixteen-year-old spending hours in the driveway working on his jump shot. Social scientists tell us that self-esteem, that sense of worth and well-being that keeps us happy and productive, is tied to having a sense of personal control and competence—a feeling of self-efficacy. In short, healthy self-esteem in a child depends on the belief that she can accomplish important tasks "by myself." Parents must, of course, be sensitive to being both overinvolved and underinvolved. Children need to be encouraged to do activities that are challenging but not too challenging. That is why parents do not try to toilet train a twelve-month-old or encourage a three-year-old to ride a two-wheeled bike. But when a child or teenager has a reasonable chance to accomplish something, they should be encouraged because the skills they develop come to have their own incentive value. We enjoy being able to do things well. I remember one evening when my youngest daughter, then six, decided that she wanted to prepare dinner for the whole family. She diligently worked to set the table, make soup, and macaroni and cheese. She did the dishes and cleaned the counters afterward. Even though it exhausted her, she was in heaven. She took so much pride in the fact that she could accomplish this adultlike task on her own. This is the feeling of pride that programs such as Outward Bound try to instill in teens with low self-esteem. They show them that they can accomplish seemingly difficult tasks such as rock climbing, white-water rafting, and solo survival camping. The enhanced sense of self-efficacy that Outward Bound graduates emerge with is priceless.

A sense of self-efficacy is important throughout life, for adults as well as children. It is important not only for self-esteem but, possibly, survival. An interesting set of studies done with the elderly in nursing homes found just that: seniors who were given more control over their lives tended to live longer than those who had their needs completely cared for by others.[6]

The experiment was straightforward. Half of the residents in a nursing home, chosen at random, were told by the staff that they were largely responsible for taking care of themselves. They were also given a plant and told that if they did not water and care for it, the plant would die. The other group was given the opposite message. They were told that the staff was there to take care of residents' every need, and that the plant in their room would be completely cared for by someone else.

Over time, the first group became more active, alert, and had a greater sense of well-being. They also lived longer. In the eighteen months following the start of the experiment, the death rate was twice as high for the group that did not have personal responsibility for their care.

One of the aspects that stands out when I have talked with groups of affluent teens is the pride they take in their solo accomplishments. For example, whenever I pose the question about whether it's good for adolescents to hold a job, they all say yes. When asked why, they say, "Because it's your own money. You've earned it yourself."

Listen to the pride in the voice of Lily in the following interview. The daughter of a mail carrier, she attends a school in suburban Chicago where most students have parents who are doctors, lawyers, or stockbrokers. Despite her relative poverty, she clearly feels a sense of self-efficacy.

Interview with Lily

DAN: How do you think you compare to the other students here?

LILY: Well, I have my own car but it isn't as nice as other kids'. It was my grandmother's old one. It's a year younger than me, seventeen years old. I think that most kids here are more spoiled in the sense that their parents haven't really given them the chance to, like, be on their own so much.

DAN: You're more independent?

LILY: Yeah. I just feel like they're more likely to run home and ask their parents for help or have their parents get them out of a jam, and I'm more likely to tell my parents to stay out of it and let me handle it.

DAN: Give me an example of something specific you've done on your own that another kid might not do.

LILY: Like when I was really young, like when I was probably first or second grade, if I got in a fight with someone my mom would call the other person's parent and the parent would deal with it. By the time I was in fifth grade I would tell my mother to stay out of it and let me deal with it on my own.

DAN: You would try to work it out by yourself?

LILY: Yeah. And I could generally take care of it myself. My parents know that if it's something serious that I can't handle I'll come to them. But for the most part they just kind of let me handle my issues myself. I think, like, other kids in school, because a lot of people's parents have good relationships with the administration, including my own, but they are more likely, if they got in trouble, to have their parents call. I mean, like Mr. Wright [the vice principal] could sometimes call my dad, but I generally won't get in trouble, and if I did I could really, like, deal with Mr. Wright by myself. My parents generally have an attitude that if the school catches me cheating or something like that, I'm the school's problem; the school will deal with me. I will face the consequences. If I could prove I wasn't cheating, I could prove I wasn't cheating.

DAN: So you think your parents have done you a favor and that all kids should be raised that way?

LILY: Yeah. I mean we'll all eventually get older, won't we? I just think that at that point they'll be more confused, like they won't know how to handle things. Like if something gets out of control and no one's going to come and save you from it, you have to save yourself. Like if you have a job and your boss accuses you of something you can't just call your parents and tell them to come in and talk to your boss. You have to learn to deal with people yourself. And my parents were never like that anyway. My parents have always told me, like, even when I was little and had projects, if you don't have it the day it's due, sorry. You deal with it.

In conversation, Lily was impressive. She had an aura of maturity that many of her peers didn't possess. She seemed willing, in a way that Connor was not, to fess up to her failings and take responsibility for her actions. It was clear that she saw herself up to almost any challenge.

Lily understood, as Connor came to understand, that facing the consequences is part of growing up. Experiencing failure, and recovering from it, learning to carry on, resolving to do better next time, and shrugging it off is an essential part of developing character. It is one of the hallmarks of maturity.

Some people who work with affluent kids feel that their world conspires against their developing a sense of self-efficacy. Jay, a college counselor at a private school, told me that he was dismayed by the amount of helplessness in many of the kids he deals with. He feels their parents are continually doing things for them that they shouldn't, and that there's no opportunity for them to learn how to do things on their own.

Interview with Jay

JAY: I was at a meeting having a few beers with Newell Browne, the dean of the faculty at St. Grottlesex, and he gave me an explanation for it. He told me that his kids, who are ten and twelve, can't do anything for themselves, and he attributes it to the fact that we organize everything for them. We have soccer moms and Little League dads. Everybody's involved in piano lessons and dancing lessons. Everything is organized for the kids so they don't know how to organize anything. You know I see that in the college application process. Some kids can do it themselves and those are the kids who, in the long run, regardless of what college takes them, seem to have a healthier understanding of what life is going to require. The other group is lost.

DAN: Parents fill out their kids' applications?

JAY: Basically, yes. They do tend to ask their kid where he wants to go to school, but it's not really a question. It's more like asking him whether he'd prefer macaroni and cheese or a PB&J for lunch. It's like, let me know and I'll go out and get it for you.

In fairness to our kids, we must also add that schools play a role in making it difficult for kids to develop ownership and efficacy. The psychologist Reed Larson has found that young people's usual experiences during schoolwork and unstructured leisure do not reflect conditions conducive to learning initiative.[7] That is, too often our children are merely hardworking plow horses dragging their burdens behind them (literally, in some cases, given the size of the school backpacks they carry). They are doing the work because they were told to and according to the exact directions they were given. Reed's conclusions stem from a creative study in which he outfitted a number of adolescents with beepers and paged them periodically throughout the day over several weeks, asking them to record their activities and feelings. He found that while they were doing schoolwork, which on average comprises almost a third of adolescents' waking hours, students often reported high levels of concentration and challenge, but also high levels of boredom and low levels of self-motivation. That is, they were working hard but felt little personal involvement with the work. They were doing it "because they had to." Larson feels that these commonplace school conditions do not foster initiative or self-direction. Students are more likely to experience these feelings while doing independent, nonrequired projects such as artwork, designing a web site, or playing in a band with a group of friends. These kinds of voluntary activities generally account for a much smaller percentage of time during an adolescent's day.

Some contemporary children and adolescents, like the self-sufficient Lily in the interview, do grow up with feelings of self-efficacy. Too many others, however, become indolent, anxious, and dependent. In most cases, this diminished sense of self-efficacy can be traced to parents who did too much and who continued to be directly involved in assisting children with activities even long after they had reached an age where they could have done it by themselves. Psychological research has consistently shown that children who have a greater sense of perceived control have parents who are warm, involved, and supportive, but who, like Lily's parents, give their children a good deal of autonomy and allow their children to do things independently (even if it also scares them both a little).[8]

Parents cannot let their own fears rule their children's lives—whether it is fear of their child's social rejection, school performance, inadequate athletic skills, or, later in life, their advancement to a college that is less than Ivy League.

Frustration Tolerance

One of the crucial ways in which our sense of self-efficacy can be undermined is when we don't have the ability to handle frustration. Indeed, one of the hallmarks of what we call emotional maturity is the ability not to be fazed by setbacks; to roll with the punches and persevere in the face of difficulties. Hope, a mother originally from the East Coast who now lives in an affluent suburb of San Francisco, is worried that she sees some signs that her fourteen-year-old daughter, Sarah, has difficulty with what I'll call frustration tolerance. Unless things come easily for her, she wants no part of them. I asked Hope if she thinks her family's affluence has contributed to this trait in Sarah.

HOPE: One of the problems we have had, as a family, in regards to overindulgence, is that Sarah has a problem tolerating people. I think that's because she is used to getting what she wants, and when she doesn't get it she becomes very unhappy with herself and those around her. I don't know if this is her age or more of a personality trait, but it makes me worry that when she gets older, no one will ever be good enough for her or she'll marry some kind of dishrag guy that she can lead around by the nose. Somebody that will give her whatever she wants.

I know Hope well. I think that she's a great mom. But her family situation, some old money from her side of the family and a husband who made a killing wisely investing in dot.com stocks, has caused them some unforeseen problems as parents. Their affluence and the fact that Sarah is attractive, athletic, and intelligent have contributed to Sarah getting what she wants when she wants it. She's not used to frustration, and, as a result, doesn't cope with it well. Perhaps she eventually will; life can sometimes teach us lessons we don't seek to learn on our own. But for now, this has made life harder for her and those around her.

Kids today can press a few keys on their computer and order up a video and dinner. They can instant message a half-dozen friends at the same time. So much appears to come to them so easily. We need to teach them how to develop skills such as frustration tolerance, and, more generally, how to cope with stress. Unfortunately, there is no magic in this. The only way a child can accomplish this is by actually experiencing frustration and stress, which is painful for him or her, and for us as parents, to watch.

In the next section, I'll turn to the topic of how we develop skills such as frustration tolerance or, more generally, how we cope with stress. Children like Sarah who have rarely had to cope with adversity due to her family's wealth and her own intellectual and athletic gifts have less of an opportunity to accommodate the problems the world throws at us all, and, as a result, can appear emotionally immature or spoiled. To make my case, I draw a parallel with a nonpsychological stress response—the immune system. The body cannot learn to adapt to stress unless it experiences it.

Coping with Stress

Most people, with some notable exceptions, would agree that experiencing substantial amounts of stress is bad for you. On the other hand, Viktor Frankl, author of the popular book *Man's Search for Meaning,* adopts the existentialist philosopher Friedrich Nietzsche's dictum: "That which does not kill me makes me stronger."[9] Frankl claims that even an experience as devastating as being interred in a Nazi concentration camp can be "good" in the sense that it leaves one with an enhanced sense of life's meaning.

Can stress really be good for a person, even children? We do know that biological "stressors," like viruses and bacteria, can actually fortify a child's immune system and increase her chance of survival.[10] Exposure to certain childhood illnesses helps train the immune system to cope with future invasion by other bugs and germs, much like leaving an infant to cry for a reasonable amount of time helps him to learn to self-regulate and cope with subsequent separations. Large or unusual assaults to the immune system can be damaging, however, just as leaving the baby to cry for too long might be more traumatic than constructive.

Young children exposed to local tropical diseases such as malaria build up a resistance and end up with milder cases of the disease when they do get sick, whereas a newcomer exposed to the same infection would be devastated. Until the emergence of the chicken pox vaccine, parents were often advised by their physicians to allow their children to be exposed to the illness in order to gain immunity when they were young, knowing that adults who contract chicken pox end up with cases that are far more serious.

Is there a parallel between becoming resistant to disease and developing immunity to stress? I've seen it among children and adolescents with whom I've worked over the years. One has to look no further than the first day of preschool for the child without any siblings and who has never had to share a toy. He is initially devastated when he can't get his way. Biting is a common negotiation strategy for such kids, but not for the middle child in a family of five who has been immunized against this stress by having had lots of practice sharing his toys with his siblings.

Indulged children are often less able to cope with stress because their parents have created an atmosphere where their whims are indulged, where they have always assumed, like Sarah and the little boy in his first day of preschool, that they're entitled and that life should be a bed of roses. A headmaster at a private school in Vermont makes it a point to tell the students in his care about his experience coping with stress and how he thinks it made him a better person.

Interview with Felton

DAN: Give me your thoughts about the role that coping with stress plays in the psychological development of the kids here at school.

FELTON: Let me tell you the story that I tell to the students here. When I was twelve, I got a call at camp from my mother telling me that my father had died. Up until the year before he'd been a teacher at a boarding school in Vermont. Not knowing what to do with me, she called the boarding school where he had worked and asked them if I could attend in September. They very nicely said of course. So for five years I got to go free to this boarding school. And the first year before I arrived in late August I ran around buying clothes. I didn't know what the hell kind of clothes to wear, my mother didn't either, and I bought all the wrong kinds of clothes. And I went to school in this double-breasted blue serge suit when every kid in school had a single-breasted gray flannel suit. I took so much shit for that suit.

DAN: I can imagine how you felt. I know other kids in that position. You must have been teased and made to feel like an outsider. I know how hard that can be on an adolescent who is struggling to fit in and belong to a peer group. They feel conspicuous, almost as though they're naked. On top of your father's death, which had already made you feel exposed, you must have felt without protection in the world.

FELTON: That's it! I suppose if I hadn't been on scholarship, we could have run out and bought a gray flannel blazer. But we didn't have any money, so I was stuck with it.

DAN: How does that affect what you do with the students here?

FELTON: I try to remind our kids that 20 percent of the students here are on scholarship and not everybody is going to have clothes from J. Crew; to try to get the kids who sit in the alcoves and talk about the Bahamas or flying to Colorado to ski to understand that not everybody can do that and maybe it isn't always a good idea to spend all your time talking about it.

DAN: You mean to protect them from taking the kind of crap that you had to take in your blue serge suit?

FELTON: In a way, yes. In those eighth and ninth and tenth grade years, especially, it's rough for a kid, I think, who doesn't have material comforts that other kids do. But, on the other hand, I often—and I believe this comes from my own background—I think they're the lucky ones. Because I think that, as a result, they develop some toughness or some perspective or something that plays out much better later on; because they've had to go through some trial. I mean, I think the blue serge suit was not great for me when I was twelve, but it didn't hurt me any in the long run—it taught me a lot of lessons, probably more important lessons than I learned in my seventh and eighth grade classes.

DAN: But when do the trials break a kid down rather than build him up? How much stress is too much stress?

FELTON: The middle ground is best. I think we all intuitively know what the extremes are. Almost anything between those extremes is okay. But I think that pertains only to other people's kids. I don't think we always intuitively know it about our own kids because intelligent people—who know that children need a degree of hardship, challenge, and discipline—spoil their own kids rotten. It's just incredible how blind we can be.

Less Is Sometimes More

Well-meaning parents can end up hurting their children by giving them too much. Too much money, too many toys, too much leeway in how they can behave, too much help, and, too often, unrealistic expectations for about how they will perform in school or on the soccer field. We've seen the dangers to our children in the atmosphere of indulgence that's been ushered in with the New Gilded Age. I'm sure many of us can identify with parents who give too much and expect too little. Many of us know children like Connor and Stephanie, who end up with a sense of entitlement. Who feel the need to perform but are also directionless. Who are crying for us to set limits—to become more involved in who they are and what they need.

In the accounts of parents, children, counselors, and teachers that are the basis for this book, there is a similar refrain—the need for us to help our children to be psychologically self-sufficient. Only when they have a sense of self-efficacy can we feel confident that they will be able to persevere in the face of adversity and forge a life that is purposeful and vibrant. As Billie Holiday sang so beautifully, "Mama may have and Papa may have, but God bless the child that's got his own."

In Part II of this book, we will explore in greater detail the kinds of problems faced by children raised in our age of indulgence. Using the traditional seven deadly sins as a jumping-off point, we'll describe seven "deadly" syndromes or problems of character that appear in kids who are indulged by busy, often affluent parents who grew up with an innate distrust of authority. We'll see how common parenting practices at the millennium such as material indulgence, permissiveness, and the kinds of overprotectiveness we've discussed in this section lead to personality traits in our children that erode the development of character.

As parents, we need to be alert and sensitive to our kids and, most important, to be honest with ourselves about how we are raising them. As Felton and many other teachers, principals, and counselors have pointed out to me, many parents can easily see the mistakes other parents make, but have blind spots when it comes to their own shortcomings. We need to understand how we as parents foster the difficulties our children face. Until we do we will be unable to change our own behavior and give them what they need. I hope we can now begin to answer in a full and conscious manner the question I posed to Annie and Bob at the beginning of Chapter 1. The happiness of our children comes from their engagement in the world; from compassion, independence, emotional maturity, and a sense of their own self-worth that is tempered by humility and a joy in being alive.

PART TWO

THE SEVEN "DEADLY" SYNDROMES

The Seven Syndromes
of Indulgence

This section focuses on the syndromes, or patterns of behavior, that are common among children in our indulgent age. The syndromes reflect both the PPM survey results, and the kinds of problems kids have that I've seen in my practice and consulting work with children in recent years. When thinking about the syndromes, I noticed their suggestive similarities to the seven deadly sins: Pride, Envy, Wrath, Sloth, Greed, Gluttony, and Lust. And it turned out that dividing the syndromes into seven types provided a straightforward, simple, yet realistic summary of the PPM findings.

A caveat! As you read through this section, please don't equate "syndrome" with "sin." I am not being moralistic. I am not saying that children who exhibit these syndromes are satanic. I borrowed from Pope St. Gregory the Great—the originator of the seven sins list—because I was attracted to the way in which he succinctly summarized a fundamental set of human problems.[1] My motivation in categorizing the PPM findings is the same: to delineate a brief, easily understandable set of fundamental behavioral syndromes or character traits that are at the root of the preponderance of the psychological problems exhibited by adolescents today.

There is a rough rather than exact correspondence in the

relationship between the sins and syndromes: Pride becomes self-centeredness; Wrath, anger; Envy, the driven quality I see in so many kids; Sloth, lack of motivation; Gluttony, eating disorders; Lust, problems with self-control; and Greed, acting spoiled. By taking some minor grammatical liberties, the first letters of the syndromes form the acronym SADNESS. This is apt given the high incidence of worry and depression seen among teenagers today and because a child afflicted with one or more of these syndromes is likely to bring sadness to those who love him.

This section, I hope, will heighten our awareness, giving us a new perspective on what lies at the root of the major emotional problems our kids face and what they need from us in order to develop the essentials of character.

CHAPTER 4

Self-Centeredness

THE EMPTINESS AT THE CENTER OF THE UNIVERSE
(Based on the sin of Pride)

Angels can fly because they take themselves lightly.
—*G. K. CHESTERTON, Orthodoxy*

In the original list of the seven deadly sins compiled by Pope Gregory the Great in the sixth century, Pride was the first sin from which all others flowed.[1] A person afflicted by the sin of pride separates himself from his proper relationship to man and God. Pride opens the door to greed, lust, and envy. A proud person is often vain. He has an excessive belief in his own abilities and an inordinate amount of self-love. He thinks of himself as the center around which the world revolves. The intense focus on ourselves, which is a symptom of Pride, tends to blind us not only to the needs of other people, but also our smallness in the face of a vast and mysterious universe.

Our children are not necessarily afflicted with Pride, but many of them are self-centered. As Pride leads to other sins, it is self-centeredness that opens the door to many of the psychological problems our kids face. It is a paradox that many of our self-centered children are not the haughty, arrogant peacocks we associate with Pride. As children grow into adolescence the amount of self-consciousness they have increases. For some this is only a phase, but many are plagued by a debilitating sense of self-consciousness: they have a heightened awareness of their shortcomings. It's as if they have an anxiety associated with being on stage and not knowing their lines. They're overconcerned with their body image and their vanity can be crippling. They have low self-esteem.

As parents, we somehow think that our children are immune from this condition because we have given them so much—so much love, so many advantages, such a good life. If we had to anticipate pitfalls for our kids, I think most of us would be concerned that they don't wind up thinking that they're better than everyone else. Instead, the opposite is true, and is perhaps due, at least in part, to the high expectations they feel from us. In one way or another, we let them know that they've had all the advantages. And, as we've discussed, they feel a crushing sense of pressure from a culture focused on excess—excessive wealth, talent, and celebrity. Somehow they feel they will never quite measure up.

One of the saddest and most frustrating aspects of being a child psychotherapist is listening to depressed children with low self-esteem talk about themselves. They are as obsessed with themselves as the most boorish narcissist, and their self-image is usually just as far off base. I see kids who are talented, attractive, and kind. They see themselves as ogres and failures; someone damaged beyond repair. I try to convince them that they're okay, that they have lots to feel good about in themselves. They just smile and thank me; my words make little or no impact. They think I'm just trying to be nice.

The initial goal of therapy is to build self-esteem in these kids. In fact, as I'm sure you're probably aware, there is a self-esteem movement in psychology; its primary tenet is that mental health is equated with feelings of self-worth. Schools have picked up on it and there are now curricula for enhancing a child's self-esteem. Some of this makes good sense. As we will discuss more fully in the chapter on "Not Motivated," if your academic self-esteem is low, you don't put much effort into your work, your grades drop, and so you get objective confirmation of your own misconception that you're a dolt.

But low self-esteem is only one side of the coin. What if you think that you're fine just the way you are? Is that unhealthy? Probably not if you really believe it and if your belief has a healthy basis in reality.

As an example of healthy self-esteem, take Cheryl Haworth, a five foot nine inch seventeen-year-old who weighs three hundred pounds. When she was in elementary school, her parents were worried: she was so big! They consulted nutritionists, physicians, and put her on a strict diet—no junk food, sweets, or second helpings. They wanted her to fit in. They knew that boys wouldn't find her attractive and they imagined that she would be miserable and friendless. For her part, Cheryl didn't seem to care about her size. She seemed to like herself fine. She had a lot of friends. She wasn't teased. She was a talented softball player. So her parents finally decided to accept her as she apparently accepted herself and they let her control her own eating. Today, Cheryl is the strongest woman in the United States and a member of the U.S. Olympic weight-lifting team. She's quoted as saying, "I never really got discouraged because I was so big. It's who I was and who I still am." By all accounts, her self-esteem is just fine.[2]

A child or an adult with fragile self-esteem is at high risk for mental illness. Like anything fragile, a fragile sense of self-worth cannot withstand stress. And when someone with low self-esteem tries to hold their world together, a world inside them that often feels on the brink of going to pieces, the means they use often exacerbate their problems.

In *Raising Cain,* I wrote about a boy named Ascher who

had few friends. He wasn't athletic, his social skills were poor, and his family was, in a word, dysfunctional. But he was quite smart and got good grades. In order to protect himself from the real pain that characterized his life, he used a time-honored psychological defense. He was hypercritical, highlighting any real or imagined imperfection in others as if to say: "They are the losers, not me." If the first-string quarterback got a D on a history test, Ascher would mercilessly attack him as a stupid jock. This neurotic defense kept Ascher from becoming really depressed about his own life, but it also limited him. He wasn't maturing and dealing with reality; and, of course, his attack-dog mentality didn't win him any friends. It reinforced the impression that he was, in fact, a loser. But with some help from me and others, and a lot of emotional courage on his part, Ascher turned out fine. As his self-esteem improved, he dropped his hostile relationship with the world.

Too Much or Not Enough?

For the child psychologist, the obvious dangers of pride pose a problem. We want our children to be proud of themselves. We want our daughters to be proud, to have a strong enough self-image to assert themselves—to be able to stand up and resist unwanted sexual advances or harassment. We want our sons to be able to have enough backbone to stand up for their rights on the playground, on the baseball diamond, and in the classroom. Don't we want our children to fly as high as they can, to reach for the stars, to be all that they can be? How else will they successfully make their way in the world? How will they be able to help others if they can't help themselves?

What we don't want is for pride to overwhelm them. We want them to be confident, but not so confident that they ignore risk and danger. We want them to be able to face and overcome challenges and have the sense of self-efficacy that we discussed in Chapter 3. We don't, however, want them to be so self-centered that they are painfully self-conscious, anxious, and ashamed. Nor do we want them to be like the unclothed emperor in the fable, who hides his nakedness with a veneer of false superiority, a set of magnificent new clothes that don't actually exist.

We want them to be aware of the needs of others as well as their own needs. Because of our child-centered world and indulgent parenting style, our kids are particularly prone to cross the line between healthy self-esteem and the excessive focus on self that we worry about in our children.

Before we talk about the natural tendency in young children and teenagers to be self-centered, I want to give you an example of a typical "normal" instance of self-centeredness in kids and one way to begin to nip it in the bud. I draw it from my own experience to show you I am not immune to the indulgent parenting style that we've been discussing.

Julia's Gym Shoes

I learned this lesson one sunny Monday morning this summer when my seven-year-old daughter, Julia, was getting dressed for day camp. She realized her gym shoes had been left at our weekend home in New Hampshire.

"You have to go back and get them," she told me and my wife, Catalina. Julia said this not in a hostile, demanding way, but in a very matter-of-fact tone, the kind that a princess or rock star might use—someone who was used to having their needs met quickly, and with a smile.

"Julia, it's two hours back to the house," said Catalina. "You'll have to wear your hiking boots. We'll get your shoes next weekend when we're back in New Hampshire."

I watched the cheery open face with which Julia usually confronts the world turn into a tight little knot of consternation and despair. "Daddy," she said, turning to me, knowing I was a soft touch. "You have to go. I need my shoes. I can't wear my hiking boots to camp all week. I can't run in them!" This last was said with a trembling voice and tears in her eyes.

How can any parent turn down such a request? Julia's wide-eyed glee brings a smile to my face even as I write this. I've learned, watching her grow up, to recognize within her my own feelings when I was her age. I could see the magnitude of the problem from her perspective—her self-consciousness at being different from the other Nike-clad campers, her worry about being teased, and her foreboding that a counselor might reprimand her for wearing shoes that weren't designed for the fast-paced activities she had planned.

The thought of her clunking around in hiking boots also pained me because, to my great joy and relief, Julia is a gifted athlete and a swift runner in a way that I never was at her age. I was very slow to develop physical coordination, and when I was seven and baseball or football teams were picked, I was often one of the last kids left. In some convoluted way, I identified with her heavy-footwear plight almost as if it were me again facing the pain of being one of the slower runners.

My wife brought me out of my reverie. Maybe she sensed that I was about to come to Julia's rescue, to be her knight in shining armor. Or maybe she was just worried that Julia would miss the bus.

"Look, Julia," she said. "No way can we go get your shoes. You'll have to wear your hiking boots to camp. But I'll make you a deal. I'll buy you new gym shoes today, and you'll be able to wear them tomorrow."

Brilliant, I thought. That should make everyone happy. But then the nagging voice of this book sounded in my head. It asked me, it seemed with a hint of sarcasm, whether buying Julia a new pair of shoes was really the right thing to do. What kind of lesson would we be teaching her? I was trapped. How could I in good conscience write a book that encourages parents to let their children learn how to cope on their own with reasonable amounts of stress, but not put that principle into practice in my own home?

"No," I said. "I think she'll survive the week without new gym shoes." My wife caught my drift right away. "It's true, Julia," Catalina chimed. "You'll have to live without them."

I wasn't worried about the cost of the shoes, and I really wasn't trying to teach our daughter a lesson about responsibility. It wasn't Julia's fault that her shoes had been left in New Hampshire—it was ours! She had been asleep when we packed. Even so, it was the right thing to do to make her cope with this problem. It was important to give her a chance to learn how to adapt to a less-than-perfect world. And we needed her to recognize that her needs were not the only ones in the universe.

How did Julia cope with this shattering of her world? Without another word of complaint. At seven, she adapted easily. And she hasn't retained any ill effects from the gym-shoe trauma. Too often we think we're psychically scarring our kids if we cause them the least bit of pain or suffering. We think we've failed as parents when they're upset with us. I was a case in point, and I should have known better. I didn't want her to experience discomfort and possible social humiliation. It's hard for us sometimes to separate our own needs from the need in children to have limits set—to learn at an early age, even if it's painful, that their needs don't always come first and that the world does not revolve around them. But this is one of the most important lessons that we can teach them.

How We Contribute to Self-Centeredness in Our Children

Even with the best of intentions, parents, especially affluent ones, can unknowingly promote self-centeredness in their children. We are so in love with our kids that we shower them with gifts and attention. We hate when they're upset and we don't want to deny ourselves the pleasure of seeing them happy. As a result, we end up making them feel that they're at the center of all universes, not just our families.

This is not to say that our kids don't deserve our praise and affirmation. They need to know that we love and respect them. They need to know when they have done a good job. But given that many of our kids have so many qualities to admire, it's easy for them to hear almost nothing but praise. The average student in the PPM survey is quite intelligent, far above average, and often very attractive. Or, as a colleague observed, "These kids come from the deep end of the gene pool." On top of this, their parents are affluent and these kids have access to advantages known to few in our society and fewer on our planet. In short, it's easy for them to think of themselves as special because, in many ways, they are—they have special talents, abilities, and privileges.

At my daughters' school, they have recently erected a new gymnasium and library. Each has the major donor's name displayed in large letters on its exterior. I sometimes wonder what it is like for the children of these donors, shooting baskets or studying under the marquee with their name on it. Do they feel that they have special rights or a special pressure to measure up to the family name? What about the gym teacher or librarian—do they treat the donor children in the same way as the other kids? In many cases, yes, just as in many cases the children won't be much affected by the flamboyant display of their surname on the school's walls.

As I write this, I realize (as is so often the case with all of us) that I am partially writing about myself here. In my early twenties I was a laborer on a construction crew, a good job for a kid my age. I was able to get the job because my father had hired the same company to build a new factory. After a few months, the size of our crew was drastically cut. We had finished a big chunk of the job and didn't need as many workers. Mine was one of the few laborer's jobs spared.

The next day the foreman and I were talking about the cuts. I told him I felt bad that so many other guys had lost their jobs while I was kept on simply because it was my father's factory. To my disbelief, the foreman said that my special status didn't have anything to do with his decision to keep me around.

"You're a good worker, kid," he said.

But to this day, the incident nags at me. I'm still not sure whether or not to believe him. Are our indulged and privileged children going to question their abilities and accomplishments in the same way?

With many parents having become enriched (or more enriched) over the last decade, they have more to spend on their most valuable asset: their child. Given the increased pressure to achieve and the increased competition for top admission to top colleges (for every student who gets into Harvard, twelve others get rejection letters), many parents find that their child's school is a great place to spend their money. A recent story in *Talk* magazine put into print what is whispered between private school parents over coffee at the school play or in the carpool line waiting for dismissal—that some of these big donors are trying to buy influence over how their child is treated.[3] The article described parents who demand that teachers be fired or that the curriculum or grading system be changed to suit their child. The important point isn't whether or how often this kind of attempted bribery takes place, but that affluent children get wind of the fact that it is an acceptable way to behave—that there are, in fact, a different set of rules for the wealthy.

Unfortunately, the blessings of talent, good looks, and wealth puts our kids at risk. It's all too easy for them to become self-centered and feel entitled when we reinforce their image of themselves as special. A child who has the sense of having been born with all the advantages often winds up with a confused and distorted sense of who he is, a sense that he is both better than others, but at the same time unable to measure up. He has a full toy box, but a sparsely furnished inner life.

As Robert Coles pointed out in his classic study of privileged children from the 1970s, many suffer from narcissistic entitlement. "Despite their specialness, their wealth and privilege," he writes, "they are unhappy, dissatisfied and empty. All the money and all the possessions, all the rugs and furniture and toys and vacations and savings accounts and insurance policies come crashing on the child's head. The child has much but wants and expects more—only to feel no great gratitude, but a desire for yet more: an inheritance the world is expected to provide. Underneath there lies apprehension, and gloom and, not least, a strain of gnawing worthlessness."[4]

The Narcissistic Child

The most extreme form of self-centeredness is narcissism. In the Greek myth that begot the term, Narcissus falls in love with his own reflection in a lake. His only relationship is with Echo, who merely reflects his words back to him. The modern narcissist is similar—he can only see the world as reflected through him. The only needs that matter are his own. A narcissist might, for example, call you at midnight in a panic. She needs to borrow a pair of shoes for a date the next day because she has just realized that the ones she had planned to wear don't match her new suit. She doesn't think to apologize for getting you out of bed or even consider that you might not want to lend her your expensive shoes. You wonder how she could be so inconsiderate. But the fact is that she isn't trying to be inconsiderate. She hasn't made a conscious decision to disregard your feelings. Rather, like Narcissus himself, she sees only herself and her own needs. It is as if, like Echo, you only exist for her.

What if you don't give her the shoes? She would probably become incredulous and hurt. When we treat an object narcissistically, we disregard its autonomy and experience it as part of ourselves. If it fails to behave as we wish or expect, we may become disappointed or offended, almost as if our arm ceased to obey us or function in the ways we take for granted. This sudden loss of control may also lead to an intense narcissistic injury and rage. But the rage is a defense against feeling the pain of acknowledging the emptiness inside ourselves; the feeling of our own worthlessness.

Seeing the Problem, Starting an Antidote

As we have seen, an excessive focus on self can lead to unhappiness and psychological dysfunction that can be mild and easily corrected, as in the case of Julia and the gym shoes, or more severe and debilitating, as in Ascher's hypercritical behavior, which alienated him from his parents and peers. In extreme instances, self-centeredness can become so severe that a child becomes narcissistic—cutting off any sense of the outer world except as it reflects his own desires and needs and projects his image of himself back to him. In the most severe instances, narcissism can have tragic results, including drug abuse and suicide.

Earlier in the chapter I asked how we as parents can distinguish between a child who is self-centered and, in order to come out of himself, needs help boosting his self-esteem, and a child who is in danger of narcissistic entitlement. It's not difficult to differentiate the more extreme instances of these types in our children. But the lines are often blurred; our kids, even as well as we know them and love them, can be hard to read, especially as they enter adolescence and start staking out their own turf and insisting—rightfully so—on a degree of autonomy and independence.

Unfortunately, there is no recipe that one can follow, no self-esteem thermometer that we can stick in our child's mouth to gauge what they need and when they need it. We must maintain a balance, critically examine what we do as parents, and discuss what we see in our kids with our kids. An increased awareness of the problem is the most important step. Just as my changed perspective about my reaction to Julia's missing gym shoes changed my response to her self-centeredness, other parents will find themselves changing their behavior in unanticipated ways after becoming more aware.

Just a couple of weeks ago I was having lunch with my friend Gary and was asking about how his eleven-year-old son, Seth, liked his new school.

"He adores it," Gary said. "Except that three times a week he's in a carpool with another sixth grader whom he doesn't like. Apparently, this kid is a little odd, a little off, and not popular. The kid makes him uneasy."

When Gary started to think aloud about whether he should drive Seth to school himself to spare him the discomfort of having to ride with this kid, I had to intercede.

"Wait a minute," I said. "Don't you think it might be a good experience for Seth to learn to understand this kid better, or at least not feel so uncomfortable in his presence? It's not like he's being bullied or threatened."

I could sense a weight being lifted off Gary's shoulders. He took a deep breath. "You're right," he said. "That's just what my dad would have said. Whenever we complained about stuff like that, he would always say that we had to do it because it built character."

Gary doesn't have to worry about Seth's self-esteem, but many parents do. A child (or an adult, for that matter) with low self-esteem cannot avoid comparing himself to others and concluding that he is less—less attractive (I'm so fat), less competent (I'm stupid), or less deserving of self-respect (I'm not worthy). He cannot internalize praise. If something good happens to him, he believes that it has nothing to do with his talent or hard work, but, rather, due to luck or circumstances. But if something bad happens, he blames himself.

This child's parents must make him aware of these "negative self-attributions," and make him conscious of the fact that he finds it difficult to take personal credit for any accomplishment. The parent must show evidence to the contrary and try to get him to substitute positive thoughts for the negative ones. Don't hesitate to seek psychotherapy if the pattern continues. In many cases a therapist can help a depressed child break the cycle of negativity.

In the case of narcissism the outlook isn't often as bright. These kids usually aren't interested in changing; they aren't as conscious of their pain as someone who's depressed. They seldom enter therapy and when they do they often don't stay long. The road for therapist and client is harder and it sometimes takes a crisis, such as a drug overdose or other injurious behavior, to begin the process of change.

The Survey Says

How did we measure self-centeredness in the PPM survey? And were the parenting practices associated with self-centered kids?

The survey results pertaining to self-centeredness in children are based on the combined responses to three survey questions: 1) "I am willing to help others when they need help," 2) "I am concerned with the well-being of others," and 3) "Are you regularly involved in community service?" The first two of these questions were scored on a three-point scale, with the high score indicating the greatest concern for others. A yes to the community-service question got a score of one, a no a zero. In order to be considered self-centered, a student needed to score a five or less. One-third of the students qualified.[5]

The next step in the research was to look at those character-istics that are associated with self-centeredness such as gender, age, family income, and the child's relationship with his par-ents. The two parent factors that related to greater self-centered-ness were whether the child had a fair or poor relationship with his father and whether they were required to do chores for their allowance.

A poor relationship with one's father is related to low self-esteem and depression. Research indicates that a father's ap-proval is important to both boys and girls. It is only after a child feels supported and loved by his father that he can develop the healthy self-esteem that is a prerequisite to devoting at least part of his attention to others. Psychologists don't have the final answers on why fathers are so important. It is probably due, at least in part, to the fact that mothers tend, on the whole, to do a better job of child rearing. They are consistently there for their kids. Fathers tend to be more variable in how they respond to their children. Also, we are still a patriarchal society and boys especially feel that a father's approval is necessary to vali-date whatever they undertake in the world. In *Raising Cain,* we highlighted the "Father Hunger" we saw in so many boys and its devastating effects on their self-esteem. These findings from the PPM survey also point to the need for fathers to get involved in their children's lives.

Doing chores for an allowance connects an adolescent to a larger group—in this case, his or her family. Participation in team sports could also provide such a connection. Kids learn that the needs of the team are more important than the needs of the individual. They're bound to hear the adage, "There is no 'I' in T-E-A-M" or "Together Everyone Achieves More."

Without this kind of connection or lifeline, kids tend to retreat into themselves, and the reality of the larger world and other people's needs recede. The child who has to be responsible for doing the dishes or picking up after himself more easily makes the connection between his actions and the needs of others.

—

CHAPTER 5

Anger

THE RAGE INSIDE THE MACHINE
(Based on the sin of Wrath)

> But unto Cain and to his offering, he [God] had not respect. And Cain was
> very angry and his countenance fell.
>
> —*GENESIS 4:5*

I've tried to keep my son from playing with toy guns, but it's almost impossible. What can I do?

I'm asked some form of this question almost every time I speak to a group of parents about *Raising Cain*. Parents who were raised in the 1960s and 1970s (especially those of us who lean even a little to the political left) are often concerned about expressions of violence in their children. When their children are small, they keep "war toys" out of their hands; when they're older, they worry about violent video games or expressions of anger.

Parents seem to expect that I will join them in their concern about the evils of toy guns and war games, but I don't. Instead, I tell them that, unless they have some fundamental religious belief that prohibits the use of these toys, it's usually not worth the effort it takes to try to make your house a demilitarized zone. It's not, I tell them, so much that I think war games are okay, but that there are too many other, more important, things about raising kids that require our time and attention.

I would tell these parents more if I had the time, but there are other hands in the air, mothers of fatherless sons, parents of sons who have been bullied, parents of boys with Attention Deficit Disorder, fathers who want to connect with boys who seem emotionally cloistered. Much of what I would tell them is here in this chapter. I would tell the parents of boys, and, maybe even more important, parents of girls, that the expressions of anger they should worry about won't come out as war play. The most dangerous and prevalent forms of anger in our kids are those that they keep buried deep inside themselves.

The common belief among parents that expressions of anger by children are something to be concerned about is relatively recent. Carol and Peter Stearns' 1986 book, *Anger: The Struggle for Emotional Control in America's History*, argues that the open expression of anger has decreased in the United States during the twentieth century,[1] partly in response to new levels of emotional control that were required at work to assure that the large groups of people assembled in urban factories and offices were able to function efficiently. There was also an element of snobbishness to it. The upper classes wanted to distinguish themselves from the waves of new immigrants, who were often very unabashed in their expressions of anger. In short, anger was seen as vulgar.

By the 1970s, guru baby doctor Benjamin Spock, influenced by his own reaction to the violence of the 1960s and his general concern about the Vietnam War, wrote that children should "learn that anger should be controlled at all times, and they should be carefully led away from indulgence in symbolic expressions of anger ranging from play with toy guns to television representation: Mature behavior consists in solving problems without anger."[2] Over the last thirty years, parents and teachers have increasingly seen expressions of anger as signs of psychological disturbance. The recent spate of suburban school shootings in places such as Columbine High have only served to heighten parental concerns about anger and violence.

In the PPM surveys, parents expressed more concern about violent media than they did about sexually explicit media or even drug or alcohol use. This response to one of our questions from a mother of two teenagers (one boy, one girl) was typical. We asked: "How wrong do you think it is for a thirteen-year-old to see an R-rated movie?" She wrote: "I can't help but add a comment since surveys kind of force you to make statements that can be misconstrued. For instance, R-rated movies with sex plus bad language we would consider not wrong at all. While those with graphic violence would be extremely wrong."

The Bible warns us against anger. The ultimate expression of anger—murder—is prohibited in the ten commandments Moses brought down from Mount Sinai. Wrath or anger is a deadly sin not only because it can lead to violence, but also because it can eat away at a person and make him miserable: "He who cools down his anger is a healer of his own heart, but wrath is the rottenness of the bones" (Proverbs 14:30). In *Raising Cain*, Michael Thompson and I used the biblical story of the first murder to illustrate what can happen when a boy has difficulty dealing with disappointment and rejection. But the aphorism that opens this chapter shows that Cain's disappointment also leads to a different manifestation of anger, namely depression. Cain's countenance fell. He became sad when God spurned him.

Our generation's commitment to nonviolence would be fine, except that too often vigilance on one front means inattention on another. Keeping tabs on the character development of our kids can be harder than being a sleep-deprived air traffic controller at O'Hare. Instead of worrying about raising little Rambos, it would be better if parents focused on talking to their kids about anger's less obvious manifestations: meanness, depression, and low self-esteem.

What Are They So Mad About?

Earlier in this book, we presented statistics from the PPM study on the rate of depression among teenagers. Over half the teenagers we surveyed said that "they were unhappy or depressed." More than one in four said that they had been so sad or hopeless at some point in the two months that they stopped doing some of their usual activities. These are potentially serious symptoms. In contrast, no child, to my knowledge, had been in a physical fight, much less charged with assault and battery, or, God forbid, attempted murder.

When parents were asked about symptoms of depression in their children, their ratings were lower. Two-thirds said that their kids were not unhappy, sad, or depressed. Thus, many parents of these affluent kids (at least a third of them) are probably missing the signs of emotional distress in their children.[3]

Not only affluent kids have these problems. Teenagers from all economic backgrounds have high rates of depression, as indicated by suicidal thoughts. Recent national data shows that in 1999, one-fifth of all high school students seriously considered or attempted suicide.[4]

Why are our children angry and depressed? Seventeen-year-old Robertino Rodriguez in a *Newsweek* article on teenagers says, succinctly: "There's a lot of anger in my generation. You can hear it in the music. Kids are angry for a lot of reasons, but mostly because parents aren't around."[5]

Robertino echoes the national survey results. A poll commissioned by Bill and Hillary Clinton quantified the parental "involvement gap." It showed that parents think they know what's going on with their kids. They say that they talk with them about important issues in their kids' lives. But their kids disagree. In fact, the number one concern expressed by kids was not having enough time together with their parents. Adolescents were three times as likely as their parents to say that this was a problem.[6] Other research shows that if teenagers don't spend time with their parents—if they don't eat dinner together as a family, for example—they're at double or even triple the risk for sexual activity at a young age, drug use, and emotional problems.[7]

Melissa

The first thing that almost everyone notices about Melissa is how beautiful she is. Her long dark hair frames an angelic face. She has long legs and a slim waist; the "perfect body" according to her best friend Allison. As if that wasn't enough, her parents are well-off. She lives in a nice house, drives a new car, and summers on Cape Cod at the family's vacation home. The gifts she has been given make her the frequent object of envy and lust. But my take on her was different. As the psychological consultant to her high school, I need to notice other things—the fact that despite her beauty and affluence, she is not very happy, for example.

I got to know Melissa informally at first. I would often show up in her first period class to visit Mike, my best friend at the school, who also happened to be her teacher for sophomore English. I liked these unscheduled visits because they gave me a better sense of the school culture that existed outside the privacy of my office. It also gave me the opportunity to get to know kids like Melissa.

Melissa would usually make it a point to say "hi" if she saw me in the hall or talk to me for a few minutes about college or some assignment she had. Eventually, she started coming by to see me in my office to talk about other things. She was worried that she might be developing an eating disorder. She had thrown up once after gorging herself on chocolate cake and had been weighing herself every day. After a few meetings it was clear that she didn't have a full-blown eating disorder (the symptoms of which we'll discuss in Chapter 9). She was not bulimic. She was dieting, but she wasn't starving herself. So we often talked about other things. On one of these occasions we talked about a weekend experience she had had about which she felt deeply troubled.[8]

DAN: So what did you do over the weekend?

MELISSA: Allison and I went to our house in Nantucket. She had never really been there before.

DAN: Were your parents there, too? Did you have a good time?

MELISSA: It was okay. Allison got kind of weirded-out by my parents though. She had actually never spent much time with them. Mostly before it was just a "hi, bye" kind of thing. But over the weekend we were with them the whole time. Or not really, I guess. That's what weirded Allison out. She couldn't believe how much they just left us alone. Like on Saturday night we were all supposed to go out to dinner together, but my parents bagged at the last minute because of some social engagement they forgot about, so they just gave us the credit card and said, like, "Go wherever you want."

DAN: Why do you think she thought that was so weird?

MELISSA: Well she has, like, perfect parents I guess. She actually talks to them about stuff. They eat dinner together as a family all the time. They almost didn't let her come with me to the house because they wanted her to go to a play with them.

DAN: So Allison thinks that your parents don't give you enough attention.

MELISSA: No, she thinks that I should like call the child abuse hot line or something. She goes like, "Your parents buy you this really expensive car because you get half-decent grades, and you can buy almost any kind of clothes you want. But—God!—they're about as warm as an ATM machine." Then she, like, apologizes because she realizes that she is being kind of harsh and we kind of drop it, but I've been thinking about it ever since.

DAN: Do you think Allison's right? I have the hot line number here somewhere.

MELISSA: Very funny, Dr. K.

DAN: Sorry. What I should have said is, "How did you feel about that?"

MELISSA: That's better, now you sound more like a real psychologist.

DAN: Thank you. I hope to get the hang of this therapy thing someday. But enough about me. Are you upset about what Allison said? Are your parents really that cold?

MELISSA: I guess that I never thought about it too much before. You know my dad has always been so busy with his real estate deals and ever since my mom got her MSW, she is always doing therapy or on the phone with some other shrink. I guess I sort of came to accept it all as normal. I mean, my little sister is always on their case about not being around, but maybe because I'm the oldest I think it shouldn't bother me or something.

DAN: Does it make you sad? Do you miss them?

MELISSA: It's hard to say. I'm not so much sad that they aren't around, but that even if they were, they'd be clueless about how to have a normal relationship with me. I'm not sure that they were cut out to be parents and it kind of makes me mad that they went ahead and had kids. I can't tell you how many nights my sister and I have dinner with the nanny. I mean, why did they bother having us?

DAN: I would think that would hurt.

MELISSA: (growing quieter) It does. I mostly feel bad for my sister.

DAN: My guess is that you feel pretty bad about it for yourself, too.

MELISSA: Yeah. Maybe I do.

Melissa's may be an extreme case, but in its essence it's one that characterizes our age. An amazing set of statistics compiled by Sandra Hofferth of the University of Michigan shows that time spent in family togetherness is becoming increasingly rare. Between 1981 and 1997, the amount of time families spent talking with one another declined 100 percent.[9] Furthermore, roughly 21 percent of children between the ages of six and twelve with employed mothers are regularly without adult supervision for some time during the week when not at school. This may be because, as parents, we're working so hard. According to a recent *Newsweek* article, fathers are working outside the home, on average, 50.9 hours a week, mothers 41.4 hours.

I am one of these statistics, too. As I type this, I am sitting at a desk two hundred miles from my home because I have gone into hiding for a few days to write. My kids were mad when I left. They complained that I go away too much, that I'm always working. Objectively, I know that I spend more time with my kids than most dads do with theirs. I try to comfort myself by thinking of the pathological fathers of kids I've seen in group counseling—absent fathers who don't call or send a birthday card, who say that they'll show up at basketball games but rarely do. Thinking about these deadbeat dads doesn't give me much comfort. I silently vow to be a more involved father when this book is done, but my unyielding conscience reminds me that I made that same vow when I was writing my last book. Then I wonder whether I'm being too indulgent. Would it be good for my kids if they always had me at their disposal? Like most fathers and many mothers, I'll continue to struggle to find the right balance between work and family.

It's clear, however, that Melissa's parents aren't even thinking about these issues. Over time, as Melissa and I talked, she came to believe that there wasn't a lot she could do to change her parents. But she did begin to realize that she could work on her reaction to them. She recognized that her brief bout of bulimia might have been a way to get their attention; her dieting, a misguided attempt to create a body they would notice. Melissa went through a grieving process, wrestling with denial, anger, and sadness. She eventually came to accept the fact that her parents aren't really there.

Melissa's case hints at the many forms anger can take. Anger is rarely a pure emotion. It is usually accompanied by other feelings, such as sadness, jealousy, fear, frustration, or irritation. One form of anger that many parents of my generation will be familiar with is the outrage expressed by young American war protesters during the Vietnam War. Some social critics theorized that those expressions of anger—occupying buildings, throwing rocks, or sit-ins—were the public expression of the private, pervasive anger that young men and women felt against their often remote, materialistic parents.

But the anger we see in our children, while it may have some of the same roots—a younger generation expressing its dissatisfaction with the complacency of its elders—is usually expressed very differently. In the last chapter of this book, I'll explore some of the social consequences of parental noninvolvement and children's reactions to it, but here I simply want to alert you to some of the varieties of anger that you, as parents, may see in your kids.

A Freudian might interpret body piercing and tattoos as signs of self-directed anger; a way of causing pain, much the same way a severe depressive will inflict nonlethal cuts on themselves with a knife or razor blade. This interpretation doesn't always apply, however. Piercing is also likely to rivet any parent's attention. It can also serve to embarrass parents—it can be a way of hurting that can be denied and justified by the child as an act of individuality, not hostility.

I'll never forget a kid I once counseled who checked into the rehab center for which his father was chairman of the board. The boy had a cocaine and alcohol problem that was out of control. But his choice of his father's center was designed to get back at the man who he felt had ignored him, who hadn't given him the help and attention he needed when he needed it. Other kids express their anger in different ways. At some level eating disorders, underachievement, or refusal to do homework can be symptoms of anger.

Some forms of anger are more justifiable than others. Jesus was angry when he swept the merchants and moneychangers out of the temple because they were defiling it. The abolitionist Frederick Douglass lambasted Americans who professed to be Christians, but failed to speak out to oppose slavery; his anger helped end slavery in this country.[10]

We admire anger when the cause is just. But it can also scare us because it is the stuff out of which revolutions are made. Just as affluent but deprived children like Melissa can be angry, so too can children who are deprived but not affluent. Sometimes the relative disparity between the haves and the have-nots provides the fuel for the anger. In a society such as ours, when the gap between the wealthy and both the middle class and the poor grows larger, I think many of us would agree that at least some forms of anger over these inequities is justified.

What Parents Can Do

Our advice here may seem contradictory. On the one hand, I have said that we shouldn't give our kids too much or overmanage their lives; we should encourage independence and self-sufficiency. We should strive to obtain some balance and distance on what for many of us is a child-centered world. On the other hand, our data on anger suggests that if we don't give our kids enough time, understanding, attention, and love, they'll become chronically angry or depressed.

Kids know how much effort it takes to be a good parent. They know when you care enough to create a structured family life that provides a regular, ritualized forum for closeness and intimacy—the family dinner, the shared vacation, participation in their interests and activities. We need to strike the balance between the mother who warms up her son's mittens before he goes skiing (or the father who's ready to rush out and buy his daughter a new pair of gym shoes) and parents who are so preoccupied with getting and spending and advancing their careers that they neglect their kids. Both parenting styles are all too prevalent today, and both have their dangers.

The PPM survey results clearly show how deprivation of this kind—not spending enough time with kids, not taking enough interest in the things they do, not being emotionally close enough to maintain a good relationship—can lead to either anger or depression. The PPM findings speak to the same parenting issues identified by the White House report we mentioned earlier and other national surveys. Adolescents want more time with their parents. Our data show that if they don't get it, they either pass on the pain they feel to others in the form of meanness or turn it against themselves in the form of depression.

The PPM surveys show a consistent pattern whether adolescents or their parents filled them out: there is less likelihood of an angry, mean, or depressed teenager in families that regularly have family dinners or attend religious services together. The risk for depression or anger is further diminished if a parent and teenager can maintain a good relationship, if they can enjoy spending time together, and if they feel comfortable talking about things that are important to them.

If this doesn't sound like your household, where should you start? Schedule regular activities such as family dinners, Sunday brunch, afternoon walks, or even watching a favorite weekly television show together. At my house, my kids know that Tuesday nights are set aside for pizza and a video. It's predictable, fun for everyone, and it doesn't take much effort.

I got this idea from a group of kids I worked with whose parents were divorced. I met with them once a week and always brought pizza. I initially thought of the pizza as a bribe for getting them to show up. Once I had them captive, I figured that we could focus on the important issues in their lives, the pain and anger that they felt over their parents' divorces. But after about a year of these meetings I realized that I was all wet.

The talking about "issues" wasn't the most important part of our meetings. What was important was that they saw that I cared enough about them to show up on time every week. I think the fact that I brought food was also important at a very deep level. If there is one constant feature of parenting throughout the animal kingdom, it is feeding our young. The mother bird dropping worms into the mouths of her voracious nestlings, the six tiny puppies rooting around to find an open nipple, the human father with pureed bananas on his tie playing "airplane" with a baby spoon—all are examples of the way we as parents nurture our children. Young animals die if their parents don't feed them. I believe that this is one reason why food—regular, predictable family dinners—means so much to kids.

I explained this once to a friend with four children, and he came up with the idea of having him and his wife take just one of their kids at a time out for dinner every Monday night (the other kids stayed home with a sitter). He said that over a short period of time it made a huge difference in the quality of his relationships with *all* his children.

But the way to good relationships with our kids doesn't have to be through food, and it certainly doesn't have to be developed only through food. I know a brilliant therapist, the head of a large hospital-based clinic, who gives the same homework assignment to each parent who comes to him with a tale of a troubled child. He tells the parent to spend one hour that week doing something together with the kid that they *both* enjoy.

"Sometimes that's all I have to do," he told me. "The parent will come back and say, 'I had forgotten that we could actually like each other. We had been doing nothing lately except arguing about homework (or body piercing, or tattoos, or loud music, or you can fill in the blank). But that hour was really great for us. It made all the difference. We're going to make a habit out of it.' "

Let's all do the same thing. Let's all resolve to make a habit of spending time with our children. There is nothing more important that we could do to help an overtly angry child, or a child who has turned his or her anger inward and become listless, anxious, and depressed.

CHAPTER 6

Driven

THE HURRIED, WORRIED CHILD
(Based on the sin of Envy)

The pressure to cope without cracking is a stress in itself, the effects of
which must be tallied with all the other effects of hurrying our children.
                                                            —DAVID ELKIND
                              The Hurried Child: Growing Up Too Fast Too Soon

"You'll never get into Harvard." Ron had heard this taunt from
his pal John countless times, but it still rankled. "It doesn't
seem fair, does it? Your grades are better than mine. Your SAT
scores higher. But I'll get in and you won't."

The taunting wouldn't have been so irksome except that
there was some truth to it. Ron was a better student than John,
but John was a legacy candidate—if accepted, he would be a
fourth-generation Harvardian.

Both boys knew how hard it was to get into Harvard. Their
college counselor had warned them that Harvard turns down
2,500 high school valedictorians every year. Last year Harvard
accepted only two kids from their top rung prep school. One
was a nationally ranked squash player who knew the Harvard
coach; the other, a girl who got in, according to Ron, because
she is one-fourth Lakota.

To accomplish his goal, Ron studied obsessively. He was always at the top of his class. He had joined his school's chess and fencing clubs, loaded his schedule with Advanced Placement (AP) classes, and woke at five each morning to practice rowing, either on the Charles River with the school crew team, or, when it was too cold for that, on a rowing machine in his basement. His summers were filled with rowing camps, community service, and internships at local software companies. He had started an e-business with a friend that provided tips and sample essays for kids applying to college.

But Ron still knew that getting into Harvard was a long shot for him and a pretty good bet for John. And he hated his friend for it.

Ron reminded me of lots of other kids in my practice— driven kids whose parents tell me they won't come down to dinner because the kids say they have too much homework. There's no question that getting into a top-ranked school is harder than it used to be (there are more kids, more of them apply to college, and there is still only one Harvard). As we've already noted, our expectations for our children have changed. Our society supports external signs of achievement—high grades, big salaries, symbols of wealth and conspicuous consumption. The bumper sticker "he who dies with the most toys wins" is ironic—to a point. Many of us snicker, but live our lives as if it was true. This is why our freshmen have a bottom-line mentality. Ron doesn't want to go to Harvard because of the brilliant teachers there who will stimulate his mind. He wants to go there for status, wealth, and to do better than his peers. So that *he* will be envied.

Ron is typical of this new breed of child. He works day and night with tunnel vision. There's a kind of edge of desperation about him; a joylessness. He seems to be running full out in a race where he's constantly looking to either side, wondering who's edging past him. (Since this writing, we learned that Ron was accepted to Harvard—and Yale!)

Envy, defined in its simplest terms, is the feeling that we want something someone else has; and we often feel we are more deserving of whatever prize it is that they possess, be it a lover, an honor, a job—or a lifestyle. When we envy a person we usually end up resenting them. We also end up resenting ourselves for our inability to obtain what they have. We focus on our lack of talent, brains, and looks. For Pope Gregory, envy was a deadly sin because it separated us from other people. When we feel envy, how can we obey the golden rule and love our neighbor as we love ourselves?

Envy causes us all kinds of psychological pain. We feel impotence, shame, anger, and anxiety. Our self-esteem is threatened. Envy is related to pride in that it assumes a certain amount of entitlement. In an age where enviousness is rampant, it is particularly sad that we don't rejoice at the good fortune or accomplishments of others. Ours is a society of comparisons— who has the most luxurious office, who drives the best cars, who has the nicest clothes, and the biggest house. I was shopping in an exclusive clothing store recently. A huge sign proclaimed: "Before they see your house, your car, and your wife's diamonds, they'll see your tie." Our kids follow suit. They compare grades, their accomplishments on the athletic field, and, eventually, like Ron, the rank of the college that accepts them.

Top college-admissions officers are beginning to see problems in what used to approvingly be called their "highly motivated" applicants. A recent *New York Times* article says admissions officers are "bemoaning the slick packaging of applicants and discussing ways they might encourage high school students to be truer to themselves rather than aspire to some model they think will get them into the Ivy League. At Harvard, the admissions office has written a paper lamenting that students seem like 'dazed survivors of some bewildering, lifelong boot camp.' "[1]

"Ratcheting Up"

A recent television commercial, aired during sporting events and aimed at Baby Boomer men, shows a sleek sports car racing along a twisting mountain road, an abyss to one side, a cliff face on the other. The camera swoops down on the flawlessly performing machine. An unseen narrator's hypnotic voice tells us that when we win in sports, business, or life, no matter how much we pretend to be gentlemen, underneath what we're really saying to ourselves is "I'm better than you are." The message of the ad is clear: drive a faster car than the other guy; play to win, even on the road. It's the same with most car commercials: earn more to be better. You are what you own.

Today's role models are people like Michael Jordan, Bill Gates, and Jennifer Lopez—people with stupendous wealth, outstanding talent, and whose names are on all our tongues. We're not emulating Jesus and Buddha. Our kids don't have pictures of the pope or Mother Teresa on their walls. We've seen a shift from a concern about character to a fixation on wealth, status, celebrity, and power.

It's only natural that our kids are looking for role models. Imitation is one of the most important ways that people learn. Is it only the rich and famous we want them to emulate? How can we instill in them a sense of healthy competition and the drive to succeed without it getting out of hand? We want them to learn to push their limits, to fulfill themselves. But how do we keep them from becoming obsessed, envious, and driven? Let's look at why this is a problem for kids today.

In the 1999 study that we referenced in the last chapter (p. 94), "Changes in American Children's Time, 1981–1997," Sandra Hofferth reports that children's free time has declined 16 percent over that sixteen-year period (from sixty-three hours per week to fifty-one hours per week) and, furthermore, time not spent in school or doing regular activities such as eating and sleeping grew more structured. Sports participation doubled. Time in school and studying time also increased.[2] In short, changes in our children's lives mirrored our own. Not only do most parents chronically feel that they don't have enough time to do what they need to do, but children are also caught in the "time crunch."

Competition has risen over the same period. Recently, Governor Gray Davis of California signed a law that raised the eligible age for kindergarten from four and a half to five, saying that tougher state standards demand more maturity. In well-off communities around the nation, the *New York Times* reported in autumn 2000 that principals and teachers were saying parents are going a step further, delaying their children's entry into kindergarten until age six in the hopes that they would be better prepared for the challenges. In 1991, 6.5 percent of parents held back their children one year. In 1995, it was 9.7 percent.

"The notion that kindergarten is a place where kids come and play is an anachronism," said Karen Lang, deputy superintendent of schools in Greenwich, Connecticut. "The expectation by the professionals is that whatever children do, it's going to be time that leads to some kind of ultimate achievement. That doesn't mean it's not fun and kindergarten doesn't look at all like it used to, but things are done for a purpose."

In 2000, North Carolina's social studies curriculum suggested that kindergartners choose samples of their work to discuss with their parents at student-led conferences. They further suggested that kids be able to identify facts in nonfiction literature. In Connecticut, the language arts curriculum requires kindergartners to read books out loud, be able to give written and oral responses to questions about books read to them, and "make valid inferences about characters and events using supporting details."

Competition starts before birth. Parents play Mozart to their kids when they're still in the womb, read aloud to their newborns, and take their two-years-olds to art museums to expose them to the Old Masters. In an effort get a head start on the competition, parents vie for spots in feeder preschools, like Crème de la Crème. Nearly all exclusive private elementary schools accept children as young as age three or four.

At some public schools, local school boards have responded to the need to "ratchet up" by cutting "extraneous" courses from kindergarten such as art and physical education and adding more reading and math. "In this business, as in any other, everybody looks down," Robert Fiersen, an assistant superintendent in Manhasset, New York, told the *New York Times*. "The high schools look to the middle schools, the middle schools look to the elementary schools, and the elementary schools look to kindergarten. Ultimately, you're going to end up with prenatal reading."

Our kids pick up on this. They want to please us, to do the right thing. They have become converts to the message that they must succeed even if the costs are high and that they have to start thinking early about their future.

The influential 1983 report from the National Committee on Excellence in Education, "A Nation at Risk," was key to the ratcheting up of the amount of homework kids do and the push for a longer school year. "History is not kind to idlers," wrote the committee. "The time is long past when America's destiny was assured simply by an abundance of natural resources and inexhaustible human enthusiasm, and by our relative isolation from the malignant problems of older civilizations. The world is indeed one global village. We live among determined, well-educated, and strongly motivated competitors. We compete with them for international standing and markets, not only with products but also with the ideas of our laboratories and neighborhood workshops. America's position in the world may once have been reasonably secure with only a few exceptionally well-trained men and women. It is no longer."[3]

Parents and schools responded to the call to arms in this report. But I think as we're beginning to see in the anxieties of our children, and the lack in many of them of what I've been calling an inner life, the results have not always been positive. As we discussed earlier in the Reed Larson study, commonplace school conditions typically don't foster initiative and self-direction in our chidlren.

What Are We Driving Ourselves Toward?

One of the pleasures of my work is the number of older, experienced educators I get to meet in the course of a school year. The following comes from a series of talks I recorded with Rick, the headmaster of a renowned Connecticut prep school. He commented on the growing amount of drive he'd noticed during his tenure.

DAN: You've been a close observer of teenagers for quite some time now. Let me ask you the question that everybody asks me: How have kids changed in the last thirty years?

RICK: The most noticeable change is that their backpacks are so much heavier now; they've changed from being one-strap backpack kids to being two-strap backpack kids. When I came here in the seventies and into the eighties, there was an informality about the way kids approached their work. Today they are so much more focused—I'm hesitant to use the word *driven*—but I think that the word applies. School for them is work. Serious, hard work.

DAN: Toward what goals are these students working so hard, in your opinion?

RICK: Well, I'm not sure they always know what the goal is. In the short term certainly, the goal is a college—I don't know that it is much clearer beyond that. They'd articulate something but I don't know how realistic it is. The strongest idea is that they've been instilled with a puritan work ethic.

DAN: Who instilled this idea of a work ethic so strongly?

RICK: Well, I think it's been put there by society. By parents. By us. You know, we're all guilty of it to a certain extent. You know, each of us in that triumvirate would, I think, blame the other two.

The Tyranny of Homework

A law passed by the California legislature in 1901 reads: "No pupil under the age of 15 in any grammar or primary school shall be required to do any home study." California wasn't alone. According to a *New York Times* report: "During the 1920s and 30s, New York City public schools banned homework until fourth grade; San Diego banned it through eighth grade; and Sacramento had a prohibition on elementary-school homework for 45 years, until 1961."[4]

This article further notes that the American Child Health Association classified homework as a form of child labor. In extreme cases, homework was seen as causing crooked spines, night terrors, and nervous breakdowns in children. "Drill and kill," they called it.

Times have certainly changed. By the mid 1980s, the Japanese were on a roll. They had purchased Rockefeller Center and the Toyota was a far better car than a Chevy or Ford; we envied the booming Japanese economy. In response, the study we looked at earlier, "A Nation at Risk," attacked our educational system, saying it was lagging behind other industrialized nations. Our children didn't study enough. So it was that homework returned to fashion. Since 1981, homework time for children under twelve has increased 50 percent.

As Rick, our seasoned headmaster, noted, the weight of increasing homework puts more pressure on kids today. Literally! They have heavier backpacks than they did twenty years ago. The American Academy of Orthopedic Surgeons has also noticed this trend, citing the epidemic of back, neck, and shoulder pain caused by too-heavy backpacks in our children.[5]

Homework, extracurriculars, AP courses, and creating a résumé that will appeal to college admissions officers—these are blips on our kids' radar screens. Trying to keep up with enormously busy schedules and the demands they place on themselves takes its toll on our kids, psychologically as well as physically. Too many of our "superproductive" kids are heading for burnout, as the following interview with Kim shows.

Interview with Kim

When I interviewed Kim as part of the PPM survey, she was a very bright, personable student at the top of her class in a suburban Boston public school. She was as popular as she was busy. What I first noticed was her incredible energy. She spoke quickly, sat on the edge of her chair, and sometimes even got up when we talked, bubbling over with enthusiasm. I soon found myself wondering how much of this was exuberant good spirits. The more she talked the more I began to worry that she was presenting me with yet another face of the driven child.

DAN: The first thing I'd like you to do is to describe yourself in terms of your likes and dislikes and kind of who you are and where you fit into the school, your group of friends, that sort of stuff.

KIM: Okay, well I'm very, very busy here. I'm here each day until nine-thirty at night. I do a lot of different stuff. In terms of classes I take a pretty well-rounded load. I take math, physics, Spanish, English, and history.

DAN: Will you be doing the AP thing?

KIM: Of course. I took AP history this past semester. In terms of extra-curricular classes and afternoon programs, I'm involved in the arts pretty big time. I've been in plays every semester since I've been here, which has been three years so far.

DAN: What grade did you start here in?

KIM: Freshman year. I've been in a play every year and this year I've been in three. I play tennis and soccer and I'm in three singing groups and I'm on the student council.

DAN: That's a lot. And you do homework sometimes?

KIM: [laughs] Yeah, sometimes I do homework. And then I also coach little boys' soccer and on the weekends I hang out with my friends. I've got a lot of good friends whom I love. I'm happy here.

DAN: So how do you manage your time?

KIM: I don't know. In the fall it was the hardest because I had soccer and then I had the lead in the play *The Breakfast Club* and I didn't sleep a lot, I got very run down. I got mono, in fact, which wasn't surprising given my schedule. I guess I just had to budget my time. I went to bed really late and I woke early, you know, used my free time at school as best I could. But I mean I made sacrifices definitely, but it was worth it, definitely worth it.

DAN: Are your parents supportive of everything that you do?

KIM: Yeah, they are. When I told them that I had gotten the part in the play, they didn't want me to take it or they wanted me to quit soccer to keep an even keel. I had matches on Saturdays and tournaments over the weekends and so they thought that that was a little bit too much to handle. But once I told them that it was something I was prepared to do, that I knew it was going to be a lot of work and they accepted that I was actually going to do it, then they were supportive. But in the beginning they kept warning me that I was going to get run down.

DAN: But as you said, you did end up getting mono.

KIM: Yeah, I did. And they kind of told me so, but I still don't regret doing it at all.

I sometimes feel like an anachronism among educators. I strongly question the assumption that we should design our children the way we design computers. The goal should not be to make children faster processors of information, to have them multitask rather than giving them the time to lose themselves in something they love.

Cheating

Pope Gregory pointed out the "trunk and branch" metaphor to describe the relationship between the deadly sins and their lesser counterparts. Lust, for example, may lead to infidelity, wrath to physical violence, and greed to thievery. The seven syndromes in Part Two of this book also have associated branches. In the present case, being driven may lead to lying, cheating, and poor health. One of the greatest problems about the driven quality that characterizes so many of today's students is that, divorced from any greater sense of meaning, it can lead to moral difficulties. As we saw in the case of Connor, many of today's kids think that winning is everything—the end justifies the means.

Interview with Keri

We asked Keri, a twenty-nine-year-old, sixth-year teacher at a high school in a suburb of Los Angeles, about the relationship between the pressure her students feel to excel and cheating. Keri is seen as one of the school's best teachers. She runs the school's peer counseling center and is the faculty member students are most likely to turn to in times of trouble.

DAN: Is cheating a problem here?

KERI: Big time.

DAN: Is that maybe because there is so much emphasis placed upon—

KERI: [Interrupts] Doing well? Yep, and they cheat all the time.

DAN: How is that dealt with? Do parents get involved?

KERI: Yeah, I had a big cheating problem here; the girl got kicked out of my class. She just blatantly cheated from the boy next to her and then she denied it, which was dumb.

DAN: Yeah.

KERI: And then she told me she studied with him the night before, so I just asked him and he said no. So they kicked her out. But if you get caught cheating once, if you wind up with a semester grade of a B they'll give you a C, if you get caught twice you get an F. I'm not sure what it's a product of—things being so fast paced, the feeling that "I gotta do well," or that they'll die if they don't get into a great college.

DAN: I would think that pressure must enter into it. I mean, if you feel like you have to get an A or whatever and you don't feel quite prepared, you'll do sort of anything to . . .

KERI: That's sad but true.

Certainly not all kids cheat, no matter how much parental pressure they have to contend with. But the increased pressure on kids today has increased the amount of cheating in the schools we surveyed, according to the anecdotal reports of both teachers like Keri and school administrators. Connor's case is not atypical. Opportunities for cheating have always existed in schools and the Internet may have increased them. But in today's cutthroat academic environment the motive to cheat has grown stronger. The increased drive for success has made taking the easy way out an irresistible temptation for too many of our children. In the PPM sample, nearly 10 percent of the students said that they lie or cheat quite often. Another 40 percent said that this is true some of the time. Amazingly, 15 percent of the students we surveyed expressed the view that cheating in school isn't even wrong.

The Importance of Sleep to Your Child

The most prevalent form of cheating is cheating on sleep. Kids need sleep, lots of it. And most of them, especially the driven ones, don't get it. According to a number of key reports, teenagers need 9.5 hours of sleep. But studies have shown that many of today's teenagers are ending up with as little as six hours of sleep on most nights. They are almost always sleep deprived, and nodding off in class is increasingly common.[6]

We typically allow our teenagers to set their own bedtimes as they get older, but as we saw with Kim, the pressure they feel to complete homework, study, and take part in sports, school plays, and clubs—not to mention trying to maintain a social life—makes sleep a low priority. Like the proverbial candle, these teens are burning sleep time at both ends of the day. They are required to rise at dawn to make it to school on time; then they stay up late to study, surf the Net, or socialize on-line. Health experts say that sleep deprivation over long periods may pose the same kinds of dangers as do other, more widely recognized, health risks such as smoking or lack of exercise.

The need for sleep is especially important since the teenagers in our survey have fairly high rates of depression and anxiety. These are problems that can be caused by too little sleep (or the stress of trying to be perfect). How do you feel when you don't get enough sleep? Don't you think the same might also be true of your teenager, who requires a lot more sleep than you do?

I've tracked this in my own home. Thursday nights were usually the worst of the week in terms of family disharmony because, by then, everyone was worn down from the combination of accumulated stress and sleep deprivation. The kids were cranky, my wife was cranky, and I was cranky. It made for some unpleasant evenings. Eventually we bit the bullet and made sure we were in bed at a reasonable hour during the week so that we could get enough rest. It was enormously helpful in maintaining good feelings in the house.

Before parents look elsewhere for the cause of their children's emotional problems, they might first look in the bedroom and see if it's being used in the proper dosage.

Research Findings and Recommendations

Although getting enough sleep may reduce some of the consequences of being driven, it doesn't get at the cause. One way to get at that is, of course, to not be driven yourself, and to let your kids know through your words and your actions that you think that there are more important things in life than getting ahead. Take a cue from David Davenport, the departing president of Pepperdine University in California. He had said that he learned more frying doughnuts in his father's bakery than in any university. So instead of sending his daughter to soccer camp he pushed her into a summer job as a chambermaid. Her summer of hard work made her see things her dad's way. "At Malibu High School, most of the students were doing marine biology camps and SAT prep classes," she said in an interview. "I don't miss that environment at all."

Fighting the prevailing current that drives kids to polish up their résumé is not easy. In talking with parents, school officials, and students around the country, I have been struck by how much agreement there is that we, as a society, have gone too far. Yet everyone blames everyone else for the inability to change. High schools say their pressure comes from pushy parents and college admissions officers. Parents blame the schools for requiring too much work. Students say that they are being robbed of their childhood, but don't see any alternative other than to play the game by the rules that have been given to them.

The PPM research findings for the driven syndrome were some of the most interesting in the survey. As with the other syndromes, our measurement of the syndrome, while imperfect, was still revealing. The survey questions concentrated on whether the children felt the need to be perfect and whether they were often worried. The majority of the teenagers surveyed, just shy of 60 percent, were driven according to these criteria, with girls more likely than boys to qualify. For the other syndromes teenagers in the survey typically rated themselves as more distraught than their parents rated them. But for the driven syndrome, the results of parents and teenagers agreed.

Driven kids also reported poorer relationships with their dads than their nondriven counterparts. As we discussed in Chapter 4 on self-centeredness, recent research has shown that a good relationship with one's father protects kids against drug use and low academic performance. It's important that a child feels that he has earned his father's respect (PPM findings showed, by the way, that this was true for both sexes). Kids who didn't feel that they had gained their father's respect were not only at risk for adverse behavior, but were often prone to anxiety. Our findings suggest that children who do not feel their father's respect doubt their self-worth. Fathers show respect by taking an interest in the activities their children enjoy, by being honest with their kids but not gratuitously critical, and by listening to what their kids have to say and how they feel with an open mind and heart.[7]

A last finding in the survey particularly intrigued me. When we looked at the extreme end of the spectrum, kids rated by their parents as both very worried and very driven, there was only one significant risk factor: whether the family had an annual income over $100,000. Kids who were affluent by this standard were over three times as likely to suffer from the driven syndrome. This was one of a handful of problems studied in the PPM survey that relate directly to wealth.

This set of findings once again underscores the magnitude of the problems facing teenagers today. Too many of them feel anxious, exhausted, and driven. Childhood should be a time of wide horizons; a period in our lives where the world opens before us and we can be carefree at least some of the time. Instead, many of our best and brightest children are narrowly focused, accomplishing much but deriving little pleasure from their accomplishments, their white knuckles clutching the steering wheel as they speed along a dangerous road toward the image of success a competitive, materialistic society has fed them.

CHAPTER 7

Not Motivated

THE LITTLE ENGINE THAT COULDN'T CARE LESS
(Based on the sin of Sloth)

> O, that this too too solid flesh would melt
> Thaw and resolve itself into a dew!
> Or that the Everlasting had not fix'd
> His canon 'gainst self-slaughter! O God! God!
> How weary, stale, flat and unprofitable,
> Seem to me all the uses of this world!
> —WILLIAM SHAKESPEARE
> (Hamlet, *Act I, Scene 2*)

The teenagers you'll meet in this chapter are at the opposite end of the spectrum from the driven, worried, high achievers of Chapter 6. They aren't striving for straight As and admission to Ivy League colleges. They're weary stragglers and unmotivated adolescents who are listless and depressed.

Take Scott, a tall, heavyset fourteen-year-old middle child living with his middle-aged parents in a middle-class suburb. His low grades belie his high IQ. He doesn't study and rarely completes assignments on time.

"I just don't care about school," he told me repeatedly in our first few sessions. "I think it's stupid."

"Having him in class is like trying to teach a large lump of clay," said Scott's history teacher, who had urged me to speak to the kid. "But I know Scott is bright. Occasionally his eyes light up and he's with me. Then he seems to sink back into a morass of numbness and lethargy. I don't mean to be unkind, but he reminds me of a sloth! He drags himself around this place in a daze. There are always a few of these kids who seem to have had the life drained out of them."

Sloth was one of Gregory's seven deadly sins. Perhaps to us sloth doesn't seem quite as deadly as pride or lust, but in Gregory's day, Christians demonstrated their devotion by ascetic practices. They knelt in prayer on the cold, stone floors of monasteries. They left their families and villages and became hermits, living in solitude in huts and caves. They fasted, prayed, and spurned the temptations of the flesh. True devotion to God required religious zeal, and for Gregory the enemy of zeal was sloth, or acedia, literally, "not caring." Without zeal, a monk would look like Scott studying for a history exam—going through the motions of prayer and fasting in a joyless way.

Along with acedia, lack of joy was the other component of sinful sloth. Gregory called it *tristitia*—melancholy, ennui, or, in today's parlance, depression. Some devout Christians still believe that joylessness reflects a lack of religious faith. A number of psychiatrists I know lament that a portion of their Christian patients interpret their melancholy as a test of faith and look for a cure through prayer, not therapy or Prozac.

Although I don't discount the power of religious faith, I have a different view of the causes of the world-weary, apathetic, and "what's the point?" attitude that afflicts kids today. As parents, we're a driven bunch, and this drive trickles down to many of the teenagers we studied. Some of them are carried away by it, as we saw in the last chapter. But there were also many adolescents that we saw in the PPM survey for whom the drive to succeed was overwhelming and who had given up as a result. I also see acedia in affluent kids, or kids who have been materially indulged. Having everything handed to them on a silver platter saps their motivation. They are like diners at the end of a seven-course meal—not very hungry.

You Can't Fire Me, I Quit

Through our sessions, I came to see Scott as a leading candidate for poster child of the not motivated syndrome. Scott is not sated from growing up with too much money. His biological parents, Rachel and Seth, were divorced when he was six. He now lives with his mother and Josh, her husband of three years. Rachel met Josh, a principal in the same district where Rachel teaches, at a public school conference. Scott doesn't get to see Seth, a bartender who winters at a Jamaican resort and summers on Nantucket, very often. Scott's older sister is an academic powerhouse and a gifted pianist. Scott's younger brother is a ten-year-old version of Scott.

Any good psychologist knows that there is always more than one reason why a person behaves as he does. Scott is a case in point. His lack of zeal has something to do with being "loyal" to his "real" father, who never had much use for school. It also derives from Rachel and Josh's intense focus on academic success. They frequently talk about how important it is to do well in school. After all, college is expensive and good grades will help their kids get scholarships. Scott's IQ proves he has the brains to excel. What his parents don't realize is that their expectations and demands are counterproductive. This was made abundantly clear to me in a moving scene at a workshop for teachers I recently led in New Jersey.

The day was winding down. One woman stood up to ask a question, not about a student of hers, but about her own son.

She looked to be in her late thirties and struck me as sincere, humble, and diligent. She was concerned because her son wasn't doing his homework. The boy was in eighth grade and had started to slack off. The fights at home over his missed school assignments were escalating. She was concerned that his bad grades would hurt his chances in life. Not only that, he attended the school where she taught. "If he fails, it's going to look bad for me, too," she said, not unreasonably. "It will be, 'How can she be a good teacher if she can't even manage her own son?'

"What should I do?" she asked me.

I advised her to back off and let the school take over. I said that I had seen too many families where almost the only thing that the parents and kids do together is fight about homework.

"It's not worth it," I said. "Your son needs more important things from you than pushing him to do his homework. I know you feel that you're in both a personal and professional bind. But try not to take it personally when he won't work."

She was clearly not convinced. The room became silent. It was clear she was in pain, and I hadn't helped her much. The tension mounted; no one knew what to say. Then an older woman stood up, a retired English teacher who looked to be in her seventies. There was weariness and pain in her voice. The topic had reminded her of her own son's painful adolescence. She turned to the younger teacher and said slowly, "Leave him alone. I used to hound my son in English. I worked with him constantly, but it did no good. I finally let go, much too late, and let him own it himself. He flunked English every year until he was a senior."

This retired teacher gave us all the benefit of her hard experience. Tears welled up in the younger teacher's eyes; she had been touched by the truth in the older woman's words. In many instances, it is not a form of indulgence to leave a kid alone when he is not doing his homework. It's important to stay involved with what's happening at school, but sometimes it's more effective to let the pressure to perform come from the school itself. Parents often don't realize how sensitive their kids are to their criticism, real or imagined. There is a deep need in our children to please us, even if it seems sometimes they couldn't care less. Criticism isn't as loaded when it comes from a teacher. The trick, as we'll see a little bit further along, is to work on other areas of your child's life, other aspects of your relationship with him. Homework and the larger issue of a lack of motivation are often symptomatic of other, deeper problems. If you're constantly fighting with your kid over homework, something's wrong. Take a step back and imagine how that time together might feel to him if you weren't fighting, but talking to him about something important to him, whether it's recent trends in ska music, the latest trades in the NBA, or Half Pipe, the awesome skateboarding course in California.

I gave Scott's parents the same advice: lay off; lighten up. But it blew right by them. Parents like Scott's need to know that effecting changes in behavior involves working on what is going on inside their kid. This is rarely accomplished by reminding a teenager how badly he's screwing up his life—disappointing you and himself—or how all he has to do is try harder. Instead, parents must do the more difficult work of determining why their child's energy has dwindled—why he seems so sad or bored and no longer seems to care if he fails.

Is That All There Is?

The PPM survey data indicated that coming from an affluent family made a teenager more likely to be driven. But some affluent kids have the opposite reaction to wealth. A prime concern of parents with substantial assets, especially nouveau riche parents, is the potentially ruinous effect of their wealth on their kids. I discussed this issue with Barbara, a therapist in West-chester County, New York, who often works with wealthy parents.

"A lot of the rich parents that I see are very worried that their kids are, in fact, not going to do anything except be rich," she said. "And that they have no values, no interests, and no politics. In this one family that I've been dealing with for years now, the parents lie to the children about how much money is in their trust fund. When the mail from the executors of the trust funds arrives, they hide it. They don't want the kids to open the letters. They're convinced their kids would just drop out of school. And in one instance, actually, they were correct to be worried. One of the kids hit the age of eighteen and said, 'Look, I just got two million dollars, so why the fuck do I need to go to college?' So, yes, the parents are worried about their kids leading empty lives because they've seen it so often among their rich peers."

Millionairess Christina Onassis, whose inheritance spun off a yearly income of about $50 million, died from a heart attack at thirty-seven, probably induced by drug abuse. As one analyst, a close friend, wrote, "Ms. Onassis had a pathetically wasted life! With all of her millions, she did absolutely no good for anyone—especially herself. Where were the foundations, the good works, attempts to help the poor, hungry, and homeless of the world? No, for her it was a tour of the road of self-indulgence. Obsessive sex, consoling herself with $300 bottles of Diet Pepsi (flown in by her private jet to her remote hide-aways) and all the rest."[1]

A wealthy parent's nightmare! Newspaper and magazine articles have recently come out entitled: "New Millionaires Worry About Raising Brats," "Brat Control on Easy Street," and "Battling Affluenza." To quote from *U.S. News and World Report*: "The latest malady afflicting the nation's super-rich appears to be affluenza. Symptoms include sloth and selfishness and a general disconnect from the average Joe."[2]

Parents' concerns have also stimulated workshops and support groups. In Manhattan, an area with 41,000 families with a net worth in the double-digit millions, a recent seminar on how to successfully raise rich kids was the talk of the town among the city's wealthiest parents. A focal point of the workshop was how to keep kids from becoming unmotivated. Merrill Lynch now offers psychological services to their clients with $100 million-plus portfolios to help their children deal with the emotional impact of wealth.

Cheese in the Maze

How do our kids, who have all the advantages, who seem poised to revel in all the riches that life has to offer, lose their motivation, their zest for life, their connection to the world? How do they fall into acedia and *tristitia*? The Greeks had a persuasive explanation for this phenomenon of world-weariness among the privileged, in this case about the most privileged you can get—the gods on Mount Olympus.

Prior to Homer, who composed his great epics in the eighth century B.C.E., the Greeks thought of their gods as a happy, hedonistic group of immortals. But by Homer's time, the gods were portrayed as moody and irritable, despite divinity's perks. Their psychology of displeasure mirrors the rich idler. The gods became jaded. They bickered over small slights and petty insults. As Solomon Schimmel writes in *The Seven Deadly Sins*: "Precisely because they have no needs, no desires that could not be instantly gratified, they also came to have no hope. Hope and longing are founded on unrealized desires, on wants for which effort and energy must be expended and luck implored. Lacking any hope, because there was no need for it, the gods became sunk in restlessness."[3]

As I mentioned in Chapter 3, this loss of hope is a major attribute of the modern syndrome that produces kids who seem overwhelmed by lassitude and consumed by aimlessness. Happiness often emanates from having goals and working toward them. We've all felt the dopamine-induced happiness that comes with moving toward a desired goal. This motivated, goal-directed happiness is the antithesis of the not motivated syndrome.

Research with lab rats in mazes clearly illustrates this point. You can train a rat to run a maze for five grams of cheese. It will run it at a certain speed. But if you double the amount of cheese, the rats will inevitably start to run the maze faster than they did for the five grams. However, once the rats get used to this bigger piece of cheese, they begin to slow down.

To anthropomorphize: the rats' behavior is energized by the bigger piece of cheese; they're eager to get the bigger reward. If, on the other hand, the reward is decreased, the rats get depressed and slow down. It's the same with our kids. They are already reaping the rewards of the richest society the world has ever known. Why should they keep running?

The rich have built up a tolerance for happiness. Henry James described this same phenomenon in his late-nineteenth-century masterpiece, *The Portrait of a Lady*:

> "I am bound to say you look wonderfully comfortable."
>
> "Well I suppose I am, in most respects." And the old man looked down at his green shawl and smoothed it over his knees. "The fact is, I have been comfortable so many years that I suppose I have got so used to it I don't know it."
>
> "Yes, that's the bore of comfort," said Lord Warburton. "We only know when we are uncomfortable."[4]

What the PPM Survey Tells Us

To gauge motivation, we asked adolescents in the PPM survey whether they felt as if they were working to their intellectual potential. One out of every four teenage boys in our sample said that they weren't; the rest said that they were working to their potential at least "some of the time." Fewer girls classified themselves as chronic underachievers, just under 15 percent. When we took a closer look at who these unmotivated teens were, a fascinating story emerged. It was as if that elder English teacher spoke to us through the numbers on the computer print-out. For both boys and girls, those who said that they were not working to their intellectual potential were those who felt that their parents were pushing them too hard—who felt that their parents' demands for academic achievement were excessive.

In an interesting Freudian twist, it was the opposite sex parent who had the most influence. In fact, for boys, the only factor that related to underachievement was whether they thought that their mother was pushing too hard. For girls, the most significant factor was the level of their father's expectations, but other factors contributed as well, including how they rated their relationship with both their parents. This is one of the most difficult challenges of parenting—knowing when to back off and when to push. In the vast majority of cases in which I've been involved, parents who pressure their kids to achieve find their plans have backfired. If you find your child is an underachiever, close communication with his school is the most important first step in figuring out when to push him at home and when to let your child find his own way with the help of his teachers.

Not surprisingly, kids who rated themselves as not working to their intellectual potential got significantly lower grades than those who said they worked to their intellectual potential at least some of the time. This was especially true among the girls where the motivated and unmotivated were separated by almost a full letter grade (B average versus a low C+ average). Kids who expressed more dissatisfaction in their relationships with parents had lower grades as well.

This finding confirms research on other representative groups of teenagers. Several large national samplings have noted the importance of the quality of the relationships between parents (especially fathers) as instrumental in promoting academic achievement. The findings from our survey also confirmed that when families ate dinner together and when parents attended to their child's interests, motivation to succeed increased.

Kids who feel too much pressure from parents often shut down. The PPM survey findings on depression presented in Chapter 5 confirm this. The factors that are associated with depression are some of the same ones that are associated with the not motivated syndrome. Unfortunately, we tend to increase, not alleviate, the pressure when our kids shut down in response to it. As one of my psychotherapy mentors once told me, "Don't expect a family to abandon a child-rearing strategy that isn't working. Expect them to do it louder and stronger." I find myself guilty of this at times, and I have seen it in my casework with families. When I try to get my children to clean up their rooms, I nag, then nag some more. After a while, the nagging becomes laced with vitriol. The rooms are still a mess. That's when I realize that I've fallen into the trap of "louder and stronger." Too often when we get frustrated we "go to the whip." We apply pressure, pump up the volume, and increase the severity of our discipline.

* * *

The teenagers who participated in the PPM research are sending us a message loud and clear: The "louder, stronger" approach doesn't work. If you want your child to respond with excitement and energy to the demands and expectations of our high-pressured world, the first step is make her feel secure and comfortable at home. This isn't done by tightening the screws, but by slowing down. When a child is filled with lassitude, when she's not performing up to her potential, when she seems disengaged and dull and shut down, what she's often telling us is, "Stop with your busy life. Spend time with me." That is the crucial first step to help her rekindle her spirit.

CHAPTER 8

Eating Problems

WHAT'S EATING OUR CHILDREN?
(Based on the sin of Gluttony)

> Gluttony is an emotional escape. It is a sign that something is eating us.
> —*PETER DEVRIES*
> *Comfort Me with Apples*

> You can never be too rich or too thin . . .
> —GLORIA VANDERBILT (attrib.)

Eating disorders are a huge problem among children today. As a culture, we are obsessed with food, eating, not eating, and our appearance. Due to the increased self-consciousness that frequently accompanies adolescent development, this obsession with food, weight, and body image is most pronounced among the young. We've seen large increases in recent years in childhood obesity. Bulimia and anorexia are rampant among teenage girls. And we're starting to see the appearance of these diseases in teenage boys, too, along with a "pumping up" craze, or "bigorexia," the unhealthy obsession with altering the body to conform to a muscular ideal.[1]

Recognizing Our Kids' Eating Problems

For dinner each night, Mike and Amy's only child, Laura, insists on peanut butter and jelly on white bread, sliced diagonally, with trimmed crusts. When her parents try to get her to eat fruit, a hamburger, or, God forbid, a vegetable, Laura screams, "I don't like that!" Inevitably her parents give in. Mike is tired from his long commute and wants to eat in peace. "By the time she's in college her diet will have changed," he tells Amy. Besides, with his busy schedule, he sees so little of his daughter that he wants dinnertime to be harmonious rather than combative. Laura is such a delight when she's happy; what's the harm in wanting warm, close, family time? Is there anything more precious?

Perhaps. The inability of her parents to guide her toward better eating habits is part of a larger pattern. They don't like to say no to Laura because it upsets her so much. So they indulge her. Like most of us today, Amy and Michael want their child to be happy more than anything else in the world. The sight of her distress is almost too much for them to bear—so what Laura wants, Laura gets.

Mike's right, Laura won't die from eating only peanut butter and jelly on white bread, at least not when she's four years old. But what about the future? Are Mike and Amy putting Laura at higher risk for health problems? Possibly. Children's eating habits are shaped by their parents—how they eat and what they feed (or don't feed) their children. When the habits children acquire are unhealthy—when their diets are unbalanced and they eat too much junk food—they're at risk for becoming a member of the growing population of the obese. Nutrition is a long-range family issue, and healthy eating habits start early. In families with a genetic propensity for heart disease and diabetes, children as young as five or six can show early warning signs of high cholesterol or poor sugar control. While Laura isn't likely to suffer in the short term, missing the opportunity to teach her to enjoy a variety of more nutritious and wholesome foods while she is still young may very well set her up for unhealthy eating habits later in life.

The Overweight Child

Pope Gregory considered gluttony a deadly sin because it turned attention away from the divine and mired you in the flesh. He advocated fasting as a way to morally cleanse oneself and approach God. Today, in most segments of our society, fasting isn't a moral imperative: gluttony is a physical rather than a spiritual problem. Eating too much or too little is bad for you—in fact, it can kill you—and it often has psychological roots.

The prevalence of obesity among children and adults has increased over the past three decades in the United States and other industrialized nations. The rise began in the early 1980s when surveys found around 5 percent of children to be obese. The rate of obesity has been accelerating with no signs of slowing. Almost 11 percent of our children today are obese. They're not alone. Epidemiologists estimate that one-third to one-half of adult Americans are significantly overweight—a percentage that has more than doubled over the past century and continues to rise. Obesity contributes to the premature deaths of approximately 300,000 Americans each year.

Concerns over the rise in childhood obesity sparked the first national summit on nutrition in thirty years. In May 2000, experts convened in Washington to discuss the problem. President Clinton gave a radio address in which he said that the vast majority of Americans don't have healthy diets. "We're eating more fast food because of our hectic schedules, and we're less physically active because of our growing reliance on modern conveniences," said the President. "As a result, more and more Americans are overweight or obese, including one in ten children."[2]

Why do we have such bad eating habits? And are indulgent parents at least partially to blame for childhood obesity? In order to begin to answer these questions we have to understand some of basics about the *feeling* of hunger and eating.

It's a cruel irony that one of the characteristics that historically has helped us survive the lean times is killing us in times of plenty. Human beings have adapted to unpredictable and often scarce food supplies by storing up energy reserves when food is available. We're drawn to foods that are high in sugar, fat, and salt because they tend to have the highest concentrations of energy (mangos and marrow versus wild leeks and carrots). All warm-blooded animals do the same thing. But now the vast majority of us in the industrialized world (and our pets) have access to a limitless supply of great-tasting food. Our bodies tell us to eat it—and that's just what we do.

It gets worse. A growing body of research suggests that even people of normal weight eat too much. People (and other animals) who eat less live longer. In experiment after experiment, reductions from 30 to 70 percent in caloric intake, while still maintaining a balanced diet, have resulted in decreases in body weight, substantial increases in longevity, and significant improvements in various indices of health: lower levels of blood glucose and insulin; lower blood pressure; higher rates of DNA repair; enhanced immune functioning; greater physical endurance; the postponement of age-related declines in protein synthesis, bone and muscle mass, learning ability, and spontaneous locomotive activity; and a delay in the onset of numerous age-related diseases, including cancer, autoimmune disease, diabetes, hypertension, and kidney disease.

Ironically, the person most at risk in modern societies for this smorgasbord of health risks has the metabolism and body type that would have been an advantage for most of human history. He has an insatiable appetite and the ability to use the energy generated from food efficiently, and to store the excess calories as fat to see him through the lean times. We are up against it from the get-go, biologically conditioned *not* to resist that extra slice of chocolate cake, and to reach for the super-sized fries.

But why the sudden increase in obesity among adults and children? No one knows for sure. Is it our sedentary lifestyle? A diet high in simple carbohydrates? Perhaps the flood of food ads, especially those for fatty or sugary foods aimed mainly at our kids, make it harder to resist temptation than it once was.

Shaping Your Children's Attitude Toward Food

Unlike most other early childhood behavior problems, overeating tends to be stable, continuing through later childhood and into adulthood. And the strongest predictor of childhood obesity is overweight parents, a reflection of the eating habits, not only the genes, that parents pass on to their kids. We shape our children's attitudes toward food—both what they eat and how much. Which brings us back to Laura, Amy, and Mike.

Research on how children develop food preferences demonstrates that indulgent parents like Amy and Mike can contribute to unhealthy eating patterns in their kids. It seems kids are born with a taste for sweet and salty foods. Fatty foods are also usually a big draw. No wonder kids like French fries and candy.[3]

Like all other omnivores, humans are neophobic when it comes to food; we don't like to sample strange foods, especially when we're young. Instinct is what turns a child's nose up at green beans, although he's never tasted them. It's maddening, I know. But we humans can learn, and, occasionally, we do. As one nutritionist says, "If kids are never exposed to broccoli, they are never gonna like it." The addition of a green vegetable into the diet of a child can seem to be a struggle akin to scaling Everest without oxygen. But take heart! Hard as it is to believe, studies show that infants who are initially disgusted by green beans reach eagerly for them after ten days of gradual exposure. Here again, the tyke fulfills his evolutionary destiny: once an animal knows through experience that a food is safe to eat, it no longer fears it.

Easier said than done. My oldest daughter, now 11, is a lifelong vegetarian. My wife and I avoided giving her meat when she started eating solid foods. It wasn't a conscious decision; it just seemed healthier. As she grew older, we started to worry about whether she was getting enough protein. Our pediatrician encouraged us to start trying new foods on her, especially meat and fish. It was a struggle to say the least. Although she wasn't bad about trying new vegetables or carbohydrates, she was adamantly opposed to meat. Even the resemblance between veggie burgers and hamburgers turned her off: she won't touch them unless they are crushed into tiny pieces and mixed with rice. We now have a child that prefers kidney beans to hamburgers, artichokes to hot dogs, and peas to tacos. As she got older her dislike of the taste of meat was transformed into a philosophical opposition. It's not that my wife and I are opposed to vegetarianism: we wholeheartedly support her. But we now realize that the choices we made for her when she was young may have ended up putting her at risk for a protein-deficient diet.

A Lean Larder, Smaller Portions

Hunger is based more on cues from the environment that on an internal state. Our hunger at mealtimes is not a response to our body's need for fuel, but our anticipation that good-tasting food will soon be available to us. As our usual mealtime approaches, our pancreas responds, like Pavlov's famous dog, and secretes insulin. This lowers our blood sugar level, and we feel hungry. If, however, we don't eat, our blood sugar soon returns to its previous state and our feeling of hunger passes. How many times have you heard someone say, "What time is it?" in response to the question "Do you want to have lunch?" Our bodies have a conditioned response to mealtimes, whether we truly require more nutrition at that time or not. Parents can help their children combat overeating by both attending to their own eating habits and by helping their children learn to listen to their bodies' messages. Trying to help your child determine whether or not he's bored, lonely, angry, or truly hungry when he tells you he's "dying of starvation" can be a first step in teaching kids to eat out of hunger, not habit.

Parents can also contribute to their kids' poor eating habits by stocking the house with lots of different kinds of junk food because, if you buy it, they will eat it, hungry or not. The term for this in hunger research is "sensory-specific satiety," which means, simply, that if we are given only one kind of food to eat we feel "full" until a different good-tasting food is offered. You may be more familiar with this as the "I can't believe I ate the whole thing" phenomenon. After gorging themselves on a big meal, many people will eat past the pain barrier when dessert arrives at the table. In fact, 81 percent of people in a recent poll said that on many occasions, when they have a lot of their favorite foods around, they will eat until they feel ill.[4]

Parents also play a big part in shaping a child's sense of how much is enough. If our plates are always piled with food, our kids will tend to think gargantuan portions are the norm. Young children learn from us what to eat, how much to eat, and what foods go together.

The lesson here is not to starve our kids. We don't want to subject them to the Spartan regimen of Gregory's monks. But we do need to take a hard look at their diets. We need to make deliberate choices and stick by them, even if they cause some initial tension. PB&J's or macaroni and cheese every night for dinner is not a good parental policy decision.

We need to realize that often, when we indulge our children around food, we are indulging ourselves. We dread their displeasure, we don't want to play the heavy, and we tell ourselves that our lives are stressful enough without turning the dinner table into a battleground. We want family time to nourish us emotionally. We want harmony and laughter. These aspirations are fine, but not when they get in the way of our kids' developing healthy habits.

Food and Money

How our bodies look—our weight in comparison to our height—is not only relevant to physical health, but, like fashion, also indicates social class. Not only can the wealthy afford to wear expensive clothes, they also have the free time and money to be serviced by health clubs and personal trainers. The rich can afford liposuction. By the late teenage years, the relationship between socioeconomic status and being overweight is set. Not only are the economically disadvantaged among us fatter—obesity is a more serious problem among poor, urban Hispanics and blacks than other socioeconomic and ethnic groups.[5] It has not always been the case that rich people were thinner; in fact, when being poor meant that one did not have as much to eat, fat was beautiful.

Among teenagers, it's hard to be both fat and popular. As one thin, blond, beautiful high school senior told us: "You don't see many fat people around here. Everyone is pretty much thin and good-looking. Otherwise you really stand out."

The kids in the schools that participated in the PPM survey are exposed not only to intense academic pressure but also incredible pressure to look good. Being overweight is a sign of being poorer than your peers, less cool, and less popular. Many of the teens at the schools we visited, therefore, went to extreme lengths to keep from getting fat.

Not Eating Enough and Body Image Dissatisfaction

When it comes to psychological problems among adolescent girls, the first thing that pops into people's minds is anorexia (self-starving) or bulimia (self-induced vomiting after one eats, to avoid gaining weight). In most people's minds, the stereotypic anorexic is a pretty, upper middle-class white girl who can only like herself if she's emaciated.

In the past, eating disorders were more common among affluent white girls, and they still are pretty much restricted to industrialized countries, but there has been a trickle down effect. Current research shows that eating disorders now cut across income lines in the United States.

We won't belabor the observation that the ideal body type for women has changed over the last three decades. I have been told that if one compares the film version of *Star Wars* (1977) with the newly released digitized version, the dancing girls have been slimmed down. By today's standards, they looked too fat.

The following interview is with Denise, a seventeen-year-old who's in great shape, and one of her large, surburban, Boston public high school's outstanding athletes. In the past, she's struggled with her body image and weight, but now feels that she has things under control; she's neither too fat nor too thin.

DAN: Do you think eating disorders are common at this school?

DENISE: I wouldn't say common, but I would say that it's a very bizarre situation because a lot of girls feel that it's an admirable trait.

DAN: Admirable to have an eating disorder?

DENISE: Yes, which is so, so warped. It's unbelievable. But you find a lot of girls saying things, such as, "Well, I only ate like a rice cake at lunch today," and, I mean, they don't necessarily have an eating disorder or some kind of personal problem, but their attitude affects other kids who might be struggling. It kind of brainwashes them into believing that starving yourself is a good thing. It's like psychological warfare.

Parents often have to fight an uphill battle against unhealthy cultural messages about body image, not only from the media but also from other family members and peers. It is easy to get sucked in, especially when a lean body has become such a big status symbol.

Narra Perfects Her Body

Narra, a graduating senior, tells a similar story about the girls at her Massachusetts prep school. She also looks like she should listen to herself more closely. Although not Calista Flockhart thin, Narra does seem to fit the description of the typical undernourished American female adolescent lamented by the people at the Centers for Disease Control and Prevention.

DAN: What is it like for girls at your school? Are there a lot of eating disorders and are they more common among the more affluent kids?

NARRA: I think that there's a ton of that here, you know— eating disorders. My very best friend is so anorexic and it's so hard to deal with. I mean I've kind of watched her go through it and it's . . . I think that it's definitely a problem. I'm sure it's a problem at most schools like this. A lot of it doesn't so much have to do with body image and control, but just because other things in her life kind of went wrong and she focused it on her body. And, I don't know, I think there's a lot of pressure, I think, that you have to be perfect. I'm sure it's that same with guys. They don't really direct it toward their bodies as much. But I don't think that as a whole people here have a lot of confidence, self-confidence. But that could be just the age, too.

DAN: You talked about this pressure to be perfect, where do you think that comes from?

NARRA: It probably comes from people's families and society—the media. I mean, you watch MTV, and God, all you see are like these tiny girls, tiny beautiful girls that are so unaverage, but that are kind of taken as the average because that's all that's on TV. Just kind of social pressure from friends and stuff. There are always comparisons between your bodies, like when you are sharing clothes and all that.

DAN: Have you had that pressure to be perfect, do you feel, or . . . ?

NARRA: Yeah, but I mean I'm definitely guilty of wanting to be perfect, but you kind of have to logically take yourself away and say, like, MTV isn't average, and, no!, I'm not gonna get influenced by that. I think, through my art, I've kind of, like, expressed a lot of my feelings toward eating disorders. And kind of getting away from what society feels someone should be. That helps.

Many writers have discussed the unhealthy cultural messages that bombard American girls. *Reviving Ophelia*[6] and other books reveal how girls with low self-esteem—no self-confidence, in Narra's words—are especially susceptible to psychological warfare.

The New Male Body

Anecdotal accounts suggest that anorexia and bulimia are on the rise among men. Estimates indicate that as many as one out of every six new cases of eating disorders is male.[7] In the PPM survey, there was a similar ratio—there were six girls with eating problems for every one boy. For those boys not concerned about losing fat, they can worry about being buff enough and become obsessed with gaining muscle mass. They want a six-pack—the rippled stomach muscles so noticeable on muscular male models.

Dr. Harrison Pope, a psychiatrist at MacLean Hospital in Belmont, Massachusetts, has done research on this trend in men toward body-muscle dismorphia. He has looked at how the GI Joe doll dimensions have changed since it was introduced in 1964. Even in the 1980s, the doll's proportions reflected those of normal men. But in the last twenty years, the image of the ideal male has changed. There is a far greater emphasis on musculature, and GI Joe has followed suit. The doll now looks like a hyper-masculine caricature with a bulked-up physique.

It is not surprising then that the boys we interviewed in the PPM survey were at risk both for starving themselves to avoid gaining too much weight and succumbing to the pressure for muscles that often results in the use of steroids or creatine.

There has been increasing concern about the use of over-the-counter diet supplements by boys who are trying to bulk up or otherwise improve their athletic performance. Indeed, a startling one out of every six boys in our sample had used creatine in the last month, and 5 percent had used steroids during the past year.

Androstenedione, or "andro" for short, is a steroid that increases the body's production of the hormone testosterone, which is responsible for the fact that men have more facial hair, lower voices, and more muscle mass than women. Andro was developed by East German researchers in the 1970s. They used it in an attempt to boost the performance of their Olympic athletes. Andro was introduced commercially in the United States in the mid-1990s. Marketers claim that a 100-milligram dose of the stuff increases testosterone by up to 300 percent and lasts for about three hours.[8]

The Association of Professional Team Physicians, composed of team doctors from professional sports teams, has recommended that andro be banned from all competitive sports because of the unfair advantage it gives and because of the health risks. Prolonged use of andro can lead to heart disease and often causes marked personality change, including a propensity for violence.

Andro is one of the common substances our teenaged boys are using to shape themselves. The other substance is creatine monohydrate, a compound produced by the body that helps release energy in muscles. Creatine is used to provide power in short bursts, such as swinging a baseball bat. Sales of some supplements received a huge boost when reporters revealed that St. Louis slugger Mark McGwire used andro and creatine during his successful bid to break Roger Maris's home run record. His main rival in the home run race, Sammy Sosa, did not use andro, but did, reportedly, use creatine.

Both creatine and androstenedione are classified as supplements under the Dietary Supplement and Health Education Act of 1994 and are available over the counter. Nevertheless, some drug chains and health food outlets are refusing to stock andro because of possible health risks. When I went to buy some (for research purposes only) I had little trouble obtaining creatine, and DHEA was also readily available (a testosterone-stimulating steroid hormone similar to andro). An Internet search revealed numerous web sites with easy mail-order access to andro, DHEA, and similar supplements. In short, these products are readily available to your son.

Things have changed for boys; they now live in a *Baywatch* world where they, too, are objectified as sexual beings. Just as they have done for so many years with women, marketers are using men's bodies to sell products. Many people (women especially) remember a Diet Coke ad that showed an office full of women with their noses pressed to the window watching a buff construction worker peel off his shirt on his lunch break. This was the first in a parade of ads that changed the way we think about men's bodies. Marketers and advertisers use anxiety about manliness and sex appeal to sell men and boys products that will relieve insecurities. Andro and creatine manufacturers are the beneficiaries of these cutural changes. Our sons are the victims.

Research Results

The findings of the PPM survey show that depending on how we interpret the data, there are either a large number of overweight kids in our sample or only a few. The index of weight most often used among nutritionists is the body mass index (BMI), which is computed in metric units and describes the ratio of weight to height. The formula is weight (in kilograms) divided by height (in meters squared). A BMI of nineteen or less is the cutoff that recent research suggests is optimal for long life, although this number represents the lowest limit of what is considered healthy for BMI by the Centers for Disease Control and Prevention. But very few of us have a BMI that low, and it is difficult to eat an adequately nutritious diet when greatly restricting calorie intake. For reference, a person who is five feet seven inches tall would need to weigh 125 pounds or less to have a BMI of nineteen. The average BMI among the teens in our study was 21.0 for girls and 22.9 for boys, well within what is usually considered normal. Nutritionists usually don't start worrying until a person's BMI clears the twenty-six barrier. Again, for reference, a person five feet seven inches tall would have a BMI of twenty-six or more if he or she weighed at least 165 pounds.

Using the BMI cutoff of twenty-six, about 15 percent of the boys and 7 percent of the girls in the sample are overweight. The BMI cutoff for obesity is generally given at around thirty (a person five feet seven inches would weigh 190 pounds).

Using this definition of obesity, 2 percent of the girls in our sample and 4 percent of boys are obese.

Because of the difficulty of determining the appropriate BMI cutoff to use, the analytical approach we employed was to simply look at which parenting factors led to a higher BMI. Although teens who had higher grades had lower BMIs on average, there was only one parenting factor related to BMI. For boys only, those who expressed a frequent wish that their fathers would spend more time with them had higher BMIs. It is difficult to resist the interpretation that these boys are "father hungry" and use food as a way of filling the void.

The average boy who saw his father as much as he wanted had a BMI of 22.5. Boys with father hunger had an average BMI of twenty-four. The average father-hungry boy weighs over ten pounds more than a boy satisfied with the amount of time he spends with his dad.

Body Beautiful

We looked at two components of disordered eating: recent severe weight-loss strategy and use of steroids or creatine. These behaviors split pretty cleanly across gender lines. Twenty-three percent of girls (a frightening statistic) and six percent of boys were classified as having disordered eating patterns. Disordered eating was defined as a child having engaged in one or more of the following extreme weight-loss strategies during the past month: 1) twenty-four hours or more of fasting, 2) vomiting/ use of laxatives, 3) use of nonprescription diet aids such as pills or powders.

We should also note that 61 percent of girls and 21 percent of boys report that they are currently trying to lose weight. In addition, fully one-third of boys and 3 percent of girls report that they are attempting to gain weight. So when we combine these figures into a body dissatisfaction sum, 64 percent of girls and 54 percent of boys are trying to change their weight.[9]

The factors that predicted creatine or steroid use in boys in the PPM study were maternal leniency and the number of siblings a boy had. This data suggests that adequate supervision is an important strategy in preventing substance abuse. It's also possible that boys who receive fewer restrictions on their behavior and perhaps less attention due to family size are more vulnerable to the pressures of society to conform to the masculine ideal of big muscles.

In the PPM research, teens with disordered eating patterns tended to be girls with something eating at them. As one of the girls we interviewed said of her eating-disordered friend—things in her life went wrong and she focused on her body. Risk factors for eating disorders were divorce and separation, having a poor relationship with mom or dad, and having lenient household rules. While there are many other reasons an individual may develop an eating disorder, parents would be wise to note these findings—if you are too lenient or don't make the time the relationship with your adolescent requires, you may find yourself watching her waste away.

CHAPTER 9

Self-Control Problems

WE WANT THE WORLD AND WE WANT IT NOW!
(Based on the sin of Lust)

> I can resist anything except temptation.
> —OSCAR WILDE, *Lady Windermere's Fan*

> They'll tempt you sir with silver
> And they'll tempt you sir with gold
> And they'll tempt you with the pleasures
> That the flesh does surely hold
> —BRUCE SPRINGSTEEN, "Pink Cadillac"

Corey has just settled down at his desk to study for the history test he has tomorrow—one of the biggest tests of his "all-important" junior year. His choice of college is on the line. Corey's grades in his other classes have been good, but American history is a thorn in his side. Mr. Lajoie, his crusty history teacher, rumored to have been teaching at this suburban school since it opened in 1910, has the reputation as the faculty's toughest grader. Corey knows that he has no chance to get an A in Lajoie's class unless he aces the test tomorrow. But just as he begins to review the details of the Dred Scott decision, his mother calls to him up the stairs, "Phoebe's on the phone!"

Phoebe has been Corey's girlfriend for the past three

months. He's crazy about her. Their relationship is a wonderful combination of friendship, fun, and passion. Tonight, passion is foremost in Phoebe's mind.

"Do you want to come over?" she coos. "My parents are going to the movies . . . and my brother is going with them. I'll be alone."

"Oh, Pheebes, I've got Lajoie's exam tomorrow. I gotta study."

"You could get up early. And don't forget your first period study hall."

"But I've still got a ton to read."

"C'mon. For a little while. I'll help you study."

"Yeah, right. If we're alone the only thing I'll study is your anatomy."

(Laughing) "Please, Corey? Just for a little while."

Corey is not the first guy to be swayed by the Siren's song. He is caught in the classic battle between willpower and desire, id and superego, short-term pleasure versus long-term gain. It doesn't take him long to decide. He grabs his car keys.

"Mom," he calls. "I'm going over to Phoebe's to study." And he's out the door.

Across town, seventeen-year-old Marney is parked in her car next to a small ranch house in a middle-class neighborhood. Like Corey, she has also just got a tempting phone call, from her friend Riff. He's got some cocaine to sell. The little bag of white powder is waiting for her now just ten yards away, inside Riff's house. She's been doing a lot of coke lately. She loves the feeling she gets from it, but she knows it's started to mess up her life. She's been missing school, and her grades have started to suffer. Cocaine has begun to be the focus of her life, taking her time and money. She's incredibly irritable after she runs through her stash of the drug. Her boyfriend, Rick, is worried about her, and two weeks ago, "made" her come see me.

"I probably do need to slow down a bit," she said to me, a jittery girl with circles under her eyes. "I'm a little out of control sometimes."

Outside Riff's, at my suggestion, Marney flicks on the interior light in the car. In its faint yellow glow she opens her purse and takes out photos of Rick and her younger sister, Emily, whom she adores. I told her to look at these pictures the next time she is tempted to buy coke, to think about how she might be hurting people she loves.

She does her best and reaches out to turn the key in the ignition and drive away. But she can taste the coke; the urge is too strong. She throws the photos back into her purse, snaps it shut, and opens the car door, telling herself she'll only buy a gram and save it until next weekend. Instead, she and Riff stay together doing coke until well past midnight.

The craving for drugs—whether cocaine, heroin, alcohol, or nicotine—is like sexual desire: it can be irresistible. Marney's story is typical of the legions who attend meetings of Narcotics Anonymous or Alcoholics Anonymous—men and women who have lied, cheated, and stolen in order to satisfy their cravings.

There are few of us who don't know someone for whom self-control is a big problem, who has put his health and happiness at risk because of his inability to resist temptation. This is one of the reasons why the government agency entrusted to keeping us healthy, the Centers for Disease Control, places so much emphasis on trying to help teenagers develop self-control. Research clearly shows that without adequate self-control, teenagers place themselves at greater risk for problems later on because healthy habits are established in childhood and adolescence.[1]

Despite public service announcements and ad campaigns, in the last ten years there has been a 33 percent increase in the number of teenagers who smoke heavily (it's unclear why this is).[2] And the earlier they start smoking, drinking, or having sex, the greater the risk to later health. In short, lack of self-control can have dire consequences.

The problem of being under the control of an overmastering appetite or craving is what Pope Gregory had in mind when he added lust to his list of the seven deadly sins. Lust and gluttony were linked in his list of sins, and they are also linked here. Both involve a lack of self-control, an inability to resist temptation—especially when it would be in one's best interest to do so.

Self-control is often vital if we hope to excel. Astounding as it may seem, scientists can predict what a preschooler's SAT scores will be when she is seventeen based on early self-control. Psychologist Walter Mischel has researched what he and his colleagues call "delay of gratification." They recently published their findings in the prestigious journal *Science*,[3] which is usually filled with impenetrable articles on neurochemistry, seismology, immunology, or genetics. It's rare for an article by a social scientist to appear in *Science*, and it indicates both the quality of Mischel's research and its importance.

Mischel and his colleagues construct experiments that are variants on a theme. They give children a simple choice: something small, not all that desirable *right now;* or, if they wait and resist the temptation of the immediate payoff, a bigger reward.

In one experiment, for example, Mischel timed how long a four-year-old was able to resist eating a marshmallow or M&M that sat within reach under a clear plastic cup. Mischel told the child that he had to leave the room, but if he was able to wait until he got back he would be given several treats, not just the one under the cup. Mischel measured how long the child was able to wait, and he collected data on the strategies the child used to hold out for the bigger payoff. The child who distracted himself by singing a song or playing some kind of game was able to wait much longer than the child who concentrated on how delicious the marshmallow was going to taste.

Mischel found that he could predict how well a four-year-old would do on his SATs by how long he was able to resist the M&M. A child who could only delay gratification for five seconds had an overall SAT score that was about sixty points lower than the child who was able to wait five minutes. When the choice was between one marshmallow immediately or two marshmallows after an unspecified waiting period, the kid who was able to wait twenty minutes for the two marshmallows had a combined SAT score that was 210 points higher than the kid who was unwilling to wait.

Not only did the children who were able to delay gratification have higher SAT scores, but they were also rated by their parents as better able to cope with stress, effectively pursue goals, and resist temptation.

Why does one child resist temptation and another succumb to it? Biology plays a role, of course. Some of us are born with a predisposition to impulsivity.[4] The neurology of children with ADHD, for example, makes it difficult for them to concentrate on their homework. But even those scientists who study how our genetic endowment affects our behavior emphasize how "plastic" the brain is; how much the neural circuitry responsible for self-regulation can be altered by our experiences.[5] This places much of the burden back onto us parents. If we overindulge our children, if we don't make them learn how to wait their turn, delay gratification, and resist temptation, the neural changes that we associate with strong character may not take place.

The most straightforward way to help our children develop self-control is to exhibit it ourselves. If we can patiently wait for forty-five minutes in line at Disney World, sit in a traffic jam without losing our cool, and remain calm while we struggle to put together a four-thousand-piece Lego Ferris wheel, the child will tend to imitate this behavior in similar circumstances.[6]

I think it's paramount to talk to your kids about the importance of delaying gratification. You may even want to explain Mischel's research to them. I have explained it to my girls. I use Mischel and his marshmallows to help them cope with frustration and temptation. "Do you want high SAT scores?" I ask them jokingly. "Then see if you can wait five minutes before you eat that candy." Or (with perhaps more success), "Let's clean up the family room before we watch TV!" When they ask, "Are we there yet?" I suggest that we divert our attention with a sing-along instead of wishing we were somewhere else.

The people of Bali have a ritualized way of inculcating early on this kind of pliability and patience in their children. When a child is twenty-one months old, a mother will "borrow" someone else's baby, and play with her and nurse her in front of her own child. Rarely does her child not become jealous and, often, he throws a tantrum. The mother remains calm, gently encouraging the child to find a way to deal with the upset. On the next occasion that a baby is borrowed, the child should react more calmly. The mother conveys how proud she is of her child. The practice recognizes that one of the first tasks of emotional maturity is to learn how to be a good brother or sister when a new baby comes along. With this approach, by the time the child is three or four, he "will have developed equanimity in the face of provocations, disappointments, or frustrations."[7]

It's important to put firm rules and structures in place for our children to follow—to insist, for example, that they clean their rooms and brush their teeth. This strategy reinforces the notion that the parents think that self-control is important and pushes kids to practice coping with the frustration of following rules. Moreover, if a parent insists on firm (but not harsh or arbitrary) rules, the child's conscience (or superego) will internalize these values.

Drug Use by Teenagers

As we saw in the examples of Corey and Marney, sex and drugs are two areas in which teenagers typically have problems with self-control. Our attitudes, as parents, can affect how our kids will respond to these temptations.

Let's look at drugs first. One of the most interesting findings of the PPM survey is that affluent parents seem far less permissive about exposing their children to violent media than they are about drug use. I was intrigued by these data. It led me to explore other data that could shed light on the relationship between income and attitudes toward drugs.

I analyzed data gathered in the summer of 1995 from nearly six thousand adults living in a diverse set of neighborhoods in Chicago by the Project on Human Development in Chicago Neighborhoods.[8] This was one of the most comprehensive social science research projects ever attempted. It studied how individual, family, and community characteristics relate to delinquency and crime. I was especially interested in one aspect of the study—how attitudes toward substance abuse by teenagers differed by income level. Do affluent families have more permissive attitudes about alcohol, tobacco, and marijuana use than middle-class or poor parents? Specifically, respondents in the project were asked how wrong they thought it was for a thirteen-year-old to use tobacco, alcohol, or marijuana. Then they were asked the same questions about a nineteen-year-old.

For my analysis, I divided the survey participants into three income groups: the first made $25,000 or less per year; the second, $50,000 to $100,000; the third, over $100,000.

My findings are presented here for the first time. The data clearly showed that the most affluent families had the most permissive attitudes for all three substances and both age groups. Of both lower- and middle-income groups, 90 percent said that it is "very wrong" for a thirteen-year-old to smoke marijuana, while this was the response of just over 80 percent of upper-income respondents. Of lower- and middle-income respondents, 60 percent said it was "very wrong" for nineteen-year-olds to drink, while only 40 percent of the most affluent group felt this way. This permissive attitude prevailed despite a much higher education level for the upper-income group—over three-quarters of them were college graduates. That was true for only one-third of the middle-income and less than a tenth of the lower-income groups.

As part of the PPM survey, I asked parents these same questions about drug and alcohol use by thirteen- and nineteen-year-olds. The average income level among this group was, of course, much higher than in the Chicago study, but the results of the two studies generally agreed, at least regarding older children.[9] In all cases, PPM parents with an annual income of over $100,000 per year had more permissive attitudes about substance use than did parents with lower incomes.

These attitudes clearly affect usage. A recent study of alcohol and drug use among twenty-five thousand high school students in America shows that these differences in attitudes toward drugs appear to translate directly into differences in drug usage across social classes. One of the conclusions of that study was that while it was not the only factor related to substance abuse, ". . . increasing family income *increased* the likelihood that youth will have a drug and/or alcohol problem."[10]

Sociologists such as Max Weber have noted the tendency for the more affluent among us to indulge in imprudent behavior, perhaps engendered by a feeling of security brought on by knowing that one can afford a good lawyer, therapist, or a bed at the Betty Ford Clinic.[11] Recent research indicates that heroin use in the United States is up, with affluent young people contributing to the increase. Quoting from one such report: "Kathryn, another upper middle-class woman who will inherit over a million dollars and receives substantial cash advances from her parents and relatives frequently throughout the year, had an outgoing nature that took her on a new adventure every night. Nowadays, however, she spends evenings at home waiting for her boyfriend to return with heroin."[12]

In the following interview with Riley, an eighteen-year-old senior at a high school in an affluent Atlanta suburb, she clearly sees that, among her friends, the ones most likely to get out of control are often those with the most indulgent parents.

DAN: So what about your friends? How will they turn out?

RILEY: I think most of them will turn out all right. They'll all have jobs and be okay. Some of them might not; they might turn out pretty bad because of the path that they are on right now.

DAN: What do you mean?

RILEY: Like drugs, and alcohol-wise. I can see some of them just being on that path and sticking to that path and not living up to their full potential.

DAN: Do you think that's a problem at your school?

RILEY: Oh, yeah. Definitely. I think it's a huge problem and I think it's a big problem in my town and especially in my class in general, the senior class. Like there are parties all the time, people are drinking all the time and I think, like, can't you find other things in your life to do so that you don't need to drink so much?

DAN: Do you see a certain type of kid who is more likely to be on that path than another?

RILEY: Yeah, actually. There's a wide variety of people who
drink and do drugs. But I think in a way it's the same
type of kids who start to drink. It's because their parents are away. My friends and I were talking about this
last week. When there's a lack of rules and stuff, its
easier to get away with things. For me, it's like my
parents are strict about drinking, and they tell me it's
not the right thing to do. A lot of parents of kids I know
are like that. But the richer you are, you actually have
fewer rules and parents don't make as much of a big
deal about drinking.

Approximately 60 percent of PPM teenagers use drugs—
alcohol, cigarettes, or marijuana—and about half of those who
use drugs have used at least two of these substances in the past
month.[13] It will come as no surprise that these students tend to
have other problems, or at least do not function as well as their
non–drug using peers. For example, drug users—both boys and
girls—get lower grades (C+/B− compared to a solid B average). Kids who use drugs are more likely to say that they don't
work to their intellectual potential, that they are mean to others,
and that they lie and cheat.

In Chapter 3, we discussed the role that dopamine plays in a
feeling of well-being. We noted that dopamine is released in the
brain when we pursue goals, and that those of us who have
nothing to strive for miss the pleasure that comes with this
chemical surge. The dopamine high that results from pursuing
a goal pales beside the flood of dopamine that bathes the brain
with the ingestion of drugs. This occurs in the case of nearly all
mind and mood altering substances used by teenagers, including the three most common: alcohol, tobacco, and marijuana.[14]

Affluent children, therefore, may become susceptible to

drugs because they think that problems can be solved by external change (such as buying something or hiring someone) rather than internal change. Not only do psychoactive drugs like Prozac and Valium fill this bill, but illicit drugs do, too. The affluent have the disposable income to buy these external fixes. And drugs fill, at least temporarily, a feeling of emptiness brought on by the lack of meaningful goal-directed activity that arises in some of our affluent kids.

But affluence is only part of the story. Teenagers are at greater risk for drug use when they have parents, whether rich or poor, who have failed to teach them self-control, the ability to tolerate delay, and how to deal with boredom—parents who have not spent enough time with them and who have not clearly communicated that they don't want their kids to take drugs.

Sex

There have been numerous stories in the media about how teenagers today are so sexually active that they make their parents, who grew up in the shadow of "free love," seem like prudes. Although there has been a slight downward trend over the last decade in the number of teenagers who have had sexual intercourse—falling from 54 percent to 49 percent[15]—there is no reliable data on other kinds of sexual behavior, especially oral sex. Based on these newspaper accounts of teenage sexuality and the reports of some of the people surveyed for the PPM, many thirteen-year-olds are having oral sex.

It's interesting that the blasé attitude toward oral sex in teenagers today stands in stark contrast to their parents. For example, as part of the PPM survey, I asked both parents and teens how wrong is it for a thirteen- or nineteen-year-old to have oral sex or sexual intercourse. Teenagers' attitudes were far more liberal toward sex in general—and they disagreed with parents about the relative wrongness of oral sex and sexual intercourse. Of parents, 95 percent said that it was "extremely wrong" for a thirteen-year-old to engage in oral sex; only 53 percent of teenagers expressed that opinion. Moreover, while parents consistently rated oral sex as "more wrong" than sexual intercourse, their children expressed the opposite view.

Often our kids are getting mixed messages about sex. Even if we tend to err on the side of caution, there are other parents whose attitude is bound to be lax. We also have trouble supervising our kids. Many parents describe the "empty house" syndrome. When they're away, their kids get permission to have "a couple of friends" over. Before you know it, word has spread on-line and over the phone that there's an empty house. Kids arrive in droves, suddenly there's a wild party, the kids get drunk, and suddenly it's *Sex and the City* with minors playing the leading roles. But nobody takes responsibility, and the same thing happens again the following weekend at a different place. This creates difficult situations for some parents. Anton, for example, was outraged that some parents at the elite private school in California that his daughter attends seem to be opening their homes to drunken teenage orgies.

DAN: Have you seen permissive attitudes among the families at Danielle's school?

ANTON: I'm appalled with the fact that just something as basic as asking parents to sign a safe-house agreement saying that if there's a party at their house they will be there to supervise, and they won't serve any alcohol, or serve anybody under age, and nobody's drinking and driving. And they shall also call and make sure when their child goes to a party that it's supervised. Something like 20 to 30 percent of parents refused to sign. There's something crazy going on. I feel like I'm fighting an uphill battle against our fourteen-year-old daughter's peer group.

It's not that I'm categorically saying that all sex is bad for our teenagers. Corey and Phoebe have a wonderful relationship. But beyond the need for teenagers to practice safe sex, to avoid contracting sexually transmitted diseases, or be part of an unwanted pregnancy, there can be high emotional costs to pay when teenagers have sex before they are emotionally ready. They can develop attitudes toward sex that won't serve them well as adults. They become furtive around sex; it can lack intimacy. And for girls particularly, sex can be lacking in pleasure. We also don't want our children to feel manipulated or exploited in their sexual relationships. And we want them to be able to wait until they feel ready.

Research Results and Prescriptions

DRUG USE

Around 60 percent of the teens who answered the PPM survey were active drug users: nearly one-half of thirteen- to fourteen-year-olds, and nearly 70 percent of seventeen- to eighteen-year-olds. Alcohol was the clear drug of choice, having been used in the past month by over 50 percent of the respondents. Marijuana and cigarettes were tied for second place: one out of four teens were active users.

To look at what kind of parenting practices relate to drug use among teenagers, I simply divided the children into those who reported that they had abstained from all drugs (cigarettes, alcohol, marijuana, and other illicit drugs) during the past thirty days and those who hadn't. Then I compared the teenagers in these two groups as to what they said about their home life.

What I found was that the kids who were using drugs were more likely to say that they were being spoiled by their parents.

Their parents were less likely to enforce rules about behavior such as swearing and weren't as vigilant about monitoring the kinds of TV shows and movies the children watched. Furthermore, echoing a recurring theme in the PPM study and other research, families who often ate dinner together were less likely to contain a teenager who was an active drug user.

Too many parents don't seem to realize that lack of supervision, lax rules, and noninvolvement provide tacit support for drug use in their children. In some cases this approval may be passive. Connor's parents, for example, chose to look the other way when they were presented with evidence of Connor's marijuana smoking. Other parents may just be misguided, thinking that alcohol and marijuana are recreational drugs that can be used without significant harm to the user. This may be true for some forms of adult use, but this line of thinking ignores both the potential legal consequences and the typical pattern of teen drug use. Teen use of alcohol is for the most part binge drinking and often involves drunk driving—one out of every five seventeen- to eighteen-year-olds who took the PPM survey had driven under the influence of alcohol in the past month. Other parents draw on their own experience and feel that it is inevitable that their teenager will try marijuana and alcohol. They did and survived. This kind of attitude often leads to lax supervision and early experimentation. These parents should know that the younger a child is when he first smokes pot or gets drunk, the higher his risk for drug *abuse*, other forms of delinquency, and unprotected sex.

SEXUAL ACTIVITY

Like early drug use, early initiation of sexual activity is correlated with undesirable outcomes, such as unwanted pregnancy and an elevated risk of STDs.

The PPM survey did not directly ask about sexual behavior.

It did, however, ask about attitudes toward sex. Do these teen-agers' attitudes translate into behavior? Probably. Research has established a clear relationship between attitude and behavior. Teenagers in our survey who condoned drug use by others were also more likely to report using drugs themselves. It is reasonable to conclude that this same correlation exists for sex.

When I divided the teens into those with permissive attitudes toward sexual intercourse and oral sex and those with less liberal attitudes and compared the kinds of parenting they have experienced, the results mirrored those for drug use. The group with the more permissive attitudes had more indulgent parents, especially about keeping their room clean. And once again, permissive sexual attitudes were more prevalent among teenagers who ate dinner less frequently with their families.

In closing, let me be clear that this chapter is not some repressive crusade against sex and drugs. It does, however, send a strong message that teenagers, especially younger ones, who use drugs or have sex are very often not prepared to handle these experiences. Parents who do not help their children resist these temptations are hurting them. Parents must be vigilant about helping their children avoid situations where it will be difficult for them to resist temptation. And we also need to honestly examine the signals our drinking, smoking, and prescription pill habits send to our kids.

CHAPTER 10

Spoiled

It Must Be Mine, All Mine
(Based on the sin of Greed)

Greed is desire run amok.
—*John Ogilvy*

If there is one word that is associated with indulgent child rearing, it is *spoiled*. We've all heard stories of the kid who gets a new BMW each time she wrecks the old one, Bar Mitzvah receptions on the *QEII*, children with personal fitness trainers and shoppers. These are, of course, extreme examples. But we've all seen kids who are spoiled. There's a greediness about them. They throw tantrums in toy stores when their parents won't buy them what they want. They always seem to want more and expect to get their own way. They have trouble sharing. The needs of family, friends, and the wider world recede like the earth in the rearview mirror of a starship.

Even the pampered movie star who throws tantrums is "like a spoiled child." We talk about a child being spoiled rotten, as though they were a rank piece of meat. We see the spoiled child as tainted and devalued. He has been overindulged and overpraised. He has not had to earn what he has: it has been given to him. An essential part of what we talk about when we talk about character is missing in him. He lacks integrity, fortitude, and a moral center.

We all tend to be critical of parents when we think they're spoiling their kids, although this kind of criticism is rarely given face-to-face.

In our age of indulgence it is almost as though our kids are being spoiled just by breathing the atmosphere. Their sense of entitlement is inbred. How many of us have watched our kids ripping into their presents on Christmas or Hanukah and then just tossing them aside. The *getting,* not the having, is what matters to them. Their behavior is a reflection of our society. *We* often seem insatiable. "Enough is enough!" we want to say to our kids. But how many of us, as parents, live *our* lives that way? Other people around the world typically view Americans as spoiled. Look at all we have, how often we take it for granted, and how, for so many of us, it doesn't seem like enough? A friend took her kids to a Washington monument. When she grew tired of waiting in the long line, she used a connection she had to get to the front of it. The next week she happened to be at her son's school, and she saw him cut to the front of a line of kids waiting for the water fountain. She was immediately stricken by guilt at the part she had played in modeling this kind of behavior.

It is almost as if the need for more and better and bigger and faster has become institutionalized. Is this part of the American character, our faith in progress? Or is it greed? Perhaps a bit of both. The line between the two has always been blurred and today the two seem synonymous.

Alexis de Tocqueville in *Democracy in America* wrote: "The love of wealth is therefore to be traced, as either a principal or accessory motive, at the bottom of all Americans do: this gives to all their passions a family likeness . . . It may be said that it is the vehemence of their desires that makes Americans so methodical; it perturbs their minds, but it disciplines their lives."

Greed was one of Gregory's seven deadly sins because, like the other sins, of pride, gluttony, and lust, it pulled attention away from the spiritual and fixed it on the material. From greed, Gregory wrote, springs "hardness of heart against compassion." The Talmud enjoins us to always give charity to beggars. Each time we are asked and we do not give, the sages say, our hearts close a little. And that's perhaps what's most distressing about the spoiled child: He seems to lack this generosity of spirit that is one of the true signs of character.

Desire Run Amok

Americans have a split national personality when it comes to greed. The Puritans believed that the desire for sensual pleasure and luxury was an obstacle to getting into heaven, and they embraced the teachings of Jesus, who said that it is easier for a camel to pass through the eye of a needle than a rich man to enter the kingdom of heaven.[1]

As a society, we still frown on excessive greed. Most of us believe too much of a good thing can be toxic; there is a dark side to the desire for wealth. We disapprove, for example, when we hear that Michael Jordan lost millions of dollars betting on golf. We gnash our teeth when we think about the greed that led Charles Keating and his cronies to defraud us all in the savings and loan scandal. We condemn Imelda Marcos and her closet full of shoes sitting in unopened boxes. "The avarice never ends!" rails Jim Carrey in the contemporary film *The Grinch Who Stole Christmas*. "I want golf clubs. I want diamonds. I want a pony so I can ride it twice, get bored, and sell it to make glue!" exclaims Carrey's Grinch.

Our ambivalence about wealth and material excess doesn't

stop us from having money on our minds. Most of us do want to be rich. Polls show that 60 percent of women and 73 percent of men say they want to be wealthy.[2] We know how easy it is to be carried away by greed—the desire for more and more and more! A glut, a surfeit of things! Our closets overflowing and our refrigerators packed. The students we interviewed seemed to have a sneaking suspicion that they live charmed lives, which most of them take for granted. They often minimized their flaws by comparing themselves to their peers. Chuck and Sandy both attend private New England high schools. Their families shower them with gifts, which they justify by comparing themselves to others who have more.

Sandy is sixteen, tall and thin, with curly brown hair. She talks to me in an earnest, concerned tone about the waste she sees around her.

DAN: Would you say you're spoiled? Could you define it and maybe tell me how you view it?

SANDY: Okay, I'm definitely spoiled. But at this school, compared to my friends and stuff, I don't think I'm that spoiled. Lots of my friends have new cars. They can buy as much clothes as they want. I have friends who, like, buy four pairs of the same pants from Abercrombie, that are like $58 each. But my parents only spoil me on things that are more necessary—like a computer or a car. You don't want to have a used car that's awful, that's going to be dangerous. I mean, I have like a cell phone, but that's if I get stuck. I have a credit card and that's because I went away, and I had it in case of an emergency.

Chuck is a grinder with a single-minded focus on grades and college. But he's nonchalant about the fact that he and his friends are spoiled. Like so many of the kids I see, he isn't particularly reflective.

DAN: You said that your parents spoil you sometimes. Are there other kids at this school in your situation?

CHUCK: Most are worse. You know, I'll go over to a friend's house and we're going to the movies and his parents hand him $150 on the way out and tell us to get dinner someplace nice. There's a lot of money floating around at this school. I don't feel spoiled compared to some of my friends. I have one friend, he'll come over to my house and he has money pouring out of every pocket.

Chuck and Sandy see how much they have, and, to different degrees, it gnaws at their consciences. And it's possible that they understand what being materially spoiled can do to their character.

It's What's Inside That Counts

We've talked about the importance of teaching our children how to cope with psychological stress, which I compared to the physical process of building immunity to a virus. The stress might be a disappointment in school, sports, or love. Coping might mean seeking support or advice from someone you trust, dealing with the disappointment "one day at a time," shifting your focus to more positive aspects of your life, or learning from the experience, resolving to do better next time, or not making the same mistake again. Helping people learn to cope is part of the work of a psychotherapist. But as Carl, a master therapist in the Boston area, relates in the following interview, a kid who's been spoiled tends to fixate on the exterior aspects of his life and seems incapable of probing his interior, his core, which, of course, is the place from which equilibrium, strength, and happiness emanate.

DAN: I know you have worked with several clients who are very well-off. What is your general impression of them?

CARL: Well, you know, the data is not great on those kids. I'm thinking of kids who I've seen who are now in their twenties. They tend to be rather materialistic, apolitical, and reclusive as they live off of their family's money. Not very happy.

DAN: Why do you think that's the case? Have they had difficult lives?

CARL: No, on the contrary. Their lives have often been too easy. I think that there has to be some adversity in one's life. I think it develops an inner sense of the capacity to adapt and prevail. And if you don't have the inner sense of the capacity to adapt and prevail, but come to rely only on external supports, mostly economic ones, then I think it's almost as though there is nobody home inside to take care of things.

DAN: An emptiness.

CARL: Yeah. It's the emptiness that makes them miserable. There is a huge externalization there. Since everything is taken care of externally. Difficulties are also externalized, so that if you fail, let's say out of art school, you say to yourself that it wasn't because I did anything wrong or didn't have the talent, it's because there was somebody on my thesis committee who really took a dislike to me. And that is why I had to leave.

DAN: It sounds like the same kind of emotional immaturity you see in alcoholics. They always blame their drinking on someone else.

CARL: Exactly, and they can't stop drinking until they can take on that responsibility.

This dynamic is illustrated in the case of Paul, a young man I saw for a short period who had good parents but still wound up in deep trouble.

Paul was the youngest of four sons born into a Philadelphia family who I first met when he was fourteen. He came to see me under duress. Paul was in danger of being kicked out of school because his grades stank and he had been caught smoking cigarettes on campus. He came to therapy with me as part of a deal his parents cut with the school so he wouldn't be expelled. His older brothers had all done reasonably well at this same school, and nobody seemed to be able to figure out why Paul had been a problem almost from the start. His mother had given me a thick folder with reports from teachers, counselors, and psychologists describing a host of problems. Paul had been stubborn in kindergarten; even as a mere tot he had decided that some of the class rules were arbitrary and capricious and refused to obey them. In first and second grade, he was tardy with his schoolwork, and he often had to stay in at recess to finish it; the list went on. He was a devilish child, no question about it. By ninth grade, he had already been to five different schools.

After a few months with me, things had not improved. He had started drinking heavily and smoking pot on weekends, activities he supported with his fifty-dollar-a-week allowance. His grades were still abysmal, so, at his request, he moved to a public school where he finished out the school year. But over the summer his drinking worsened and he instigated violent arguments with his father. His parents hired an educational consultant who suggested a private school in Arizona. Perhaps Paul's love of the outdoors, the distance from his father, and a fresh start would finally do the trick. Instead, he fell in with Diego, another wayward youth, and they started spending their days together eating peyote in the mountains. After two months of this, they lit out for San Francisco.

Paul's parents had to make a very difficult and courageous decision at this point. They used their money one last time on their son's behalf. They hired a former policeman turned teen-runaway retriever to hunt him down and deliver him to an expensive no-nonsense drug rehab–therapeutic school where he lived for the next three years.

Paul's parents' money was both a blessing and a curse. It helped him get into trouble and it helped him get out of it. By the ability of his parents to keep buying expensive new schools for him, Paul was able to avoid the internal work that he needed to do more easily than some of his less affluent peers. Like Carl the therapist said, the cure was always external. Paul had been spoiled. Whenever something wasn't working out, his parents would buy him entrée into a new life. It wasn't because they were lazy or didn't care about him. They were neither of those things. They had options for external cures that most of us don't have and they took advantage. But in the process Paul didn't have to assume responsibility for his actions. He was intent on pleasing only himself, and he assumed that if he fell from the high-wire act that often characterized his life, the safety net of his parents' money would catch him. Changing the externals in his life became a panacea, but it prevented him from developing the inner poise and purpose we associate with character.

Chuck describes how these external cures can become habitual: "The really rich kids around here are generally impatient—I've got a little bit of that myself. It's pretty clear to me that I tend to get sick of people pretty quickly. They try to sort of do things with their money instead of trying to learn a skill themselves. I worked with a kid here named Joseph making these little beaded hats for the school play. When we got done we decided to make some for ourselves. He made a design, and I drew up a design and started working on it. One day he told me he hadn't even started working on his, but he still really wanted one. He offered me sixty dollars to make it for him. To, you know, make his design. I kind of think of that as just an extreme example of how impatient people here are. He basically came up with an idea and threw money at the problem."

Joseph got the hat, but not the pride of accomplishment that would have come if he had made it himself. He avoided the necessity of dealing with the shame or self-recrimination if he had failed. Either experience would have helped him mature, but he was able to buy his way out.

Being a Brat

Although having money often makes it easier to externalize both problems and cures, parents without a lot of money can do the same thing. By not requiring their children to take sufficient responsibility for their actions or giving in easily to their demands, one can also spoil children without spending a dime. The students we interviewed used the term "brat" to describe this type of kid.

I met with Andrea in the spacious, sunny, carpeted lunchroom of her school in suburban Atlanta. It was a far cry from others I had visited when I had been a traveling psychologist for hire in a large urban school district. In those schools, the cafeterias all had a characteristic, unappetizing smell, little light, and worn, tile floors. They were never big enough. The students always seemed to be jammed in together, looking like extras in a bad coed prison movie. The schools I visited for the PPM survey were another story. Appetizing aromas wafted from their kitchens. Their cafeterias and dining rooms were, by and large, colorful, cheerful places.

Andrea was typical of many of the affluent high school students I interviewed. She was polite, engaging, and sincere. Although she didn't strike me as a brat, she was still happily ignorant about the way most people live.

DAN: So, do you consider yourself spoiled?

ANDREA: Not in the conventional sense of spoiled.

DAN: Well, what do you think *spoiled* means?

ANDREA: I think *spoiled* has to do with getting everything you
          want, all the time, no matter what. I'm not quite that
          extreme. But I have had a lot of opportunity that
          other people don't have. I don't have to have a
          job—my parents have said that I can't get a job dur-
          ing the school year because school is my job. They
          give me an allowance. They send me to really great
          camps where I have all these great experiences and
          meet all these interesting people. But they say no to
          me sometimes. I don't get away with whatever I
          want. They expect things of me. I have to do some
          housework; I have to have some responsibility. They
          don't let me do everything all the time. I can't go out
          until three o'clock in the morning. I do have friends
          who can get away with anything. Like their father
          will be outside in the cold shoveling their walk and
          they'll be inside in slippers, drinking hot chocolate.
          I think that's spoiled.

Kids we talked to often made this distinction: spoiled was
not necessarily a surfeit of money or material possessions; it
was an attitude of not helping, not participating, not chipping
in—of doing only what we want to, when we want to. Many of
the students we interviewed had a sneaking suspicion that they
were indulged—spoiled in the sense that they led a cushy life.
But they knew they had to guard against the brattiness that they
saw in some of their peers. The exchanges I had with Joyce,
Gwen and Marty, all seniors at a public high school outside
Charleston, South Carolina, are typical. Joyce and Marty came
from wealthy families; Gwen's parents were middle class.

JOYCE

DAN: So kids like you who have a lot of things—your own cars, fast computers. You go on great vacations. Are you all spoiled?

JOYCE: There is a difference between being spoiled and being a brat. Like if something doesn't go my way, I can handle it. Or if I can't have something, then that's fine and I understand that, but I think a lot of people at this school don't. Because they are so used to getting everything they want all the time that when some little thing happens or they can't have something they want they're like, "What?!"

GWEN

DAN: What does it mean to act spoiled?

GWEN: A lot of times you can just tell that a kid is spoiled if they expect to get away with everything. Like eating in class. Or if you hang out with them, they expect to get everything because they always do. So you can kind of tell the way people act, like just in general when they are walking down the halls.

DAN: Like in class, do they expect to get good grades without working?

GWEN: Yeah. And they expect to, like, if they think they have the right answer, they expect their teacher to agree with them, you know, if they are arguing or something. And they expect the teacher to make or do special favors for them, like give them an extension on an assignment. Something like that.

DAN: Just because they've gotten that all along?

GWEN: Yeah.

DAN: That's interesting. And what happens if the teacher doesn't give in?

GWEN: After a while they give up, but then you know then they walk outside and say, "Oh, so and so, she's so mean!" That kind of stuff.

MARTY

DAN: Are you spoiled?

MARTY: Um, I'm definitely spoiled, I know that. But is that to say I'm unappreciative? Definitely not. Especially this year because this past summer I did a community-service trip in South Africa. That's given me a perspective on the world. I see how much I have compared to how little other people have. I mean, I know I'm spoiled. Look where I go to school. Look at the car I drive, my house, the things in my room. I know I'm spoiled, but I think my parents have done a good job in making sure I'm appreciative of that. And I don't think that's the case of everyone at school.

DAN: Are there people here that are spoiled?

MARTY: Almost everyone.

DAN: And what do you think will be the consequences from that later in life?

MARTY: Well, they'll be clueless, like when they get out of school or whatever. Because they've been on a free ticket.

Many of us adopt a similar child-in-a-bubble strategy, keeping our kids away from psychological or physical pain, exposing them to the wider world in doses calculated to awaken their sense of how fortunate they are without subjecting them to undue stress or upset. A stint with the Tutsi is well and good, but then it's back to suburban Pleasant Valley. We run the risk of creating a brat, a child who is used to getting her way and will continue to expect it. How can we expect a child to be any different when the world in which they've been raised is obstacle free? One mother, Linda, I talked to about this issue gave me the following example. She was part of a group of parents attending an evening presentation at their eighth graders' suburban middle school. The event was an information session about an upcoming overnight "mini–Outward Bound" camping trip.

"It was extraordinary," said Linda. "We talked about the trip and what the kids were going to do. They were going to camp overnight. One anxious mother stood up and asked in all seriousness, 'But what if my daughter doesn't like what they serve for dinner?' "

Who Spoils Their Children?

Nearly two out of three parents who filled out the PPM survey said that their children were at least "somewhat spoiled," although fewer than one in twelve said that their child was "very spoiled." The spoiled quotient was identical for preteens and teenagers, boys and girls, firstborn, middle, or youngest children. It made no difference whether the parents were divorced or together or where they lived.

But our data did show that there were some things that parents did (or didn't do) that led to spoiling, at least in the parents' minds. Parents who said they were more interested and involved in their children's lives were less likely to say they had a spoiled child. They also rated their kids as more likely to be spoiled if they rated themselves as less strict than their parents had been. Finally, if the family's annual income was more than $100,000 per year, parents were more likely to rate their child as spoiled.

When we asked teenagers whether they were spoiled, we got a slightly different story. More of them, especially the girls (one out of nine), said that they were "very spoiled." There were demographic differences, too. Like their parents, kids who said that their families were more well-off than average for their school were also more likely to say that they were spoiled. Finally, girls rated themselves at greater risk for being "very spoiled" if their fathers tended to be indulgent, and they didn't have to obey rules, such as being in by a certain hour.

Both parents and kids said getting an allowance without having to do chores was related to being spoiled (especially for girls), as was having a mother whom they perceived as being too lenient (especially for boys).

What Our Children Are Trying to Tell Us

Perhaps the most important finding that came out of our research on the spoiled syndrome was that kids recognize that their parents are often too soft on them—that we let them get away with more than they should. They know that in order to be strong, to face the challenges of life, to become the people they want to become, they need our help in building character; in fighting against the atmosphere of indulgence that comes part and parcel with living in the richest society the world has ever known.

We need to be aware that aside from creating obnoxious kids, there are other dangers to being spoiled. The PPM data clearly shows that being spoiled is part of a pattern that may have dangerous consequences. Girls who say they are "very spoiled" are three times as likely to have driven drunk and about twice as likely to have smoked marijuana in the past month. They are at risk for a host of other problems, including academic underachievement, bulimia, cigarette smoking, cheating on tests, and skipping school.

Boys who were "very spoiled" were also at higher risk for behavioral problems such as lying, cheating, being anxious or depressed, skipping school, underachieving at school, using creatine or steroids, and drunk driving.

Keeping Your Child Syndrome Free

As a final note, eighty-one (forty-six females, thirty-five males) of the 639 teens with complete data in the PPM survey manifested none of the seven deadly syndromes: they didn't drink, smoke cigarettes or marijuana; they weren't depressed, mean, spoiled, or self-centered; they didn't suffer from eating problems; they said it was wrong for thirteen-year-olds to have sex; and they worked to their intellectual potential in school without being overly driven.

What separated these too-good-to-be-true teens from their peers? According to our data, five things: their families frequently ate dinner together, their parents were not divorced or separated, they had to keep their rooms clean, they didn't have a phone in their room, and they did community service.

In the last part of this book, I'll offer practical suggestions for how to help your kids avoid the seven syndromes that undermine their character, and to which they're particularly susceptible in this age of indulgence. But as we will see, these practical guidelines are only part of the solution—the external part. In order to help our children change, we need to explore our own psychology and heighten our awareness of our own motivations—why we act the way we do with our kids. We've already mentioned that we often confuse our needs with those of our kids. I now want to delve more deeply into this concept with an eye to helping us strengthen our parenting skills by cultivating our inner parent.

PART THREE

PARENTING IN THE AGE OF INDULGENCE

CHAPTER 11

———

Finding Your Inner Parent

A JOURNEY INTO OUR OWN CHILDHOODS

> And so we beat on, boats against the current,
> borne back ceaselessly into the past . . .
> —F. SCOTT FITZGERALD, *The Great Gatsby*

Just over 10 percent of us are completely satisfied with our parenting skills, according to the PPM survey.[1] I was moved by one father of a nine-year-old boy in the PPM group who wrote in tiny letters, "I have no talent for parenting." Most of us wouldn't go that far, but we know that there are things we do as parents that we shouldn't, and things we don't do that we should.

Asked to identify the obstacles to better parenting, one weary mother summed up what many of us feel: "Sleep deprivation," she said. "Too much to do; too little time." Parents also wrote that work obligations, the negative influences of peers, their child's difficult temperament, and lack of emotional support from a spouse or partner all undermined their parenting skills. I know when I'm tired, struggling to make a writing deadline, or at odds with my wife, it saps my patience and erodes the quality of the attention I give to my children.

But there is one fundamental obstacle to good parenting that many of us ignore, or, perhaps, of which we're not even aware. Our psychological makeup as parents—our attitudes, hot buttons, hang-ups, and neuroses—play a central role in how we become the parents we are. When we think about the ways in which we could become better parents (if only we didn't have to work so hard, if only our spouses would cooperate a little more, if only the culture wasn't pushing them to grow up too fast, if only! if only!) we look to the external world. How often do we look to the place where all change begins—inside ourselves?

As I have described in previous chapters, overindulgence is one of our most prevalent failings as parents and the origins of indulgence come, for the most part, from inside us.

Books and articles that offer advice on how to avoid being an indulgent parent often have "brat" in their title.[2] A recent *Parenting* magazine article takes a more humane approach. It offers us "loving ways to set limits" and suggests strategies for getting your kids to clean up after themselves, dress when they're supposed to, and go to bed without a fight. The article lists the top three reasons we have trouble setting limits: ignorance about the kinds of behavior that are "normal," fear that your child won't love you anymore, and concern that limits will constrict his creativity and stifle his spirit.

This is a great start, but there is a more subtle level of "why" we have trouble setting limits that needs to be explored. Why are we afraid that our child won't love us if we tell them they can't have candy? Why are we afraid that we might crush their spirits by telling them to clean up the Legos that crunch underfoot each time we cross our living rooms? Why are we afraid that they'll be angry at us or that they won't love us anymore?

A good place to start looking for these deeper whys is in the past; to the interactions you had as a child or teenager with your parents or anyone else who was intimately involved in your upbringing. We can't avoid the influence of the people who raised us in the way we parent our kids—for better or worse.

Each of us carries idealized images of good parents and bad parents inside us. Psychoanalysts refer to these idealized images as internalized objects. In important ways, we react to these inner parents as if they were living people. They influence our feelings and can have enormous power.

These inner parents belong to us alone, constructed from memories of our own childhood and inhabiting our psyches. These are not memories of incidents as they actually happened, but memories filtered through the lens of our childhood personality, with its unique needs, temperament, strengths, and deficiencies. For example, a child who is the star or hero in a dysfunctional family, perhaps a very responsible and talented firstborn who feels the need to compensate for a parent's drinking, will have her memories colored by the burden of the adult-like role she assumed in the family. This would be a very different memory filter than that of a child who could never measure up and lived in the shadow of a high-performing brother or sister. A hypersensitive or painfully shy child will remember interactions with his parents differently than an outgoing, extroverted kid for whom childhood was a fearless, playful romp. Even though we can update or remodel our inner parents from time to time, they are always constructed on the foundation that was laid down in childhood.

Identifying the Good Inner Parent

Let's visit these inner parents on their home turf, inside our heads. We'll start with a good inner parent. Begin by thinking about an experience with your mother that brings back positive feelings. If you can't think of one, don't worry—you're not alone. Instead, pick another relative—your father or grandparent, for instance. Try to remember as many details about the experience as you can.

When I asked Fatima, a forty-two-year-old mother of three who grew up in Jordan and now works as a doctor in the Boston area, she recalled the loving care of her father during her frequent and severe gastrointestinal illnesses. "It's somewhat indelicate," she said, "but the memory that comes immediately to mind is me in the bathroom, vomiting until I thought I was going to turn inside out, and my father cleaning up, holding me, telling me that I was going to be fine. I remember cool blue tiles of the floor on my knees, the milky flicker of the fluorescent light, and the chain with its wooden handle dangling from the raised tank of the commode. My father was a doctor, too, you know. And I think the combination of love and care he showed in those moments inspired me to choose a career in medicine. I was so miserable so much of the time growing up, and his attention never left me. He saw me through. You might think it odd, but it is my father who I remember caring for me in this way. When my children need me, it's his presence, his love, that I feel inside me. My mother was so absorbed in her social life, her parties, and her duties at the university. My illnesses scared her. She was largely absent. But my father was there when I needed him."

When I asked Rhonda, an executive with an HMO outside Denver, Colorado, in her late thirties, to identify her good inner parent she fondly recalled shopping trips with her mom. "We lived outside New Haven at the time," said Rhonda. "I was around eleven or twelve. I remember coming down to breakfast one Saturday morning. I think it was spring, but, you know, as I think about it I may be transposing the sense of excitement, newness, freshness that comes with spring onto the experience. 'Today is a special day,' my mother said. 'I'm going to teach you to shop, just the way my mother taught me.' We took the train into Manhattan. It became our activity together. We would have so much fun together going into New York on a Saturday or Sunday. She just loved to shop and wanted to share that feeling with me; maybe it's the female equivalent of a sports-crazy dad taking his kid to a baseball game. She would tell me which stores were good for which kinds of merchandise, taking me to one store to look at a blouse, then another to show me the exact same blouse at a lower price. She taught me about what was good or bad about different kinds of fabrics, how to spot sewing flaws, that kind of thing. That first trip I remember feeling like I was being initiated into the adult world—sort of a Bas Mitzvah at Bloomingdales. It was like these were shopping secrets only my mom knew and now she was passing them along to me. I felt very grown up."

When I myself think back, I have a fond memory of my mother making eggs and bacon for me as I was getting ready to go to high school one morning. She stands by the stove, sleepy-eyed, in her pink, terry cloth bathrobe. It's just getting light on a bitterly cold Chicago morning. Outside it is silent. The arctic air has frozen sound. But inside the kitchen it is warm! Eggs are popping in the pan. Bacon sizzles. The aroma of the cooking meat is overwhelmingly delicious. My mother is not a morning person, and I now know what a chore those crack-of-dawn breakfasts must have been for her. But I also think she knew how much I appreciated getting a solid meal before school. I'm not sure I could have articulated it at the time, but I know now that it really made me feel that she loved me and cared for me that she dragged herself out of bed to cook.

It makes no difference whether my mom or Fatima's dad were as saintly as we remember them. What's important is that we believe that they were. At some level children need to idealize their parents, to imbue them with saintly qualities because it makes children feel as if their parents can protect them from all harm. The same is true for all of us; our good inner parents have idealized qualities that are specific to our own experiences.

These good inner parents stand next to us as we raise our own children; we try to emulate and please them. Fatima told me her story after she stayed up all night, nursing her daughter through a stomach flu. It was deeply affirming for her to be able to care for her daughter in the same way her father had cared for her. I tap into the good inner parent of my mother when I make pancakes for my kids on winter dawns before we go ski-ing. The warm nourishing food is a concrete expression of my love for them. I fill them with my love in the same way my mother filled me. They carry my glowing bundle of sustenance inside them on the frigid slopes in the same way I carried my mother's food inside me as I struggled through the snowdrifts on my long walk to school (which, by the way, was fifteen miles away and uphill in both directions). Cooking for my kids draws praise from my good inner parent, it allows me to think of myself as a good father in a deeper, more satisfying way than tak-ing them shopping or even caring for them when they're sick.

The Dangers of the Good Inner Parent

Our good inner parents, however, are not only about the warm, glowing feeling that come from comforting a sick child or whipping up pancakes on snowy mornings. They can also pro-voke anger at our spouses or partners when the demands of their inner parents don't match the demands of ours. When, for example, they don't believe that a hot breakfast is absolutely crucial for their child's well-being and performance. These inner parents can also make us feel bad (guilty mostly) about the way we parent. I know a woman who remembers her mother as always having a tissue or handkerchief ready for her or her sisters when they had a runny nose. She feels guilty when she is not as prepared for her children's sniffles. Similarly, Fatima has never quite forgiven herself for being at a weeklong medical conference when her daughter came down with a bad case of chicken pox. Our good inner parents can motivate us to be more like them, which sometimes makes us better parents, but they can also make us indulgent, as in the case of Kate.

Kate, a petite woman with straight blond hair, cut short, is the mother of Matthew and Isaiah, twin thirteen-year-olds. We are sitting in her well-appointed kitchen outside Houston, Texas. She is most at home there; a good cook descended from good cooks. Her great-grandfather emigrated to Galveston, Texas, in the mid-nineteenth century and started a successful bakery. Five years ago, she divorced Kurt, a successful mutual fund manager, and his alimony and child support payments allow her to be a stay-at-home mom. She spends large chunks of her day gardening or cooking while the twins are at school.

Kate rarely sees Kurt anymore. He moved to New York shortly after their divorce, but she stayed in touch with Kurt's mom, Eleni, whom she had always adored. They shared a love of cooking, and before Eleni died, she had given Kate a legacy—hundreds of recipes, which Kate kept on three-by-five-inch index cards in two battered metal filing cases.

Kate showed them off to me. They were shaped like narrow shoe boxes and looked out of place next to the gleaming, modern appliances in Kate's kitchen. She clearly treasured them. Eleni's mother and grandmother had cooked with many of those same recipes, refining them over the years. The recipes that sat inside those cases were like spells and potions, passed down through the years by women who had developed a kind of secret, highly personalized knowledge.

Now that knowledge was Kate's. I could sense as we talked that they were the medium through which Kate communed with Eleni; cooking from them had about it the aura of a séance with the dead woman's presence being conjured. Kate shared a closeness with Eleni that, as the youngest of seven kids, she had never really had with her mom.

It was no surprise, then, that as we talked, I came to see that Kate's good inner parent looked a lot like the Eleni she so fondly remembered. Kate rose from the kitchen table now and then to stir the chili she was making in a large, cast-iron pot. It was a brilliantly sunny winter day, and with so much light streaming into the room all I could see was her dark silhouette. Showing me the recipes reminded her of something that had been bothering her and she started to tell me about an incident that had happened just before Christmas.

Matthew's class had decided that they wanted to exchange holiday gifts. The teacher, sensitive to the disparity in wealth among the children and their different religious backgrounds, laid out strict ground rules for the "Secret Snowman" gift exchange. The gift had to be handmade and cost no more than five dollars. Matthew wasn't interested in being anyone's Secret Snowman after he learned that he wasn't going to be giving a gift to the girl he had his eye on. When Kate suggested that he make some gingerbread cookies, Matthew said sure. Kate had wanted to try a recipe for gingerbread she had spotted among the cards in Eleni's file. When she told Matthew she would help him out, Matthew wasn't too enthused, and he went to bed the night before the gift exchange without having done any baking. "So I made the cookies for him," she told me. "It would have been so perfect if Matthew had been able to make something from one of his grandmother's old recipes; but he was so busy that I did it for him. Do you think I shouldn't have?"

"Yes!" I wanted to say. I did think she had been overindulgent. He hadn't even asked her to bake for him! But I didn't want to add to her woes. It was clear to me that making those cookies was a way for Kate to connect with Eleni; to do something that would have made Eleni proud of her, something that she would have loved to do at thirteen if she had been Eleni's daughter. Kate was also trying to connect Matthew with his dead grandmother. Helping Matthew bake cookies from scratch would have pleased Kate's good inner parent. But Matthew didn't cooperate, so she did the next best thing and made them herself, satisfying some of her own needs. She felt competent because she had pleased her good inner parent, and she could ease the grief she still felt over Eleni's death by bringing her back to life through her recipe. But she didn't help Matthew grow up very much. She missed a chance to help him develop character, to experience the consequences—the embarassment and shame at being the only one in his class who didn't make a gift—for his self-centered thoughtlessness.

The Dangers of the Bad Inner Parent

Trying to please a good inner parent can blind us to our children's real needs, but trying to keep from being like a bad inner parent can often be even more self-defeating and destructive. For an introduction to your bad inner parent, simply do the opposite of our first exercise. Recall a painful or traumatic experience with one of your parents, an incident in which you felt furious, abandoned, or betrayed.

It's ironic that many of us indulge our kids because we want to avoid any resemblance to our bad inner parents. Phil is a case in point.

Interview with Phil

Phil, the father of two boys and a girl, enjoys his work running a landscaping business, in large part because it allows him to spend time with his kids. He is one of the more involved fathers I know. He makes it a point to attend his kids' hockey games, school plays, and piano recitals. I talked with him over lunch at a local coffee shop in suburban Boston.

DAN: Do you do anything differently in terms of raising your three kids than your parents did?

PHIL: Totally. I learned more from my dad what *not* to do. He was a very structured, scheduled person. He would run Monday, Wednesday, and Friday mornings. He'd eat eggs Tuesdays and Thursdays, and cereal Monday, Wednesday, and Friday. If I wanted to see my dad I had to do it on his schedule, in his den, between eight and eight-thirty on weeknights. I'd stand on the threshold of that dark, wood-paneled room, my heart in my throat, and he'd look up from reading his book, or doing his stamp collection, or whatever he did. It was horrible. So now I'm all over the place with my kids. We're absorbed with all these totally random activities. I bend to their schedules because I don't ever want them to feel the way I felt with my dad.

DAN: Anything else?

PHIL: The thing that I probably worked the hardest at as a father is to make sure that I maintain an emotional, physical relationship with my sons. I mean, with my dad, when I was age twelve the hug went to a handshake and I don't know what the hell happened. Honest to God, I don't know what happened. Maybe he read in the *Wall Street Journal* one day that when your son turns twelve you should only shake his hand and not hug him because he's going to be gay or something. I wouldn't put it past my dad. But I'm terrified to think that could happen with my kids at the age of twelve or thirteen. I'm going to make sure it doesn't.

There is, of course, nothing wrong with Phil's desire to be involved with his kids in a way his father never was—to hug his sons, and to be available to them on their schedule, not his. But notice the word he used, *terrified,* a word that carries more intensity than the situation warrants. The terror comes from reliving, as we all do, his own childhood as he raises his kids. He dreads the loneliness he felt as the child of an emotionally and physically distant father. Moreover, although he didn't mention it in our interview, I know that he was devastated when, while he was away at college, his father had a fatal heart attack. He still broods about not being closer to him when he died. He wants to protect his children from that pain as well. If he were to die suddenly, he doesn't want his children to wonder if they were loved. But just as significantly Phil wants to protect himself. When he hugs his fourteen-year-old son, Phil is getting one of the hugs his father never gave him.

On the whole, trying to avoid being like his bad inner dad has made Phil a better father. But the intensity of his relationship with his inner father has also had unintended results. It can make him too accommodating, too willing to bend over backward to make sure his kids' lives are perfect. His children can sense this and when they try to coax him into giving them an unearned privilege or undeserved treat, they instinctively probe the weakest area of his defenses. They know where he's vulnerable and they exploit their knowledge. They effectively feign emotional withdrawal from him or overdramatize how they will be emotionally scarred if their request is denied, and he is likely to accede to their coercion.

Phil is similar to Craig's father, whom we met in Chapter 3, a man who was sometimes too much of a friend to his son. Like Craig's dad, Phil relishes the emotional closeness he has with his kids and he needs it; sometimes too much. Because of this need, which comes from his relationship with his bad inner parent, he sometimes expects too little from his kids and gives them too much.

The Unconscious Effects of Our Bad Inner Parents

The unconscious ways our parenting styles are affected by our bad inner parent is illustrated by the relationship of Carla, the twenty-nine-year-old mother of Diane, a precious five-year-old.

Carla started therapy with me because her daughter was difficult to manage. We were about ten minutes into one of our first sessions. I had to take a phone call, which is something a therapist should never do. I kept the call very short and apologized profusely, assuring her that I never take calls during sessions except under extreme circumstances. She didn't seem too upset and the incident stimulated a useful discussion. Carla was reminded of an incident from her childhood.

"We had a strict rule in our house about interrupting our parents while they were on the telephone." she said. "It was a no-nonsense policy. No exceptions. One day, playing outside, I was hit in the face with a soccer ball. I ran inside to have my mom look at it. It hurt like hell. I thought my nose was broken. I was nine years old, and I was really sensitive about my looks. I had an uncle who had played a lot of hockey in school and had had his nose broken about five times. I remember thinking that I was going to look like him. I thought I'd been disfigured. When I came in, my mom was on the phone, and I didn't dare interrupt her. So I sat there scared and in pain while she blabbed on and on about something stupid with one of her friends. I was mad at her, too, but I kept quiet until she got off the phone."

In one of those magical moments of insight that happens sometimes in therapy, Carla suddenly made a connection between that incident and her own behavior with Diane, who she said never even bothers to pause when she breaks in on one of Carla's phone calls. She realized that by not setting firm limits on being interrupted when she's on the phone, she was trying to protect Diane from the pain and fear that she felt as a child. She was able to bring this bad inner parent out in the open.

"It's kind of stupid when you think about it," she said. "There's a big difference between butting in on your parent's phone call because you've severed an artery, and interrupting because you need help snapping the blond hair onto your Play-mobile princess. I'll bet even Diane could learn that distinc-tion."

This moment of insight turned out to be the key to helping Carla better manage her daughter. Now that she was conscious of an important reason why it was hard for her to set limits, she became a much more consistent parent. Carla didn't feel as guilty when Diane cried after not getting her way; she could view her attempts to build Diane's character clearly now. The bad inner parent that had been looming over her as she parented Diane became far less ominous. Not only could Diane make the distinction between a right and a wrong time to interrupt, but Carla could also make the distinction between herself and her bad inner parent. And in doing so the bad inner parent no longer ruled her.

Revamping Your Inner Parent

Visiting our good and bad inner parents can help us gain insight on why we raise our children the way we do. Our fear of being like our parents, passing on a karmic load that we know our kids would be better without, often causes us to contort in ways that are counterproductive to giving our kids the tools they need to become independent and form healthy relationships of their own. Our fear of being like our bad inner parents is "kind of stupid when you think about it," as Carla said—but only from a rational, adult perspective, not when you experienced the power of the bad inner parent as a relatively powerless child.

It is possible to remodel these inner parents, or, at least, to reduce their power over us. Just by getting to know them, by simply being conscious of them, we diminish their influence. We realize that they are not living, breathing entities (the conundrum of how to deal with our living, breathing, very real "outer" parents will have to wait for another book). Our inner parents' power to make us feel good or bad comes from inside us, not from anything real; by visiting them, we can begin to come to terms with the incidents that formed them, giving us the perspective to be able to be the kind of parents we want to be, instead of automatically reacting to figments and projections inside ourselves.

Why Us?

As we noted earlier, one of the reasons that inner parents—both good and bad—have so much power over us is that our generation has had the most extended childhood and adolescence in history. More of us went to college and graduate school, waited longer to get married, and remained financially dependent on our parents well into our twenties and sometimes thirties. And unlike children in previous generations, we were largely extraneous to the family. We did not contribute to the family in any material way. We did not have to care for younger siblings, work outside the home to bring in money, or help with the farm chores. Given that such a long period of our lives was spent in a state of relative dependence, it is no surprise, then, that we should be so affected by the psychological issues we dealt with as children.

For the most part, our parents were happy to have us dependent on them. Their lives had been very different. As one man in his seventies told me: "We had it so hard. I think that's why we were so soft with our children." Our parents had to struggle through the Great Depression, World War II, and the Korean War. When we were born into a period of relative peace and prosperity, the parents of us Baby Boomers wanted to forget war, poverty, and hardship. They wanted to immerse themselves in the peace of their family and material comforts. We played our part as best we could. We squealed with delight on Christmas morning, we stared in awe at the new color TV, and, dressed as Zorro or Cinderella, we collected pounds of Halloween candy.

Now, as we raise our children, we revisit our childhood. We want to re-create the magic of our childhood for our children. And we are vigilant about making sure that they don't have to relive the difficult and frightening parts of being a child that we all experienced. It is easier, in some ways, because times are good. Many of us can afford the trip to Disney World; we can rent a beach house and buy our kids expensive birthday presents. And so can our friends.

Our children are lucky that they mean so much to us and that we have so much to give. But it is important to be able to distinguish between when we are parenting them and when we are reparenting ourselves as children. Unless we raise them with the help of an inner parent who knows when to say no and be unyielding, our children will never develop the core of strength, independence, and fortitude they will need to be happy. They will, in short, lack character; that unshakable sense of self that sees us through life's vicissitudes, and is the foundation of all our meaningful relationships.

CHAPTER 12

Techniques and Tools

PRACTICAL ADVICE ON ALLOWANCE, CHORES, RULES, INHERITANCE, AND MORE

As a generation, we often have trouble navigating the boundary between being a friend to our kids and being their parents. We are like Craig's dad, who went ahead and bought his son a CD burner even though he hadn't earned it. Too often, we want them to like us and feel comfortable with us, at the expense of helping them learn lessons in responsibility. Like Stephanie's parents, we are too often lax in our vigilance about what our kids are doing and with whom. We need to teach our children accountability, the hard lesson Connor learned—in spite of the overly protective attitude of his parents.

We indulge our kids and coddle them. No wonder 85 percent of respondents in a recent AOL Time Warner poll said kids in America are spoiled. Too many of us—responding unconsciously to the demands of our inner parents—seem to be seeking our children's approval, a deep affirmation in them of ourselves and our worth. We shower our kids with love, and, in turn, we want to be loved by them. This reciprocation of feeling is the foundation of our lives. But too often it happens at the expense of teaching our children the hard lessons entailed in growing up.

Give Them More T.L.C.

Many of the specific recommendations in this chapter emphasize setting appropriate limits, being strict about certain rules,
and setting inflexible standards for behavior. Though these are
important recommendations, it is important that we remember
what the PPM findings clearly show: what is most crucial for
avoiding the seven deadly syndromes is the quality of the relationships within the family.[1]

Beside limits, children also need time and caring. Time,
Limits, and Caring, or T.L.C., is the holy trinity of child care.
Time—just being there for our kids, being around, being present, being available, spending time with our kids. Limits—
being able to say no, incur our children's wrath, and push them
to do things that are often difficult for them to do. And Caring—taking an active interest in our children's lives, being willing to listen to what's on their minds and participate in their
activities, even if they're not inherently interesting to us.[2]

It's impossible to raise children well unless we spend time
with them. The PPM survey results and research by others is
clear on this point. My research shows that children in families
that eat dinner together at least a few times per week tend to be
less depressed, have less permissive attitudes toward sex, are
less likely to use drugs, and are more likely to work to their
intellectual potential in school. These shared meals, especially
when they permit open communication and mutual enjoyment,
can be the glue that holds families together and that provides
children with a sense of security and belonging that reduces
harmful risk taking and promotes better mental health.

Caring for children consists partly in taking their interests
seriously. This is sometimes easier to do when they're toddlers
and want us to listen to what their teddy bears are telling them
than when our adolescents want us to attend to a disquisition
on why members of 'NSync are cuter than the Backstreet Boys.

But their motivation in both instances is the same. To have our interests taken seriously is a validation of our worth as people. And our teenagers are often more sensitive than we realize about needing the kind of validation that only we, as parents, can give them.

Parents in the PPM survey who often spoke to their children about these adolescent interests were less likely to have a child who was depressed or spoiled and more likely to have one who was working to his or her intellectual potential.

Setting limits for our kids is often what is toughest for us as parents. The PPM survey gave us useful data on how setting limits helps them avoid eating disorders, risky sexual behavior, and drug use. We also saw in the survey how parents can help kids manage chores and allowance that will help them react in a positive way to the inheritance that many of us will leave them.

General Guidelines for Limit Setting

One of the most important PPM findings is that when teens rated their parents, especially mothers, as too lenient—however they wished to define *lenient*—they were at risk, not only for being spoiled, but also for eating disorders, underachievement, creatine/steroid use, meanness, and having permissive attitudes when it came to thirteen-year-olds having sex. Although this should provide sufficient motivation for indulgent parents to start setting firmer limits, many of us balk because we believe it will destroy the closeness we have with our children and take all the fun out of parenting.

One parent, a single mother and an advertising executive in a high-powered, Chicago-based firm, took issue when I asked her the survey question, "How good are you at setting limits and enforcing rules with your child?"

"I have never raised my child that way," June told me. "Since Caroline has been little and her father and I split up, I have felt that mutual respect is inconsistent with 'setting limits,' which is a power relationship."

How many of us feel this way, to a greater or lesser degree? Such an attitude is endemic in our generation for reasons we discussed earlier in the book.

Caroline was seventeen when I interviewed June. It was a Friday afternoon at Caroline's private school. At the end of the interview with June, Caroline appeared, fresh from practice on the school's tennis team. She struck me as a lovely young woman, level-headed and responsible. And the relationship with her mother was obviously close and full of the mutual respect that June had worked hard to develop. Wouldn't it be nice if it always worked out this way?

Unfortunately, it doesn't. Although trust and mutual respect may be more important in the long term than limit setting for a child, I strongly disagree with the philosophy that says that it is always bad to assert power over our children.

Start with an extreme case. If our two-year-old wants to stick his finger in the electrical outlet, we assert our power and pull him away, even if he throws a fit. What's the difference if our fourteen-year-old pleads with us to let her go to a three-day rock festival with an unsupervised group that includes a cadre of seventeen-year-olds? We may try to discuss the issue, but in the end we may need to assert our authority and simply refuse permission to let her go.

We all need limits, adults and children. We are human. We can't always be trusted, even when our intentions are good. Our children may say in all honesty that they're not going to take drugs or have sex at the rock festival, but once there the temptation and peer pressure may sway them. Without laws against speeding or drunk driving, the majority of us would be at higher risk for committing vehicular homicide. Our marriage vows help keep families intact against the divisive forces of sexual temptation, boredom, and hurt feelings. Without grades, almost all of us would have learned less in college. If there were no penalties for work absences, the nation's GDP would fall as fast as a rock tossed from the Sears Tower.

So when a child tries to get your okay to do something they're not ready for by saying, "Don't you trust me?" I recommend responding, "No! And I wouldn't have trusted myself at your age either. Part of my job as a parent is to protect you from risky situations."

When my kids ask me, "How am I ever going to learn if you never let me do anything?" I reply, "I'll have to be the judge of when you're ready."

These responses may anger our children, but our firmness also sends them the message that we care enough about them to hold the line, risk their displeasure, and create conflict and friction. They know it would be easier for us to give in. They are testing us.

How do we know when they're ready? How can we gauge when to loosen the reins? When in doubt, err on the side of caution. Even if you are convinced that your child will someday get drunk, smoke pot, and be sexually active, the longer they wait until that happens, the better off they'll be. I don't think it hurts here to reiterate the point we made earlier—the research is quite clear. The earlier a child begins these activities, the higher their risk in later life of substance dependence, unplanned pregnancy, and delinquency.

An immature child can quickly get in over her head. Irrespective of any physical or emotional harm that may accrue, the psychological adaptation to her situation is most often counterproductive. In order to justify what she's done, she often gets in even deeper. She may, for example, have to lie to cover her tracks. It was striking in the PPM interviews how teens described their lives almost like someone with multiple personalities. There was the life of school, sports, and friends they told their parents they were living, and another, hidden life, of sex, drugs, and lies.

One can exert power, set limits in this way, and still have fun with the kids. In our sample, most kids who said their moms or dads were "pretty strict" or "too strict" also said they had fun with their parents most or all of the time.

We shouldn't be afraid to switch hats or be inconsistent. One minute we can be a playmate and the next the voice of authority. Our children can easily make the distinction when we have switched over to "parent mode." I know with my own children, they can be teasing me, abusing me, calling me names, tackling me and generally being little bundles of seemingly uncontrollable mischief. I can protest, whimper, and whine. But should things get out of hand, they cross a certain line, they become too aggressive, or they start to breach certain boundaries of decency and respect, then I need to put an edge of steel in my voice; when they hear this tone, they most often begin to simmer down and fall into line.

Consistency

Consistency is probably the word most frequently used in articles that give parents advice about setting limits; but let's face it—it's hard, if not impossible, to be consistently consistent in parenting about everything. In two-parent households, one parent is probably more lenient than the other. Sometimes we can't remember the specifics of policy decisions that we (or our partner) have made. Sometimes we are just too tired to battle with our kids and we concede.

This said, consistency is important. I generally recommend parents pick three limits, or rules, about which they're always consistent. Sit down with your partner, spouse, or yourself, and agree on these limits and what the punishment will be for your kids if they've transgressed. Then discuss them with your kids. Convene a family meeting that functions the way a staff meeting does at an office. Present the limits and discuss them. In subsequent meetings, the limits can be altered. If the established limits are being automatically adhered to, one or two more could be added. Families are not democracies, and these meetings are not democratic. We should listen carefully to our kids' opinions, but the final word is ours.

As an example in my family, saying "shut up" to another family member exacts an automatic $.50 deduction in the offender's allowance. Before we put this rule in place, we would chastise our children when they said "shut up," but we had no official penalty. I occasionally used the word myself, most often in a joking way. But then "shut up" started to become a regular part of our kids' vocabulary, and my wife and I felt it had gone too far. We originally instituted a penalty of three dollars, but when the younger daughter, Julia, started pushing her buttons, Diana lost her whole allowance in fifteen minutes. So we had another meeting and settled on the fifty-cent penalty. After a week of having this rule in place, "shut up" almost completely disappeared from our home. My children, being sharp negotiators, wanted parity. If a parent used the word or was overheard using a swear word, fifty cents would be added to each of their allowances. We agreed. They accept the rule as fair now, and enforcing it has become effortless.

Penalties

If you are going to be consistent and set limits, it's usually necessary to have some kind of punishment in place. Some non-indulgent parents can avoid punishments or "consequences" (as we like to call them in my house); usually those who have both a philosophical opposition to punishment and a lot of free time. We interviewed one boy of fourteen in suburban Chicago who had such parents. We asked Alex if his parents grounded him when he did something wrong.

"Umm, I've never been grounded," he said. "Usually when I do something extremely horrible, my parents sit me down and we talk for hours and hours on end and just work through what's going on. We sit and talk through everything. Like my family is not the kind to punish my brother and me. They don't think it's the right way. They think that if you sit down and you work at it and you talk, it will help it for the next time."

Time out is usually effective for younger kids as a consequence or punishment. As kids get older, their rooms are generally where they want to be. I stopped using time-outs as punishment when my kids turned seven.

Talking it out, the way Alex's parents do, is important, but I think rules are usually more effective if there are real consequences to breaking them, and it's important that the consequences are spelled out in advance. I take my inspiration from professional sports and the criminal courts. When a professional athlete commits some infraction, such as rough play, arguing with the referee, or using performance-enhancing drugs, the penalty usually takes the form of a time-out (suspension, the penalty box, fouling out of a game), or a fine. The courts take the same approach, but also add community service, reeducation and counseling.

In theory, using positive reinforcement is much more effective than punishment in getting people or animals to do what you want them to. Unfortunately, a parent trying to get her child to be more courteous does not have the kind of control over the environment that a dolphin trainer does. In my experience parents who try to put the philosophy of behavior modification into practice usually fall short of their goal because they try to do too much. Those who maintain charts that keep a tally of a child's good behavior (i.e., whenever a child has refrained from using the words "shut up" for one hour, he or she gets a point or token redeemable for treats at week's end) often find it demands too much of their time and that they can't maintain the consistency they need to make the program effective. I heartily approve of positive reinforcement and the principles of behavior modification.[3] It is vitally important that we use positive reinforcement, such as praise, whenever we catch our children being good. But, realistically, we often have to use punishment or consequences as well. This leaves parents with a lot of options. Philosophically, I like community service, doing tasks that aren't a normal part of a child's responsibilities, such as stacking firewood, sweeping out the garage, or washing windows. Grounding (house arrest) is popular among parents and often effective; the loss of phone privileges can be effective, too. But be cautious about setting penalties that are too severe. For one thing, it limits your ability to punish for anything else. Once I worked with a set of parents who, in response to various infractions, removed nearly everything from their son's room—stereo, television, computer, and phone—until they no longer had any disciplinary leverage.

Chores and Allowance

An allowance can provide children with some important early lessons in financial planning. Some experts suggest making a child divide his or her allowance into the same three (not necessarily equal) parts that adults do: savings, spending, and retirement.[4] The children can use their savings for expensive purchases, but the retirement account is never touched. The spending portion of the allowance is disposable income: they can spend it immediately on whatever they want. For older children some parents find that a monthly stipend to be used for designated expenses such as clothes or school lunches works well in helping their teenagers learn how to manage their money.

How much money should your kids get? A useful rule of thumb is a dollar per week for each year of age. This could be adjusted, depending on how much the child needs for fixed expenses (school lunches, etc.), or if a large portion of the allowance is to be designated for a savings plan, such as a college fund, charitable donations, or investments. Think about how much money your child really needs. Too much disposable income makes it easier for them to buy cigarettes, alcohol, or drugs. In my clinical practice I've seen a direct relationship between a large disposable income and drug use.

Should children be required to do chores for allowance? This question elicits strong responses. Some experts recommend that allowance not be tied to chores. They suggest that this can reduce a child's intrinsic motivation, teaching them that they should never do anything unless there is an external reward. I know at least one set of parents who are split on this issue. "I don't think that children should get paid for doing household chores," the mother told me. "The chores should simply be a part of their responsibility as a part of being in the household. My husband disagrees. So they get an allowance, but he tells them it's for their chores and I tell them it's not."

My children don't get their allowance if they haven't done their chores. The reason I have come down on this side of the fence is that it is hard for me to discount the PPM research that shows that children who get an allowance but do not have to do chores to earn it are at risk for depression, tend to be self-centered, and have more permissive attitudes toward thirteen-year-olds having sex than their peers for whom an allowance is tied to a set of proscribed responsibilities. Moreover, teens who don't do chores are also more likely to see themselves as spoiled: they know they're getting something for nothing.

Trust Funds—the Unearned Windfall

If you are fortunate enough to be able to leave a hefty inheritance to your children, you face some of the same decisions that you had to think about with respect to allowance—except there are more zeros involved. You may be worried that giving your children too much money might ruin them. You're right to worry. Andrew Carnegie said on the subject of inheritance, "I would as soon leave my son a curse as the almighty dollar."

I interviewed a number of attorneys and accountants, specialists who work with wealthy families to figure out how best to transfer wealth from one generation to the next, who share some of Carnegie's concerns. Their primary responsibility is to figure out how best to minimize gift and estate taxes, set up trust funds, and preserve as much of their clients' capital as possible, but they also recognize the psychological issues with which they have to contend. They all told me *many* sad stories about people whose wealth had been a curse rather than a blessing.

They clearly saw instances where a large inheritance or trust fund can remove incentives and diminish achievement in a child. One estate planner told me: "For a lot of people—and this is something that I spend a fair amount of time counseling clients with—is that they somehow have to indoctrinate in their kids how their wealth can be a liberating force rather than a constraint. People who are enormously talented but somehow see there's this big pot of gold, and they don't want to wander very far from it. One guy who had worked all his life running this big family business, but never liked it. He really wanted to be a doctor, but instead was running this widget company. He's in his late fifties now, and he has been fighting with the rest of the family for years about the business. But he never had any interest in the business in the first place. Believe me, there was plenty of money! He could have been a doctor and traveled and lived where he wanted. Instead, the wealth put blinders on him and he couldn't see what he really wanted to do. I have three other clients whom I've watched grow from youth into middle age in the same situation. Their wealth is an albatross around their necks."

In other instances, people who inherit big chunks of money or who get control of a family business feel that in order to prove their self-worth, they need to prove that they are worthy of the money and position. This sometimes comes about when a child is given too much control over money and power they aren't able to handle. This can be analogous to the parent who gives a child a big allowance or gifts in order to allay guilt about not spending enough time with a child. A tax attorney/estate planner says he sees this all the time.

"I think it's fairly common to see successful entrepreneurs who are workaholics, if you will. They come to the conclusion that they're going to make up for the time they didn't spend with their kids by showering them with money—wealth. Over and over I've seen that the wealth has a negative rather than a positive influence on the child's life. The child, never having developed the discipline or business acumen that the father did, nonetheless feels compelled to make his mark and prove his self-worth to the father by trying to do things with the wealth that are beyond his own abilities. What often happens is that the kids fall into the hands of all kinds of promoters who are looking for funds to pursue their own ideas—their own business ventures. So they'll assume business risks with the heir's wealth, risks they would never take with their own money, and the heir buys into it because he thinks this guy is really smart and that he's going to show his father that he's smarter than his dad 'cause he's gonna make all this dough. A lot of people think that one of the things that you need to do with wealth is to be careful about kids getting their hands on it 'cause they'll spend it all, and I find that with clients of really substantial means, the far greater risk is that the money is lost through investment rather than spending. Families of really significant means can't make a real dent in their capital by buying things. On the other hand, they can blow $50 million overnight due to bad investments. I've seen this happen more than once.

"I counsel clients to let their kids go out and do something on their own and then come back into the family business or whatever so that they've tested the waters and understand their own abilities and limitations. I tell my clients not to just dump money on their kids—keep it in the trust and let the trustee mature and have an orientation period where he or she begins to better understand the wealth."

After interviewing a number of people who work in the field, I got a clear sense of how important it is for parents to bring in professional help when they're passing money on to their kids. They have to make sure to set appropriate limits and make sure their wealth has the intended effect and guards their children against at least some of life's difficulties. Money should also make their kids' lives fuller and richer, and not just in the material sense.

Sex

Another area where it's clear we have to set limits as parents is about sex. We want to raise kids who are sexually responsible, but it's often hard for us to think of our kids as sexual beings. It makes us uncomfortable. We often fail to recognize the intensity of their emerging sexuality because we're scared of it. Some parents feel that talking too much about sex with their teens just makes it more likely that they'll have sex. Because of our discomfort and denial we too often don't take an active enough role in shaping our children's attitude toward their emerging sexuality.

Sex can be wonderful or horrible depending on when, how, and why it happens. But all too often it is less than wonderful for teenagers. In fact, most teens who are sexually active—both boys and girls—wish they had waited.[5]

I spoke to Sam, a senior at a suburban public high school outside Boston, who said he had fallen desperately in love when he was twelve. He had pursued the girl, a couple of years older than he was, before she finally relented and slept with him.

"I pursued her and pursued her and pursued her," he said. "I wanted to marry her. We were going to run away to Mississippi where we had heard it was legal to get married at fourteen. Our parents let us sleep together when she came to visit, or when I went over to her house. Her mother helped her get birth control pills. Our sexual relationship was completely out in the open."

Sam described what started out as an idyllic love affair for both of them. But after about a year the relationship shifted. He began to realize he was no longer in love. It was devastating for both of them.

"I felt so awful," he said. "I just realized my feelings had changed. I wasn't ready to make the kind of commitment I had made to her. I was very much in the process of growing up, changing, and becoming. She had no idea what had happened. She became reinvolved quickly. With our history teacher, as it turned out. He lost his job, and she went on to have a series of boyfriends through high school. But it made me distrust myself. I haven't had any girlfriends since we broke up. I think we had sex way too early, and I, at least, wish we had waited."

Waiting is what parents should try to instill. Remember, you are not trying to prohibit your child from ever having sex or brainwashing them into believing sex is bad; you are simply trying to get them to wait to have sex until they are mature enough to handle it.

Here are some specific tips to help your kids wait until they're ready for sex. The first and most important step is to clearly communicate your own values about sex. The PPM research as well as other studies show that parental attitudes about sex get translated to their kids.

For example, parental approval of birth control by teens can lead to earlier sexual experiences by their children unless there is also a discussion about other values associated with sex. We need to let our kids know that sex is special, a form of love and caring, and that it is as powerful in its ability to make us feel rage, self-loathing, and loneliness as it is to bring us joy and intimacy.

Don't be afraid to tell your child that a relationship should never be contingent on sex, that if a boyfriend or girlfriend is pressuring them to have sex, that they should find someone else. Don't be afraid to tell them that they'll be happier if they wait. The PPM survey clearly shows that as teenagers get older (and more of them become sexually experienced), they understand the need to wait. While nearly half of thirteen- and fourteen-year-olds surveyed didn't think it was wrong for a thirteen-year-old to have oral sex, the seventeen- and eighteen-year-olds were far less permissive—less than one in five expressed that attitude.

We don't want to panic our kids, but we also want them to have a real sense of the physical danger as well as the psychological confusion associated with having sex. We need to be sure they're aware of HIV and STDs. And we need to stress to them that waiting until they're ready and sure is the best way of protecting themselves against the physical dangers of sex.

It's important that we carefully monitor and supervise our kids, especially during after-school hours. Research shows that most teenage girls get pregnant between 3:00 and 6:00 P.M.

These are also the hours that most juvenile crime occurs. Why? Because these are the hours when teenagers are most likely to be unsupervised. Make sure you know where your children are. Communicate closely with their friends' parents. On weekends, set a reasonable curfew. Don't make it too easy for your son or daughter to stay out late drinking. Alcohol use and teenage sex go hand in hand.

Discourage early steady dating. One mother I know has a daughter not quite fifteen. The girl persuaded her parents to let her bring her boyfriend along on a ski weekend to their Vermont vacation home. The parents figured they were there to chaperone the young couple, and they said why not. They liked the boy. He often ate dinner with them, and he seemed like an upright lad. But the parents were also clear that they didn't want their daughter sleeping with her guy, so they gave them separate rooms. But, surprise, the daughter and her boyfriend managed to have sex anyway! The mother feels horribly guilty now.

"She should have realized that she was legitimizing their relationship," said a psychologist friend of mine who was privy to the story. "She was endowing the relationship with a maturity it simply didn't have. She should have realized how intense it was to bring a boyfriend to her weekend home. She was giving implicit consent to their sexual experimentation by allowing them to spend the night together under the same roof. And thinking that they were mature enough to resist temptation was simply naive.

"Eventually, the daughter told her mother about how a group of kids would party at the house of whoever's parents were away for the weekend. She said the urge to party was due in part to the pressured lives the kids led doing sports and hours of homework every day. They just wanted to blow off steam—to get loaded and laid."

Teen relationships can get serious in a hurry. Exclusive, committed relationships among children under sixteen can quickly lead to adult situations that are beyond their emotional maturity. You should also discourage your son or daughter from becoming involved with older or younger people. Teen relationships where there is an age difference of two years or more can put too much pressure on the younger partner and should be discouraged.

Eating Problems

In Chapter 8, we focused on issues relating to poor nutrition and our children's dissatisfaction with their body image. Here are some guidelines for helping your kids steer clear of eating disorders.

- Prepare balanced meals
- Introduce new foods slowly
- Don't worry that you might be starving your child. Appetite and hunger are two different things
- Parents should decide what to buy and what will be offered
- Don't be the food police—at every age it is up to your child to determine what she wants from the food that's offered and decide how much or how little to eat at a meal
- If you are worried that your child might be anorexic or have some other problem with eating, contact your physician, don't start a fight
- Make sure your child knows you're not making a moral issue about his or her food choices

If All Else Fails, Hire Someone to Help

What if you find that it's impossible to set the limits you know you should? Perhaps you find it impossible to remodel your inner parents, or because of your other commitments, you just can't make the necessary time. You can hire someone to help you. This is not an all or nothing proposition. Even in families where there is little indulgence, exposing your child to a no-nonsense nanny, a strict school, or an exacting coach can have its benefits.

A friend told me about the saga of her son, who was about to take an exam in his Tae Kwon Do to move up to the next level, a black stripe on his red belt.

"The instructor called me at home," she said, "to warn me that this exam was a difficult one, and that my son might fail. My son would have had to perform certain movements that are very precise. Lots of memorization was involved. He said my son was moving to the next level rather quickly."

"Are you really, really sure you want him to take the exam?" the instructor had asked.

"What are the consequences of him taking it and failing?" she had replied.

"None."

"So why not just let him try?"

"Well, he might fail and then be upset. Some parents get upset when their kid doesn't make it. I just wanted to let you know."

"I urged him to let my son take the exam, and to fail him if he isn't prepared. Unfortunately, I related this story to my son and he opted, on his own, to wait until he was more prepared to take the exam. In a way, I wish he had taken it, failed, and then learned that he had to work harder. The instructor said I wouldn't believe the cranky parents and children who cry and rant if they don't make it to the next rank—some quit altogether. He said there was always pressure on him to pass kids who weren't ready to advance."

In my own house, I recently saw the benefits of having my kid deal with failure. For reasons that are still not completely clear to me, my eleven-year-old daughter wanted to join a local hockey team, despite the fact that she would be the least experienced member. During a recent school vacation, she decided to enroll in a three-day hockey camp. She was subjected to three nonstop hours of rigorous hockey drills with twenty-five other kids, most of whom were older boys. She told me that she finished last in every race they had; after each session she was so worn out she almost had to crawl off the ice. I would never have been able to work her that hard at anything, even if she would have agreed to let me try. But her coaches were able to extract a level of effort she didn't even know she had. No wonder she was proud of herself! I could see the blossoming of her confidence and self-esteem.

This is one of the same reasons that programs such as Outward Bound or the Peace Corps work so well for so many people. There are obstacles to overcome, hardships to endure, and, by being successful, participants develop self-confidence. We need the manufactured hardships of hockey camps, survival training, and two years of helping out at a health clinic in sub-Saharan Africa. For most American kids, physical and psychological hardships of this magnitude are not part of their experience.

The Future?

Let's turn now to the future. What will become of the children of the Age of Indulgence? What kind of contribution will our kids—who have been raised with more wealth and fewer limits than any generation in history—make to the world?

Talkin' About My Generation

THE MILLENNIAL FUTURE

> You better start swimming
> or you'll sink like a stone
> for the times they are a-changin'
> —*BOB DYLAN*

What will the "Millennials"—the children born in the last twenty years of the twentieth century who are the focus of this book—be like as adults? Will they be happy and successful? Will they be able to create solid marriages and raise psychologically sound kids? As adults, will they possess the healthy attitudes, good habits, and ethical behavior that are character's core? Will they change society for the better?

The PPM research shows us that our kids are at risk for the seven syndromes, at least partially because many of us don't give them the time, limits, and caring they need. These risks don't just apply to the kids in the PPM survey—they apply to millions of other middle- and upper-class children who are the core of the Millennial generation. Millennials are highly competitive, prone to self-centeredness, depression, anxiety, and anger. Even when they're driven they often seem adrift. They like to party—drugs, alcohol, and cigarettes fuel their social life and too many of them are getting involved in sexual relationships at too young an age.

The children in the PPM sample and the millions of other advantaged youth like them will (unless our political system changes drastically) have the inside track on the most influential positions in our society. They will network at elite colleges; graduate and professional schools. They will be recruited by the big corporations, investment houses, and law firms. By the year 2040 the Millennials will be in charge—it will be the beginning of an era in which they will predominate the legislature, judiciary, executive offices, and boardrooms of banking and business.

I worry about how these Millennials will fare. I worry about the effects of their upbringing not only on their own health but on the health of our nation. Unless we change, I'm afraid that our kids won't be able to handle the challenges that they'll face. I worry that we—their parents and teachers—haven't instilled in them the character they'll need to adequately cope with adversity.

It is hard to resist comparing the Millennials—the children of our New Gilded Age—to the kids who grew up in the original Gilded Age. Their births are exactly one hundred years apart (1880 to 1900; 1980 to 2000), and the oldest members of each of these two generations came of age at the turn of a century. Each generation lived in a time when new technology created vast wealth for a segment of society and fundamental change for nearly all of it.

The children of the Old Gilded Age were the first to embrace the automobile and airplane, inventions that made the world a smaller place. The Millennials were born during the infancy of the Internet, which promises to connect us all in its web and shrink the world even further.

Indulgent child rearing and a dramatic rise in society's concern with the needs of children marked each historical period.

In the most influential late-nineteenth-century child-rearing manual, *Gentle Measures in the Training of the Young*, Jacob Abbot wrote:

> It seems to me that children are not generally indulged enough. They are thwarted and restrained in respect to the gratification of their harmless wishes a great deal too much. Indeed, as a general rule, the more that children are gratified in respect to their childish fancies and impulses, and even their caprices, when no evil or danger is to be apprehended, the better.[1]

The children of the Gilded Age were defined by the horror of the First World War, which changed the balance of political power in the world, and the Spanish flu epidemic of 1918, which killed over 20 million people around the world, including more than half a million Americans. After the Great War, many who had grown up in the Gilded Age had difficulty adapting to the new world in which they found themselves. They had trouble getting their bearings from cultural landmarks that no longer existed; because of this, they are often referred to as the Lost Generation.

The children of the Gilded Age reacted in different ways to the combination of the indulgent, affluent environment in which they had been raised and these cataclysmic events. They became the hedonistic flappers and bootleggers, expatriates such as Ernest Hemingway and F. Scott Fitzgerald. Or, like Dorothy Tiffany Burlingham, the heir to the Tiffany glass, silver, and diamond fortune who fled her Victorian world of external opulence for a life with Sigmund and Anna Freud in Vienna and London, they immersed themselves in the inner world of psychoanalysis or other nonmaterialistic pursuits.[2]

It is impossible to predict what cataclysms, if any, our Millennial children will face. There are those who predict that the Millennial future will bring the outbreak of deadly disease epidemics due to the collapse of the public health infrastructure around the world.[3] And following the dot.com boom, some prognosticators are predicting a deep recession that may foreshadow a period of great economic hardship, especially for the middle class. Others predict that the growing gap between rich and poor (individuals and nations) will create substantial unrest and fuel terrorism and political upheaval.[4]

But even if there are no such societal cataclysms, nearly all Millennials will have to contend with personal misfortunes—death, illness, financial hardship, and failure. Will they have the strength of character to respond?[5]

One thing is certain: Millennials will be faced with high levels of competition for college, job placement, and professional advancement. On July 1, 2025, the U.S. Census Bureau estimates that there will be 107,517,000 Millennials living in America. In contrast there were about half that many American Baby Boomers alive on July 1, 2000.[6] And if that were not enough fuel to stoke the fires of competition, the Millennials are the generation with the highest expectations for achievement—more of them envision that they will complete four years of college, attend graduate or professional school, and land prestigious, high-paying jobs.[7] They are also likely to frequently switch jobs, change careers and locations. Friendships will also probably be more transitory. Perhaps more than any previous generation, the Millennials will need enormous inner resources—character—to compensate for the breakdown of social cohesion and support in a world that will be multicultural, without borders and established social norms, and in the process of rapid and radical transformation.

The outcome for the Millennial generation in large part depends on us. If we as their parents raise them to be compassionate, charitable, and honest with themselves and others, instill in them a respect and appreciation for the privileged world in which they have been born, give them the psychological tools with which to adapt to stress and transcend adversity—in short, if we help them develop the essential traits of character—they will have a bright future. Let's do a favor for our kids, our grandchildren, and all those who will come after us. Let's take the time, focus our attention, and help our children become the strong, loving, and vital people we know they can be.

———

Methodology and Selected Results from the Parenting Practices at the Millennium Study

Sampling Method

Eleven schools were contacted for participation in the PPM study. We (myself and my research assistants) chose schools that served upper-middle to upper socioeconomic status (SES) communities in the Northeast, Mid-Atlantic, Southeast, Midwest, and far West of the United States. We did this because we wanted a sample of students and parents that was geographically diverse and, given our desire to focus on advantaged families, one that oversampled children and parents in upper SES groups. All eleven schools agreed to participate. However, due to scheduling problems or other logistical reasons, data was collected at only nine of these. The schools represent a convenience sample in the sense that in all but two instances someone we knew had a personal connection at the school. Despite its convenient nature, we feel that these schools—two large suburban high schools and seven independent schools—are typical of their kind and in that sense the sample is representative of upper-middle and upper-income families in the United States.

Even though we sampled schools, in all cases the unit of analysis was the individual student or parent. We understand that contextual effects such as those at the level of the school or classroom are often important (Bryk & Raudenbush, 1992) but hierarchical statistical models require a larger number of "level two" units and the primary focus of our study was at "level one"—an investigation of the relationships between parenting behavior and student outcome.

There are 1078 parents and 654 teenagers in the final survey sample. In the spring of 2000, 2509 anonymous surveys (described below) were mailed to parents of elementary, middle, and high school students. 1078 parents returned the surveys directly to us, for a very acceptable response rate of 43 percent. Due to concerns about the validity of responses (Breton et al., 1995), the student survey sample was only filled out by children over the age of twelve. Trained interviewers administered 654 student surveys (described below) to selected classes within schools or, in one instance, the entire school. In order to obtain a representative sample of students within schools, we chose classes within schools that had a typical student composition (i.e., nonelective classes). Students under eighteen years of age had to obtain permission to fill out the survey from a parent or guardian (parental refusal rate was less than 1 percent). Students were instructed to fill out the anonymous questionnaires on their own, and the interviewer remained in the room during the entire process and collected the surveys immediately after administering them to preserve confidentiality.

Tables 1 and 2 (on page 225) present demographic data on the parent and child sample. This data shows that the parent sample is largely white, affluent, and the modal respondent is a married woman. The distribution of family income in this sample is skewed toward the upper end. The adolescent sample ap-

Table 1—Selected Demographics—PPM Parents
N = (1078)

Relationship to Child	
Mother	80%
Father	19%
Other	1%
Single Parent	16%
Race/ethnicity	
Black	3%
Hispanic	3%
White	92%
Other	2%
Average household pretax yearly income*	
Less than $50,000	10%
$50,001 to $100,000	26%
$100,001 to $200,000	26%
$200,001 to $500,000	24%
More than $500,000	14%
Average number of children	
in household	2.4

*n = 1007

Table 2—Selected Demographics—PPM Adolescents
N = 654

Sex	
Female	54%
Male	46%
Age	
13–14	13%
15	23%
16	22%
17	28%
18	14%
Race/ethnicity	
Black	6%
Hispanic	6%
White	80%
Other	8%

pears to have a higher percentage of nonwhite members, but this is due, at least in part, to the students' greater propensity to write in responses such as "human" in the "Other" category. The disjuncture between parents and adolescents with respect to race/ethnicity raises the question of whether they are representative of the same population, so we investigated whether other discrepancies existed.

The student sample is epidemiological in the sense that we were able to randomly select whole classrooms and in one case surveyed every student in a school.

On the other hand, even though we mailed questionnaires to all parents (or in the cases of very large schools, a random sample), the 43 percent who returned questionnaires may constitute a nonrandom sample of the parents at these schools. To examine this question, we looked at the concordance between student and parent samples on a number of indicators. It is well known that children and their parents do not show high levels of agreement on behavior checklists and other diagnostic instruments and the dilemma of how to combine information from multiple informants is one of the biggest methodological headaches in the social sciences (Achenbach, T., 1991; Kindlon, Kuo, & Mohler, 1991). Because of this, we chose the most concrete items on the PPM survey—questions about owned possessions, allowance, and demographics, that should show the highest levels of agreement—and compared the two groups. Given that there was variance between schools on these parameters, we stratified the analysis by school and limited it to the four schools (one public, two independent, one parochial) in which there was a large number of students and parents of students in all age groups between thirteen and eighteen. The N for this analysis is 1089 (480 teens, 609 parents). Table 3 (on page 227) contains the findings from these analyses.

What these results show is that there is a general agreement between parents and students on most of the parameters. For

Table 3—Comparison of Agreement Between Parent and Student Samples

	PARENTS	ADOLESCENTS
School 1 (N = 203)		
Sex of child		
Male	55%	57%
Female	45%	43%
Child receives an allowance*	89%	74%
Number of Children in Family		
1	17%	13%
2	39%	40%
3	29%	27%
4 or more	15%	20%
Child owns a horse	3%	1%
Child has a car	29%	33%
Child has cell phone	33%	40%
Child has a parent-financed credit card	12%	14%
Child has Nintendo or video game system	52%	59%
Child has TV in bedroom	50%	56%
Child has a phone in bedroom	45%	53%
Child has computer in bedroom	27%	39%
School 2 (N = 414)		
Sex of child		
Male	48%	49%
Female	52%	51%
Child receives an allowance*	93%	83%
Number of Children in Family		
1	10%	9%
2	47%	51%
3	30%	23%
4 or more	13%	16%
Child owns a horse	2%	3%
Child has a car*	24%	35%
Child has cell phone	30%	35%
Child has a parent-financed credit card	28%	29%
Child has Nintendo or video game system*	38%	61%
Child has TV in bedroom*	22%	33%
Child has a phone in bedroom*	60%	72%
Child has computer in bedroom	50%	55%

Table 3 (continued)

	PARENTS	ADOLESCENTS
School 3 (N = 154)		
Sex of child		
Male	46%	46%
Female	54%	54%
Child receives an allowance*	92%	78%
Number of Children in Family		
1	12%	14%
2	47%	42%
3	25%	22%
4 or more	16%	22%
Child owns a horse	6%	16%
Child has a car	43%	53%
Child has cell phone	42%	35%
Child has a parent-financed credit card	22%	27%
Child has Nintendo or video game system	38%	50%
Child has TV in bedroom	41%	51%
Child has a phone in bedroom	67%	75%
Child has computer in bedroom	31%	28%
School 4 (N = 317)		
Sex of child		
Male	46%	43%
Female	54%	57%
Child receives an allowance*	80%	69%
Number of Children in Family		
1	12%	8%
2	49%	50%
3	29%	28%
4 or more	10%	14%
Child owns a horse	2%	3%
Child has a car	22%	24%
Child has cell phone	14%	16%
Child has a parent-financed credit card*	9%	16%
Child has Nintendo or video game system	50%	54%
Child has TV in bedroom	54%	63%
Child has a phone in bedroom*	65%	76%
Child has computer in bedroom	33%	34%

*Chi-Square test of association shows a difference between parent and student samples significant at $p < .05$

example, in no instance is there a statistically significant difference between parents' and adolescents' reports of sex ratio or family size. In all instances adolescents were less likely to report receiving an allowance, and when significant group differences were reported about the percentage of children owning a given possession (six out of thirty-six comparisons), these were always in the direction of children being more likely to report owning the object. These results, although not conclusive, suggest that the parents and children are drawn from the same population.

Both parent survey and adolescent survey results were used in the analyses and the results are presented separately. For some syndromes, data from only one of the two informants was used. For example, drug-use questions were answered by teens only. In cases where large gender differences exist, results are presented separately for boys and girls. Table 4 (on page 230) gives the operational definitions of the syndromes and the percentage of adolescents who exhibit the syndrome.

The Parenting Practices at the Millennium Survey

Both a parent and adolescent version of the Parenting Practices at the Millennium Survey were developed for the purposes of this study. The parent version consisted of thirty-eight questions, many of which were answered using a yes/no, or Likert scale, format. No open-ended questions were asked on either the parent or student survey. In addition to demographic information, such as relationship to child, race/ethnicity, and annual household income, parents were asked a variety of questions about the rules, chores, and disciplinary practices they established with their children. Some of these questions involved asking parents to

Table 4—Dependent Variables

		PERCENT OF CHILDREN WHO EXHIBITED THE SYNDROME	
SYNDROME	DEFINITION OF ANALYSIS VARIABLE(S)	PARENT REPORT	TEEN REPORT
Self-centered (Pride)	*For adolescent report:* Combined responses to three survey questions: 1) "I am willing to help others when they need help," 2) "I am concerned with the well-being of others," and 3) "Are you regularly involved in community service?" The first two of these questions were scored on a 3-point scale (1–3), with higher scores indicating greater concern for others. A "yes" to the community service question got a score of one, a "no" a zero. A score of less than 5 was defined as self-centeredness.	N/A	32.6%
Anger (Wrath)	**Mean to others:** *For both adolescent and parent reports:* A "very true" or "somewhat true" response to, "I am (My child is) mean to others."	29.4%	28.4%
	Depression: *For adolescent report:* A "very true" response to, "I am unhappy, sad, or depressed" *or* a "yes" to "During the past 2 months did you ever feel so sad or hopeless that almost every day for two weeks or more you stopped doing some usual activities?" For parent report: A "very true" or "somewhat true" response to, "My child is unhappy, sad, or depressed."	15.7%	Boys—24.3% Girls—31.7%

Table 4 (continued)

		PERCENT OF CHILDREN WHO EXHIBITED THE SYNDROME	
		PARENT	TEEN
SYNDROME	DEFINITION OF ANALYSIS VARIABLE(S)	REPORT	REPORT
Driven (Envy)	*For adolescent report:* Combined results from two survey questions: A "very true" response to "I worry a lot" *and* a "somewhat true" or "very true" response to "I feel that I have to be perfect." *For parent report:* Combined results from two survey questions: A "very true" response to "I worry a lot" *and* a "very true" response to "I feel that I have to be perfect."	5.1%	24.8%
Not Motivated (Sloth)	*For adolescent and parent report:* A "not true" response to "I (my child) work(s) up to my (his) intellectual potential in school."	12.4%	Boys—25.8% Girls—14.9%
Eating Problems (Gluttony)	**Body Mass Index:** *adolescent variable only:* Weight (in kilos)/height in meters^2	N/A	N/A
	Disordered Eating: *adolescent variable only:* (one or more of the following extreme weight-loss strategies during the past month: 1) Twenty-four hours or more of fasting, 2) vomiting/use of laxatives, 3) use of nonprescription diet aids such as pills or powders.	N/A	Boys—6.4% Girls—23.5%
	Creatine/steroid use: *adolescent variable only:* Use of either creatine *or* nonprescription steroids during the past year.	N/A	Boys—18.7% Girls—.85%

Table 4 (continued)

SYNDROME	DEFINITION OF ANALYSIS VARIABLE(S)	PERCENT OF CHILDREN WHO EXHIBITED THE SYNDROME	
		PARENT REPORT	TEEN REPORT
Self-Control Problems (Lust)	**Drug Behavior:** *adolescent variable only:* Has used alcohol, marijuana, other illicit drugs or cigarettes during the past month.	N/A	58.9%
	Permissive sexual attitudes: *adolescent variable only:* Combination of 4 attitude items relating to the "wrongness" of oral sex and sexual intercourse for 13- and 19-year-olds. A permissive attitude is defined by responses of "not wrong at all" for sex by 19-year-olds *and* a response of either "not very wrong" or "not wrong at all" regarding sex by 13-year-olds.	N/A	21.3%
Spoiled (Greed)	*For adolescent report:* Response of "very true" to "I am spoiled." *For parent report:* Response of "very true" or "somewhat true" to "My child is spoiled."	57.7%	Boys—11.0% Girls—19.8%

imagine certain scenarios, such as catching a child using alcohol, and then checking off what their response would likely be (e.g., discuss it with the child, ground him/her, etc.). We also asked parents to evaluate their relationship with the index child (e.g., about how often in the past month have you shown physical affection to your child? How would you describe your relationship with your child?). Parents were also asked to check off whether their child had a variety of personal material possessions, such as a television set, computer, car, or horse. Lastly, parents were asked a series of behavioral questions about their child that were similar in format to those used on diagnostic behavior checklists, such as: shows respect to adults, worries a lot, or is mean to others (possible answers were "not true," "somewhat or sometimes true," and "very true"). The parent survey took approximately ten to twelve minutes to answer.

We developed two versions of the student survey: one that omitted five sex-related questions, intended for middle or junior high school students (per request of the participating schools), and one that included the sexual attitude questions for students in grades nine through twelve. The adolescent survey consisted of 57 questions, many of which were identical to or very similar to questions asked on the parent version described above. In addition to the questions common to both surveys (those relating to chores, rules, material possessions, behavior, and actions in hypothetical situations), students were asked questions adapted from the Youth Risk Behavior Surveillance used in the annual research by the Centers for Disease Control and Prevention regarding risk behaviors such as drug and alcohol use, smoking, and restrictive eating (U.S. Department of Health and Human Services, 1999). We chose not to ask about personal sexual behavior on the student survey in order to make it more acceptable to parents and school administrators. Students were also asked a more detailed series of questions regarding their relationships with both their mother and father. The student survey took about fifteen minutes to complete. While surveys were administered in the students' classroom, at either individual desks or group tables, every effort was made to ensure that answers were kept as confidential as possible throughout the survey process. In most cases, the classroom teacher remained in the room during the survey, but only the interviewer administered the survey and collected the completed questionnaires.

In addition to administering paper and pencil questionnaires, we tape-recorded twenty- to thirty-minute interviews with a nonrandom sample of twenty students at four of the nine schools. The interviews consisted of mostly open-ended questions regarding how the students viewed the way in which they and their peers were being raised, with a focus on whether they considered themselves "spoiled" and what that term meant to them. Parental permission was obtained for all students under the age of eighteen. Students were randomly chosen from the classes we surveyed and then asked if they were interested in being interviewed. Students that expressed interest and obtained parental permission were interviewed at their school during a free period or after classes.

Statistical Analyses and Results

We first examined the bivariate relationships between predictors and the dichotomous dependent variables. Then, using logistic regression, we modeled the linear relationship between the outcomes and those predictors that were significantly related to the outcomes using a forward selection procedure (SAS 6.12). This process involves choosing the most important predictor (the most highly correlated variable) and then continuing step by step to add variables in descending order of importance while controlling for variables already selected. We used $p = 1.0$ as the criterion for retention in the selection procedure, to ensure that we analyzed the maximum information for choosing the best model (see Kleinbaum et al. *Applied Regression Analysis and Other Multivariate Methods*. 1998. Duxbury Press, Boston: 396–400). However, the final models reported in the text were determined by including only those variables that retained their significant relationship at the .05 level of significance with the dependent measure in the presence of the other predictors. Ordinary least squares linear regression was used to model the body mass index.

Results of the final regression analyses are presented in Table 5 on pages 235–240.

Table 5—Final Regression Models

Self-Centered—Final logistic regression model

VARIABLE	PARAMETER ESTIMATE	SE	CHI-SQUARE	ODDS RATIO
Intercept	3.9029	1.2768	9.3433	—
Age	−0.2772	0.0796	12.1320	0.758
Female gender	−1.1249	0.2051	30.0727	0.325
Fair or poor relationship with dad	0.5218	0.2219	5.5303	1.685
No chores for allowance	0.4649	0.2038	5.2043	1.592

Note: all chi-square tests significant at p<.05 N=495

Depressed (adolescent report)—Final logistic regression model

VARIABLE	PARAMETER ESTIMATE	SE	CHI-SQUARE	ODDS RATIO
Intercept	−0.5298	0.2070	6.5521	—
No chores for allowance	−0.4448	0.2095	4.5072	0.641
Family* eats dinner together at least a few times per week	−0.6696	0.2172	9.5015	0.512
Relationship with mom is fair or poor	1.3435	0.2651	25.6893	3.832

Note: All chi-square tests significant at p<.05 N=505
*Family includes respondent, and *both* parents (if live together)

Depressed (parent report)—Final logistic regression model

VARIABLE	PARAMETER ESTIMATE	SE	CHI-SQUARE	ODDS RATIO
Intercept	−0.1066	0.6215	—	—
Child's age (4–18)	0.1260	0.0243	27.0139	1.134
Family attends religious services together about once a week	−0.2966	0.1512	3.8478	0.743
Family* eats dinner together at least a few times per week	−0.6165	0.1936	10.1433	0.540
Relationship with child is good to excellent	−1.2785	0.4485	8.1242	0.278
Talk with child about his/her special interests at least once a week	−0.7441	0.3222	5.3333	0.475

Note: All chi-square tests significant at p<.05 N= 1047
*Family includes respondent, and *both* parents (if live together)

Table 5 (continued)

Mean to others (adolescent report—boys only)—Final logistic regression model

VARIABLE	PARAMETER ESTIMATE	SE	CHI-SQUARE	ODDS RATIO
Intercept	0.4440	0.1953	5.1676	—
View parents as not strict about punishment for drinking	−0.6159	0.2434	6.4047	0.540
Child lives in more than one household (e.g., divorce)	−0.8938	0.3491	6.5556	0.409
Wished mom spent more time with you "most of the time" or "almost always"	−1.2666	0.5898	4.6123	0.282

Note: All chi-square tests significant at p<.05 N=297

Mean to others (adolescent report—girls only)—Final logistic regression model

VARIABLE	PARAMETER ESTIMATE	SE	CHI-SQUARE	ODDS RATIO
Intercept	−0.7326	0.1701	18.5442	—
Parents not strict about helping with dishes	−0.6322	0.2555	6.1238	0.531
Mom is seen as "too lenient" or "pretty lenient"	0.8143	0.2782	8.5653	2.258
Relationship with mom is "fair" or "poor"	0.7876	0.3133	6.3200	2.198

Note: All chi-square tests significant at p<.05 N=335

Mean to others (parent report)—Final logistic regression model

VARIABLE	PARAMETER ESTIMATE	SE	CHI-SQUARE	ODDS RATIO
Intercept	−0.3157	0.3941	—	—
Family* eats dinner together at least a few times per week	−0.4417	0.2209	3.9972	0.643
Relationship with child is good to excellent	−1.0249	0.4064	6.3615	0.359

Note: All chi-square tests significant at p<.05 N=1051
*Family includes respondent, and *both* parents (if live together)

Table 5 (continued)

Driven (adolescent report)—Final logistic regression model

VARIABLE	PARAMETER ESTIMATE	SE	CHI-SQUARE	ODDS RATIO
Intercept	− 2.3563	0.2086	127.6279	—
Female	1.6751	0.2216	57.1191	5.339
Fair or poor relationship with dad	0.5446	0.2052	7.0455	1.724

Note: All chi-square tests significant at p<.05 N=651

Driven (parent report)—Final logistic regression model

VARIABLE	PARAMETER ESTIMATE	SE	CHI-SQUARE	ODDS RATIO
Intercept	− 3.9149	0.3817	105.1861	—
Yearly income >$100,000	1.2249	0.4144	8.7354	3.404

Note: All chi-square tests significant at p<.05 N=1003

Not Motivated (adolescent report—boys only)—Final logistic regression model

VARIABLE	PARAMETER ESTIMATE	SE	CHI-SQUARE	ODDS RATIO
Intercept	− 1.2879	0.1630	62.3980	—
Mother "expects too much" in terms of school performance	0.7618	0.2963	6.6114	2.142

Note: All chi-square tests significant at p<.05 N=298

Not Motivated (adolescent report—girls only)—Final logistic regression model

VARIABLE	PARAMETER ESTIMATE	SE	CHI-SQUARE	ODDS RATIO
Intercept	− 3.0575	0.3102	97.1409	—
Fair or poor relationship with dad	0.7287	0.3379	4.6507	2.072
Mom is seen as "too lenient" or "pretty lenient"	0.8211	0.3453	5.6540	2.273
Relationship with mom is "fair" or "poor"	0.8961	0.3892	5.3012	2.450
Mother "expects too much" in terms of school performance	0.6984	0.3554	3.8621	2.011
Dad "expects too much" in terms of school performance	0.9547	0.3334	8.1995	2.598

Note: All chi-square tests significant at p<.05 N=350

Table 5 (continued)

Not Motivated (parent report)—Final logistic regression model

VARIABLE	PARAMETER ESTIMATE	SE	CHI-SQUARE	ODDS RATIO
Intercept	0.5021	0.2190	—	—
Female	−0.8269	0.2190	14.2562	0.437
Yearly income >$100,000	0.4690	0.2114	4.9232	0.626
Talk with child about his/her special interests at least once a week	−0.5040	0.2418	4.3422	0.604
Family* eats dinner together at least a few times per week	−0.3836	0.1244	9.5037	0.681

Note: All chi-square tests significant at p<.05 N = 1007

Body Mass Index (adolescent report—boys only)—Final OLS regression model*

VARIABLE	PARAMETER ESTIMATE	SE	T STATISTIC
Intercept	24.912	1.075	23.18
Grade Point Average	−0.756	0.337	−2.24
Wished dad spent more time with you "most of the time" or "almost always"	1.285	0.543	2.37

Note: All T-statistic significant at p<.05 N = 290
*None of the predictors for BMI in girls was statistically significant

Disordered Eating (adolescent report)—Final logistic regression model

VARIABLE	PARAMETER ESTIMATE	SE	CHI-SQUARE	ODDS RATIO
Intercept	−3.9427	0.3465	129.4692	—
Fair or poor relationship with dad	0.5783	0.2631	4.8317	1.783
Female	1.6516	0.3024	29.8225	5.216
Child lives in more than one household (e.g., divorce)	0.6972	0.3197	4.7549	2.008
Mom is seen as "too lenient" or "pretty lenient"	0.6030	0.2669	5.1044	1.828
Relationship with mom is "fair" or "poor"	0.8740	0.2995	8.5144	2.396
Wished dad spent more time with you "most of the time" or "almost always"	0.5458	0.2625	4.3223	1.726
Has a job during the school year	0.6254	0.2515	6.1864	1.869

Note: All chi-square tests significant at p<.05 N = 612

Table 5 (continued)

Creatine/steroid use (adolescent report)—Final logistic regression model

VARIABLE	PARAMETER ESTIMATE	SE	CHI-SQUARE	ODDS RATIO
Intercept	−3.3971	0.4573	55.1882	—
Number of children living in home	−3.3971	0.2937	4.4885	1.388
Mom is seen as "too lenient" or "pretty lenient"	0.6236	0.2937	4.5083	1.866

Note: All chi-square tests significant at p<.05 N=647

Past month drug use (adolescent report)—Final logistic regression model

VARIABLE	PARAMETER ESTIMATE	SE	CHI-SQUARE	ODDS RATIO
Intercept	−3.3541	1.1345	8.7402	—
Age (13–18)	0.1993	0.0716	7.7438	1.221
Parents not strict about child swearing	0.3632	0.1777	4.1780	1.438
Family* eats dinner together at least a few times per week	−0.3987	0.1930	4.2704	0.671
Parents have never forbidden child from playing really violent video game or seeing an R rated movie	0.4761	0.1779	7.1602	1.610
Child says that it is "very true" that he/she is spoiled	0.7592	0.2565	8.7604	2.137
Summer job	0.4032	0.1929	4.3708	1.497

Note: All chi-square tests significant at p<.05 N=647
Family includes respondent, and *both* parents (if live together)

Permissive sexual attitudes (adolescent report)—Final logistic regression model

VARIABLE	PARAMETER ESTIMATE	SE	CHI-SQUARE	ODDS RATIO
Intercept	6.4660	1.4279	20.5048	—
Age (13–18)	−0.4925	0.0898	30.0600	0.611
Female	−1.9371	0.2373	66.6113	0.144
Parents are not strict about having child keep room clean	0.5431	0.2755	3.8868	1.721
Family* eats dinner together at least a few times per week	−0.5652	0.2326	5.9060	0.568
Parents are indulgent**	0.1201	0.0487	6.0900	*1.128*

Note: All chi-square tests significant at p<.05 N=645
*Family includes respondent, and *both* parents (if live together)
**Sum of fourteen items (range 0–14) based on perceived parental strictness on three chores and four household rules, chores for allowance, monitoring violent media, general parental leniency, spoiling, and perceived parental leniency regarding drug and alcohol use.

Table 5 (continued)

Spoiled (adolescent report—boys only)—Final logistic regression model

VARIABLE	PARAMETER ESTIMATE	SE	CHI-SQUARE	ODDS RATIO
Intercept	−1.1246	0.5576	4.0681	—
Number of children living in home	−0.5839	0.3835	8.1374	2.986
Mom is seen as "too lenient" or "pretty lenient"	1.0939	0.2339	6.2330	0.558

Note: All chi-square tests significant at p<.05 N=294

Spoiled (adolescent report—girls only)—Final logistic regression model

VARIABLE	PARAMETER ESTIMATE	SE	CHI-SQUARE	ODDS RATIO
Intercept	−4.6149	0.8690	28.2024	—
Parents aren't strict about "other" listed rules	0.9149	0.4537	4.0672	2.497
View parents as not strict about punishment for drinking	0.7422	0.3204	5.3662	2.101
No chores for allowance	1.2480	0.3354	13.8476	3.484
Perceives family as having more money than others in school	0.7105	0.3127	5.1605	2.035

Note: All chi-square tests significant at p<.05 N=274

Spoiled (parent report)—Final logistic regression model

VARIABLE	PARAMETER ESTIMATE	SE	CHI-SQUARE	ODDS RATIO
Intercept	1.8836	0.5545	11.5368	—
Relationship with child is good to excellent	−1.0394	0.5134	4.0994	0.354
Yearly income >$100,000	0.4778	0.1349	12.5424	1.613
Talk with child about his/her special interests at least once a week	−0.9451	0.3454	7.4849	0.389

Note: All chi-square tests significant at p<.05 N=999

Technical Appendix References

Breton, J., L. Bergeron, J. Valla, S. Lepine, L. Houde, and N. Gaudet. "Do children aged 9 through 11 years understand the DISC version 2.25 questions?" *Journal of the American Academy of Child and Adolescent Psychiatry* 34, 946–954.

Bryk, A., and S. Raudenbush, *Hierarchical Linear Models for Social and Behavioral Research: Applications and Data Analysis Methods.* Newbury Park, CA: Sage.

Kindlon, D., M. Kuo, and B. Mohler. "Methodological Challenges in Urban Longitudinal Research: Multi-culturalism, Developmental Variation and Multiple Informants." Symposium presented at the Society for Research in Child Development biannual meeting, Albuquerque, NM, April 1999.

Kleinbaum, et al. *Applied Regression Analysis and Other Multivariate Methods.* Boston: Duxbury Press, 1998.

U.S. Department of Health and Human Services, Centers for Disease Control and Prevention, *Youth Risk Behavior Surveillance—United States, 1999.* Washington, DC: Available: *www.cdc.gov/epo/mmwr/preview/mmwrhtml/ss4905a1.htm*

ENDNOTES

INTRODUCTION

1. Robert Coles (1977) *Privileged Ones: Volume V of Children of Crisis,* Boston, MA: Atlantic, Little Brown. Pages *x–xi*.

CHAPTER 1

1. Details of the results of four survey questions are as follows:

SURVEY QUESTION	NOT TRUE	SOMEWHAT TRUE	VERY TRUE
I am unhappy, sad, or depressed	47%	40%	13%
I worry a lot	29%	38%	33%
I feel that I have to be perfect	41%	38%	21%

	TRUE
So sad or hopeless that stopped doing usual activities for at least two weeks	26.4%

Respondents are 654 adolescents ages 13–19 years.

2. Barry Mano, president of the National Association of Sports Officials, quoted on National Public Radio (2000) "Talk of the Nation," Lynn Neary, Host, July 18, 2000. Transcript produced by Burrelle's Information Services, Box 7, Livingston, NJ 07039.

3. The full results from the strictness question of the Parenting Practices at the Millennium Survey (by geographical region, annual income, and child's age) are given in the table below. None of the differences seen are statistically significant.

REGION	LESS STRICT	ABOUT THE SAME	MORE STRICT
Northeast	48.6%	30.9%	20.5%
South	39.9%	29.4%	30.7%
Midwest	43.9%	33.3%	22.8%
West	44.7%	29.1%	26.2%

Chi-square = 10.67; df 6, p = .099

ANNUAL HOUSEHOLD INCOME	LESS STRICT	ABOUT THE SAME	MORE STRICT
Less than $75,000	47.6%	30.1%	22.4%
$75,000 to $100,000	38.6%	34.1%	27.3%
$100,000 to $200,000	43.8%	30.8%	25.5%
$200,000 to $500,000	43.0%	30.0%	27.0%
$500,000 to $1,000,000	43.0%	31.4%	25.6%
More than $1,000,000	55.1%	28.6%	16.3%

Chi-square = 5.30; df 10; p = .870

CHILD'S AGE	LESS STRICT	ABOUT THE SAME	MORE STRICT
Ages 5 to 12	46.6%	26.5%	26.9%
Ages 13 to 19	43.8%	32.0%	24.1%

Chi-square = 2.76; df 2; p = .252

4. The PPM Survey results for the hypothetical questions regarding parental response to alcohol or marijuana use are:

LIKELY CONSEQUENCES FOR GETTING CAUGHT		DRINKING	SMOKING MARIJUANA
Spank/hit	Parents of Teens	1%	1%
	Teenagers	7%	12%
Ground	Parents of Teens	66%	67%
	Teenagers	52%	59%
Scream at/lecture	Parents of Teens	20%	24%
	Teenagers	44%	58%
Discuss calmly	Parents of Teens	93%	90%
	Teenagers	63%	52%
Get counseling	Parents of Teens	19%	32%
	Teenagers	9%	23%
Call police	Parents of Teens	< 1%	3%
	Teenagers	2%	5%
Try to make you feel guilty	Parents of Teens	NA	NA
	Teenagers	26%	28%

CHAPTER 2

1. Articles in that series include: Powell, M. (1999) "A bull by the horns; the smart & the lucky are on one crazy ride. Eat their dust." *Washington Post*, Friday, July 9, 1999, Page C01; Gowen, A. (1999) "The *New Gilded Age*: Rise of the slacker millionaires; for Hal McCabe, AOL peon, getting rich was the easy part. It's the happy-ever-after he can't seem to manage." *Washington Post*, Sunday, August 1, 1999, Page F01; Frey, J. (1999) "Striking it Ritz; for the er, richly deserving, a not-so-humble abode." *Washington Post*, Tuesday, August 24, 1999, Page C01; and Stepp, L. S. (2000) "Beyond the silver spoon; affluent parents are spending themselves silly. But will it buy kids happiness?" *Washington Post*, Tuesday, January 4, 2000, Page C01. See also Remick, D. (Ed.), (2000), *The New Gilded Age:* The New Yorker *Looks at the Culture of Affluence*, New York: Random House.

2. See, Frank, R. H. (1999) *Luxury Fever: Why money fails to satisfy in an era of excess*, New York: The Free Press. He writes for example that John D. Rockefeller's net worth was about 2% of America's annual income whereas that same figure for Bill Gates, the richest American, is $1/2$ of 1%. The economist Dr. Frank also notes that in 1982 there were 13 billionaires in America, in 1997 there were 170 and that the number of millionaires (now about 5 million in number) doubled between 1992 and 1996.

3. Quoted in Brown, P. L. (2000) "Teaching Johnny Values where money is king," *New York Times,* March 10, 2000, A1, and A14.

4. The Dow Jones Industrial Average closed at 1,315 on May 31, 1985. On May 31, 1990 the DJ Industrials closed at 2876.66. On May 31, 1995, the Index was 4465. On May 31, 2000, that index stood at 10,522. Source: *Wall Street Journal*.

5. Shapiro, I., Greenstein, R., (1999) "The widening income gulf, Center on Budget and Policy Priorities report," September 4, 1999. *www.cbpp.org/9-4-99tax-rep.htm.*

6. For lawyers' salaries, see the article by Michael Orey: "Law firms ponder major changes to fund leap in starting salaries," which appeared in the *Wall Street Journal*, Friday, May 12, 2000. The information on CEO compensation comes from studies done by William M. Mercer Inc. and reported in the *Wall Street Journal* on Thursday, April 6, 2000, Pages R9–R13.

7. Home prices were taken from an article by Nguyen, L. N. (2000) "America's 250 Richest Towns: 5th annual survey," *Worth: The Business of You* 9, no. 6, June 2000, 88–104 and a May 7, 2000 article: Zorn, F. H. "Where wealth knows no bounds." Available at *Worth: Online, www.worth.com/articles/z0005l01.html.*

8. For example, according to information on CEO compensation from studies done by William M. Mercer Inc. and reported in the *Wall Street Journal* on Thursday, April 6, 2000, Pages R9–R13, John Welch, Jr., CEO of General Electric, had salary plus bonus compensation in 1999 of $13,325,000. In addition to other compensation, primarily stock options, this results in total direct compensation potential of $529,494,100. The country of Eritrea, on the other hand, has annual budget revenue of $225 million. This figure is taken from *The World Factbook, 1999* available online at: *http://www.odci.gov/cia/publications/factbook/er.html#econ*

9. See, Frank, R. H. (1999) *Luxury Fever: Why money fails to satisfy in an era of excess*, New York: The Free Press.

10. This quote is attributed to the Talmud in Winokur, J. (1996) *The Rich Are Different,* New York: Pantheon, p. xv. See also the Dalai Lama quoted in *The Art of Happiness*, New York: Riverhead Books, 1998, p. 24. "Now all of these factors [health, material wealth, friends] are, in fact, sources of happiness. But in order for an individual to be able to fully utilize them towards the goal of enjoying a happy and fulfilling life, *your state of mind is key*. It's crucial."

11. The breakdown of number of parents in each income category is as follows:

YEARLY INCOME	LESS THAN $50,000	$50,000 TO $75,000	$75,000 TO $100,000	$100,001 TO $200,000	$200,001 TO $500,000	$500,000 TO $1 MILLION	MORE THAN 1 MILLION
Number	96	134	129	261	243	89	49
(Percent)	(9.5%)	(13.3%)	(12.9%)	(26.1%)	(24.3%)	(8.9%)	(4.9%)

12. The text in the chapter that describes what kids own is based on the responses of 250 parents of children ages 5 to 12 and 754 parents of adolescents ages 13–19. Because children were considered to be unreliable reporters of their parents' income, the use of only parent data allows for a more fine-grained analysis of the relations between income and possession. There were, however, no notable differences between parents and teens in terms of the percentage of respondents indicating that they owned these items. Selected data for both parent and teen report is given in the tables below.

WHAT PARENTS SAY THEIR KIDS HAVE BY YEARLY INCOME LEVEL	UP TO $75,000 N=230	75,000 TO 100,000 N=129	100,000 TO 200,000 N=261	200,00 TO 500,000 N=243	500,000 TO 1,000,000 N=89	MORE THAN 1 MILLION N=49	TOTAL N=1,001
Computer in Room (all ages)	81 (35%)	39 (30.2%)	102 (39.2%)	100 (41%)	53 (59.6%)	28 (57.1%)	403 (40.2%)
Computer in Room (preteens)	15 (35.7%)	9 (47.4%)	20 (36.4%)	23 (29.9%)	19 (48.7%)	8 (47%)	94 (37.8%)

Computer in Room (teens only)	66 (34.9%)	30 (27.3%)	82 (40.0%)	77 (46.1%)	34 (66.7%)	20 (62.5%)	309 (41.0%)
TV in Room (all ages)	129 (55.8%)	53 (41.1%)	91 (34.9%)	72 (29.5%)	20 (22.2%)	17 (34.7%)	382 (38.1%)
Phone in room (all ages)	116 (50.0%)	65 (50.4%)	145 (55.6%)	129 (53.1%)	43 (47.8%)	29 (59.2%)	527 (52.5%)
Credit Card paid by parents (teens only)	24 (13%)	14 (12.8%)	32 (15.7%)	45 (27.0%)	12 (23.5%)	11 (34.4%)	138 (18.4%)
Cell Phone (teens only)	43 (24%)	27 (24.6%)	52 (25.5%)	50 (29.9%)	19 (37.3%)	20 (62.5%)	211 (28.1%)
Car or motorcycle (ages 16–19)	40 (34.2%)	29 (42.7%)	50 (43.1%)	34 (39.5%)	13 (52.0%)	9 (50.0%)	175 (40.7%)
Car or motorcycle (ages 17–19)	34 (45.9%)	23 (56.1%)	35 (49.3%)	24 (53.3%)	10 (71.4%)	8 (66.77%)	134 (52.1%)
Horse (teens only)	8 (2.2%)	2 (1.8%)	7 (3.4%)	8 (4.8%)	1 (2.0%)	5 (15.6%)	31 (4.1%)

WHAT TEENAGERS SAY THEY OWN BY HOW MUCH MONEY THEIR FAMILY HAS IN COMPARISON TO OTHERS AT SCHOOL	LESS MONEY	ABOUT THE SAME AMOUNT OF MONEY	MORE MONEY	TOTAL
Computer in room	58 (39.2%)	195 (46.1%)	43 (59.7%)	296 (46.0%)
TV in room	83 (55.7%)	187 (44.4%)	36 (51.4%)	306 (47.8%)
Phone in room	86 (57.7%)	301 (71.2%)	59 (81.9%)	446 (69.5%)
Credit card paid by parents	16 (10.7%)	113 (26.7%)	27 (38.6%)	156 (24.3%)

Cell phone	34	140	39	213
	(22.8%)	(33.1%)	(55.7%)	(33.2%)
Car or motorcycle (ages 16 to	35	138	37	229
19 only)	(36.5%)	(53.7%)	(67.3%)	(35.7%)
Horse	3	21	3	27
	(2.0%)	(5.0%)	(4.2%)	(4.2%)

13. Aldrich, N. W. Jr. (1988) *Old Money: The Mythology of America's Upper Class*, New York: Knopf.

14. For another report of allowance amount see the "National Longitudinal Survey of Youth" report by Jay Zagorsky, research scientist at Ohio State University's Center for Human Resource Research. Dr. Zagorsky's research was reported in many newspapers and magazines such as *American Demographics*, typically focusing on the finding that about half of American teenagers get an allowance from their parents, and most typically get about $50 a week with children of the wealthy getting in the neighborhood of $175.00 per week. These articles would then highlight the fact that about 9.8 million U.S. teenagers are given $1.05 billion to spend each week. I wrote to Dr. Zagorsky asking him why he thought his findings showed that his teens had higher allowance levels then did ours in the PPM study. In part, I wrote "I realize that your analysis of the NLSY data was different in that you asked about money for all expenditures, but I'd like to know if you did a breakdown of the source of the spending money (e.g., allowance versus money for clothes, versus lunch money)." I repeat his response below. In essence, he says that he thinks the NLSY figures may be too high. This gives me confidence that our findings are valid. Dr. Zagorsky's response: *To answer your question, no, we did not ask for any breakdown of source of spending money in the NLS survey. The NLSY97 is a huge survey focusing on schooling, training, and work. The allowance questions are basically a small afterthought. However, if we knew how much interest there was in allowances, we probably would have asked a few more questions. I don't know if you saw the article, but Carol Meeks of Iowa State recently published a paper using the Survey of Families and Households. She found boys got an average (mean) of $40 and girls an average of $36 back in the early 1990s. It is interesting that you found a smaller figure in an economically better time. I just finished reading a book (All Souls), which is an autobiography about growing up in the slum projects of south Boston. The author has a short section on how much allowance he got (some days $5 in the 1970s) compared to his rich cousins in the suburbs, who were only getting pocket change. The author suggested his mother gave him a big allowance to compensate for growing up in a slum, but his cousins, who lived in a nice house/neighborhood, didn't get or need compensation. Lastly, I believe the numbers published in the* American

Demographics *article are too high. Somewhere in the article is a quote that I felt some respondents were lying to impress the interviewer. In other NLS surveys we ask sexual activity questions. If you believe all the responses then some of the interviewees never leave the bedroom. Another potential difference is that in my research, almost half of all kids stated they got no money from their parents. While* American Demographics *thought it made good press to focus on only those who get an allowance, this is not an accurate representation of life in America since it immediately removes half of all teens from the picture. Including these missing teens drops all figures dramatically. Finally, after the tables were published I determined another reason why some high values exist. In most of the NLS survey we ask the respondent a "how much" question and then ask in what time unit that value was just reported. For the allowance numbers, we ask how much but then we ask "How do you receive your allowance? Weekly, Monthly, etc." We do NOT directly ask if the dollar amount they just reported was in weekly, monthly, or other terms. Hence, there are some kids who are reporting a yearly total, but saying they get their allowance weekly. For people who do this I overcalculate their transfer amounts because I adjusted all amounts by the time unit reported. I doubt many are falling into this category since if I assumed everyone was reporting total annual allowance, then many teens get pocket change (i.e., 75 cents a week), over ⅓ get less than $2 a week, and the very richest teenagers in the 95th percentile get only $13 per week. These numbers appear much too low compared to other people's research. Nevertheless, even if a few interpret the questions as distinct, their answers will upwardly bias the amounts I report. My guess is some of the really high figures might fall into this case.*

15. This finding is taken from page 2 of Owings, J., Madigan, T. & Daniel, B. (1998) "Who Goes to America's Highly Ranked 'National' Universities?" National Center for Education Statistics, Statistics in brief, November 1998.

16. This information was obtained from the Crème de la Crème web site: www. cremechildcare.com and a telephone call requesting price information in May 2000.

17. See Sax, J. L., Astin, A. W., Korn, W. S., & Mahoney, K. M. (1998) *The American Freshmen: National Norms for Fall, 1998*, Los Angeles: Higher Education research Institute University of California at Los Angeles.

18. There has been quite a bit written on this topic. The figures given here are taken from several sources, including: the projections for 1999 supplied by the Congressional Budget Office (*www.cbo.gov*) and analyzed in Shapiro, I. & Greenstein, R., (1999) "The Widening Income Gulf." Center on Budget and Policy Priorities report, September 4, 1999. *www.cbpp.org/9-4-99tax-rep.htm*. These reports say, in part, that: "The CBO data indicate that after-tax income is more heavily concentrated among the richest 1 percent of the population—and also among the most affluent 20 percent of the population—than at any time from 1977 to 1995, the years for which historic CBO data are available."

CHAPTER 3

1. *American Psychologist* 55, 56–67 (2000). See especially the article by D. G. Myers, "The Funds, Friends and Faith of Happy People." This section also relies on the work of Mihalyi Csikzentmihalyi, most notably: "If We Are So Rich, Why Aren't We Happy?" *American Psychologist* 54, (1999): 821–827. Other research reviewed in these articles shows that women are no happier than men and young people are no happier than older people. Religiosity contributes to happiness and, not surprisingly, intimate human contact also contributes to happiness. In general, having more friends leads to greater happiness and married people, at least those who are not in "bad" marriages, are happier than unmarried people.

2. For stories about lottery winners, see Tresniowski, A. (1991) "Payday or May-day? Sure, rich is better than poor, but those who've hit it big know the dough can cause problems." *People Weekly* 51, May 17, 1999, p. 128 + (1) and Angelo, B. (1991) "Life at the end of the rainbow," *Time* 138, Nov. 4, 1991 n18 p. 80 (2). "Take William Curry, a 37-year-old cafeteria worker who dropped dead of a heart attack brought on by the stress of being hounded after his win of $3.6 million was made public."

3. The work of Jeffery Gray forms the basis for much of our understanding of the BAS. See Gray, J. (1987) "Perspectives on Anxiety and Impulsivity." *Journal of Research in Personality* 21 493–509. Gray, J. (1982), *The Neuropsychology of Anxiety: An Enquiry into the Functions of the Septal-Hippocampal System.* Oxford: Oxford University Press, 1982. Gray, J. (1975) *Elements of a two-process theory of learning.* New York, Academic Press. I have collaborated on scientific papers with Enrico Mezzacappa and Tony Earls in which we discuss how Gray's work on the BAS and related brain systems contributes to our understanding of impulsivity and aggression. See Kindlon, D., Mezzacappa, E., Earls, F. (1995). "Psychometric Properties of Impulsivity Measures: Temporal Stability, Validity, and Factor Structure." *Journal of Child Psychology and Psychiatry and Allied Disciplines*, 645–661 and Kindlon, D. J., Tremblay, R. E., Mezza-cappa, E., Earls, F., Laurent, D., & Schaal, B. (1995) "Longitudinal patterns of heart rate and fighting behavior in 9- through 12-year-old boys," *Journal of the American Academy of Child and Adolescent Psychiatry 34*, 371–377.

4. Material for this section on the neurobiology of happiness draws from the following articles: Spanagel, R. & Weiss, F. (1999) "The Dopamine Hypothesis of Reward: Past and Current Status," *Trends in Neurosciences*, 22, 521–527. Wise, R. A. (1996) "Neurobiology of Addiction," *Current Opinion in Neurobiology*, 6, 243–251. Wise, R. A. (1996) "Addictive Drugs and Brain Stimulation Reward," *American Review of Neuroscience*, 19, 319–340.

5. The classic article on effectance motivation is found in White, R. H. (1959) "Motivation Reconsidered: The Concept of Competence," *Psychological Review, 66,*

297–333. For a source reflecting more recent views see: Bandura, A. (1994) *Self-effi-cacy: The Exercise of Control.* New York: Freeman.

6. For details of this research see: Langer, E. J. & Rodin, J. (1976) "The Effect of Choice and Enhanced Personal Responsibility for the Aged: A Field Experiment in an Institutional Setting," *Journal of Personality and Social Psychology, 34,* 191–198, and Rodin, J. & Langer, E. J. (1977) "Long-Term Effects of a Control-Relevant Intervention with the Institutional Aged," *Journal of Personality and Social Psychology, 35,* 897–902. The overall death rate in the nursing home in the 18 months prior to the start of the study was 25%. In the 18 months following it was 30% for the no-responsibility group and only 15% for the self-responsible group.

7. Quoted from page 78 in Larson, R. W. (2000) "Toward a Positive Psychology of Positive Youth Development," *American Psychologist, 55,* 170–183.

8. For a review and commentary on the research literature concerning the develop-ment of perceived control and self-efficacy see: Skinner, E. A., Zimmer-Gembeck, M. J., & Connell, J. P. (1998) "Individual Differences and the Development of Perceived Control." *Monographs of the Society for Research in Child Development, 63,* Nos. 2–3, Serial No. 254. See also: Landry, S. H., Smith, K. E., Swank, P. R., Miller-Loncar, C. L. (2000) "Early Maternal and Child Influences on Children's Later Independent and Cognitive Social Functioning." *Child Development, 71,* 358–375. This recent study of 2- to 4-year-old children shows that early directive interaction with children supports later independent cognitive and social functioning, but that if it persists too long it will undermine these abilities. These authors conclude that as children age, "directiveness needs to decrease in relation to children's increasing competencies." See also: Ryan, R. M. & Deci, E. L. (2000) "Self-Determination Theory and the Facilitation of Intrinsic Motivation, Social Development, and Well-Being." *American Psychologist, 55,* 68–78. These authors review a wide array of research and conclude that there are "three innate psychological needs—competence, autonomy, and relatedness—which when satisfied yield enhanced self-motivation and mental health and when thwarted lead to diminished motivation and well-being." (p. 68)

9. This quote is from *Twilight of the Idols,* published in 1888. A revised and up-dated version of Frankl's book *Man's Search for Meaning* (1998) is available from Washington Square Press. This book describes Frankl's experiences in Auschwitz and other concentration camps, and how through his suffering, he found meaning for his life.

10. See Strachan, D. P., Harkins, L. S., Johnston, I. D. A., & Andersen, H. R. (1997) "Clinical Aspects of Allergic Disease: Childhood Antecedents of Allergic Sensi-tization in Young British Adults," *Journal of Allergy and Clinical Immunology, 99,* 6–12. Rogers, Naomi. *Dirt and Disease: Polio Before FDR.* New Brunswick, NJ: Rut-gers University Press, 1992. Ikwueke, K. "The Changing Pattern of Infectious Disease."

British Medical Journal 1984; 289: 1355–1358. Harvard Medical School Office of Public Affairs, News Release. "Harvard Researchers Find Genetic Key to T-Cell Differentiation." Available at: *www.hms.harvard.edu/news/releases/696tcell.html.*; Prescott, S. L., Macaubus, C., Smallcombe, T., Holt, B. J., Sly, P. D., Holt, P. G. "Development of Allergen-Specific T-cell Memory in Atopic and Normal Children." *Lancet* 1999; 353: 196–200.

INTRODUCTION TO PART II

1. Much of the material on the origin of the 7 deadly sins is taken from Schimmel, S. (1997) *The Seven Deadly Sins: Jewish, Christian, and Classical Reflections on Human Psychology*, New York: Oxford University Press; Lyman, S. M. (1989) *The Seven Deadly Sins: Revised and Expanded Edition*, Dix Hills, NY: General Hall, and Solomon, R.C. (1999) *Wicked Pleasures: Meditations on the Seven "Deadly" Sins*, Lanham, MD: Rowman & Littlefield. The list that came to be the most influential was developed by Pope St. Gregory the Great (540–605): superbia (pride) avaritia (greed), luxuria (luxury, later lust), invidia (envy), gula (gluttony), ira (anger) and acedia (sloth). If the reader is interested in biblical references to these sins, the most fertile ground to investigate may be in Matthew chapters 5 through 7. The seven deadly sins have influenced much art and literature, most notably Dante's *Divine Comedy* and the painting "The Seven Deadly Sins" by Hieronymus Bosch.

CHAPTER 4

1. Pride was the first sin. When Adam and Eve ate the apple, the act was disobedient, but the sin was pride. The relevant biblical quote in relation to eating the forbidden fruit is "The serpent said, 'Of course you will not die. God knows that as soon as you eat it, your eyes will be opened and you will be like gods . . .'" Genesis 2:3. Genesis goes on to say that Adam and Eve thought eating the apple would make them godlike; instead, it made them human and for the first time they became self-conscious and as such, capable of shame. In the biblical account, Adam hides after eating the fruit saying "I was afraid because I was naked." God replies "Who told you that you were naked? Have you eaten from the tree which I forbade you?" The relationship of pride with shame and neurosis is discussed in Allport, G. (1950) *The Individual and His Religion*, New York: Macmillan. For more information on neurotic coping, see the classic work: Shapiro, D. (1965) *Neurotic Styles*, New York: Basic Books.

2. See article by Bob Duffy, "She'll always be a strong favorite," *Boston Globe,* Thursday, Sept. 21, 2000 page E12. Cheryl won a bronze medal at the 2000 Summer Olympics in Sydney, Australia. But there are many cases of young people who say that they like themselves who are, in fact, troubled. I got an inkling of this in my first job as

a psychologist. I was part of a federally funded research project studying children's mental health on the island of Martha's Vineyard. We spent a month interviewing and testing most of the seven-year-olds on the island, about a hundred overall. One of the tests we used, the Pictorial Scale of Perceived Competence and Acceptance, measured children's self-esteem. The tests used pictures to help children rate how competent they felt in a variety of contexts. For example, the child was shown two pictures of kids sitting at desks in school; they were told that the kid in picture A was good in math, but not the kid in picture B. Which kid are you more like? we asked. If the child chose A, we asked: Are you really good at math or just pretty good at math? In general, the seven-year-olds with the highest self-esteem had the best mental health as rated by their parents, teachers and by another psychologist and myself. There was one exception to this rule—a group of kids who had very high scores on the self-esteem test but who were seen as the most psychologically troubled. These children would, for example, rate themselves as very good at math when in fact they weren't (we gave a math test as part of the research). In addition, they also misrepresented reality on a Lie Scale we gave them. This test asked questions such as, "Do you like everyone you know? Have you ever done anything bad?," questions that must be honestly answered "No" by just about everyone. In short, the most troubled seven-year-olds were the ones who couldn't accept themselves. They lied to others about who they were, and, most likely, they lied to themselves as well. The details of this research may be found in: Garrison, W., Earls, F., & Kindlon, D. (1983) "An Application of the Pictorial Scale of Perceived Competence and Acceptance Within an Epidemiological Survey." *Journal of Abnormal Child Psychology*, *11*: 367–377.

3. Schwartz, M. (2000), "You Can't Get Them Out with a Bomb," *Talk*, November, 2000; pages 69–71.

4. Robert Coles (1977) *Privileged Ones: Volume V of Children of Crisis*, Boston, MA: Atlantic, Little Brown.

5. The operational definition of this syndrome and the others in Part II are like all attempts at measuring abstract psychological concepts—imperfect. Readers interested in the numerical details of the findings can find them in the Technical Appendix.

CHAPTER 5

1. Stearns, C. Z. & Stearns, P. N. (1986) *Anger: The Struggle for Emotional Control in America's History*, Chicago: University of Chicago Press.

2. In the earlier editions of Benjamin Spock's *The Commonsense Book of Baby and Child Care* (e.g. 1945), he takes a relatively tolerant view of anger expression in children, but by the third edition in the 1970s, his view had changed.

3. The results for parents and teens on the question about sadness and depression is as follows:

		NOT TRUE	SOMEWHAT OR SOMETIMES TRUE	VERY TRUE
Child is Sad or	Parent (of teens) report	64.6%	32.0%	3.4%
Depressed	Teen report	46.6%	40.7%	12.7%

4. The statistics concerning suicidal ideation and attempts among teenagers is found in Prevention, National Center for Health Statistics, *Health, United States, 2000: Adolescent Health Chartbook*, Washington, D.C. (Author), during 1999 ⅕ of all high school students reported seriously considering or attempting suicide.

5. *Newsweek,* August, 2000.

6. See: "White House Conference on Teenagers: Raising Responsible and Resourceful Youth." Available: *http://www.whitehouse.gov/WH/EOP/First_Lady/html/teens/transcript.html* and Global Strategy Group Inc. "Talking with Teens: The YMCA Parent and Teen Survey Final Report" *http://www.whitehouse.gov/WH/EOP/First_Lady/html/teens/survey.html*

7. Council of Economic Advisers: "Teens and their Parents in the 21st Century: An Examination of the Trends in Teen Behavior and the Role of Parental Involvement." Available: *http://www.whitehouse.gov/media/pdf/CEAreport.pdf*

8. This interview with Melissa is not a wholly verbatim transcript, but is factual.

9. Hofferth, S.L. (1999) "Changes in Children's Time 1981–1997," *Center Survey, 9,* no. 1.

10. Douglass, F. (1845/1994) *Narrative of the Life of Frederick Douglass, An American Slave* (p. 99) New York: The Library of America. "Dark and terrible as is this picture, I hold it to be strictly true of the overwhelming mass of professed Christians in America. They strain at a gnat and swallow a camel . . . They would be shocked at the proposition of fellowshipping a *sheep*-stealer; and at the same time they hug to their communion *a man-stealer.*"

CHAPTER 6

1. Quoted in: Zernike, K. (2000) "Ease Up, Top Colleges Tell Stressed Applicants," *New York Times*, Thursday December 7, 2000, National Desk. (From *NY Times* on-line archive)

2. Hofferth, S.L. (1999) "Changes in Children's Time 1981–1997," *Center Survey,* 9, no. 1. Hofferth reports on her research conducted at the University of Michigan over the course of 16 years beginning in 1981. Children's free time has declined 16 percent over this period (from 63 hours per week to 51 hours per week) and time not spent in school or doing regular activities such as eating and sleeping is more structured. Church-going declined 40 percent during this period. Most remarkable was that "household conversation just sitting and conversing declined by 100 percent over this period. Sports participation doubled. Time in school and studying time also increased." She says that these changes in children's time is tied to the fact that women have entered the workforce in large numbers. In 1950, 12 percent of moms worked, in 1980 47 percent of mothers worked, and in 1997 67 percent of mothers worked.

3. See The National Commission on Education (1984): *Nation at Risk: The Full Account*, Portland, OR: USA Research.

4. News articles on homework used in this chapter include: Zernike, K. (2000) As "Homework Load Grows, One District Says 'Enough,' " *New York Times*, Tuesday, October 10, 2000, Metropolitan Desk (From *NY Times* on-line archive). Nussbaum, D. "How a Speeded-Up Society Trickles Down to Children; From Infancy to Academics, the Race Is On." *New York Times*, October 31, 1999, Sunday New Jersey Weekly Desk.

5. See: Wineripe, M. (1999) "Homework Bound," *New York Times*, January 3, 1999, *Sunday Education Life Supplement*; Kralovec, E. & Buell, J. (2000) *The End of Homework: How Homework Disrupts Families, Overburdens Children, and Limits Learning*, Boston: Beacon Press. See also Guyer, R.L. (2001) "Backpack = Back Pain," *American Journal of Public Health, 91*, 16–19.

6. An excellent source for information on the effects of sleep loss see: Dement, W. C. & Vaughn, C. (1999) *The Promise of Sleep*, New York: Delacorte Press. Also, Brody, J. (1999) "Personal Health; Paying the Price for Cheating on Sleep," *New York Times,* December 28, 1999, Tuesday Health & Fitness; Brink, S. (2000) "Sleepless Society," *U.S. News and World Report*, October 16, 2000. pps. 62–72.

7. There are numerous recent studies on the important role fathers play in the lives of their children. The interested reader may wish to consult: Duncan, G. J., Hill, M & Yeung, J. (1996) "Fathers' Activities and Child Attainments," paper presented at the NICHD Family and Child Well-Being Network's Conference on Father Involvement, Washington, D.C. Oct. 10–11, 1996; Pleck, J. H. (1997) "Paternal Involvement: Levels Sources and Consequences." In M. E. Lamb, (ed.) *The Role of the Father in Child Development* (pps. 68–103), New York: Wiley. Yogman, M. W., Kindlon, D., & Earls, F. (1995) "Father Involvement and Cognitive/Behavioral Outcomes of Preterm Infants," *Journal of the American Academy of Child and Adolescent Psychiatry, 27,* 58–66; and Capaldi, D. M., Crosby, L. & Stoomiller, M. (1996) "Predicting the Timing of First Sexual Intercourse for At-Risk Males," *Child Development, 67,* 344–359.

CHAPTER 7

1. Originally taken from a letter to the *Chicago Tribune*, quoted in Jon Winokur (1996) *The Rich Are Different*, New York: Pantheon Books. Page 92.

2. See Hall, J. (2000) "New Millionaires Worry about Raising Brats," *Detroit Free Press*, Tuesday January 11, 2000, Religion Section. Also Harden, B. (2000) "Brat Control on Easy Street," *New York Times,* Monday, June 12, 2000, Metropolitan desk. Roane, K.R. "Affluenza Strikes Kids: Financial Services for Children of Rich Parents Provided by Merrill Lynch," *U.S. News and World Report*, March 20, 2000, *128*, p. 55.

3. In S. Schimmel, *The Seven Deadly Sins*, Oxford Univ. Press, 1997.

4. Quote from opening scene of *The Portrait of a Lady* (1881/1917) by Henry James, NY: P. F. Collier & Son—Harvard Classics Shelf of Fiction.

CHAPTER 8

1. See Troiano, R. P. &, Flegal, K. M. (1998) "Overweight Children and Adolescents: Description, Epidemiology and Demographics," *Pediatrics, 101* 497–504; Pope, H., Jr., et al *The Adonis Complex* and Pinel, J. P. J., Assanand, S. & Lehman, D. R. (2000) "Hunger, Eating, and Health," *American Psychologist, 55*, 1105–1116; Scaglioni, S. Agostoni, C., DeNotaris, R., Radaelli, G., Radice, N., Valenti, M., Giovannini, M., & Riva, E. (2000) "Early Macronutrient Intake and Overweight at Five Years of Age," *International Journal of Obesity, 24*, 777–781, and Maffeis, C., Provera, S., Filippi, L., Sidoti, G., Schenea, S., Pinelli, L. & Tato, L. (2000) "Distribution of Food Intake as a Risk Factor for Childhood Obesity," *International Journal of Obesity, 24*, 75–80.

2. This quote was found in the article: American Public Health Association (2000) "Nutrition Takes Center Stage on National Agenda," *The Nation's Health*, July, 2000. 1, 10.

3. This section of food preferences among the young is taken from the talk by LeAnn Birch on food preferences among children at *Dietary Behavior: Why We Choose the Foods We Eat* (November 3, 1999) *http://www.usda.gov/cnpp/*. See also articles by Birch and others: Cutting, T. M., Fisher, J. O., Grimm-Thomas, K., & Birch, L. L. (1999) "Like Mother, like Daughter: Familial Patterns of Overweight Are Mediated by Mothers' Dietary Disinhibition." *American Journal of Clinical Nutrition, 69*, 608–613. Fisher, J. O., & Birch, L.L. (1999). "Restricting Access to a Palatable Food Affects Children's Behavioral Response, Food Selection and Intake." *American Journal of Clinical Nutrition, 69*, 1264–1272. Birch L. L. (1999). "Development of Food Preferences." *Annual Review of Nutrition, 19*, 41–62.

4. See Pinel, J. P. J., Assanand, S. & Lehman, D. R. (2000) "Hunger, Eating, and Health," *American Psychologist, 55*, 1105–1116.

5. For information on the relationship between SES and eating problems see: Kolata, G. (2000) "While Children Grow Fatter, Experts Search for Solutions," *New York Times*, Thursday October 19, 2000, National Desk; Lindquist, C. H., Reynolds, K. D.,

Goran, M. I. (1999) "Sociocultural Determinants of Physical Activity Among Children," *Preventive Medicine, 29,* 305–312; Goodman, E. (1999) "The Role of Socioeconomic Status Gradients in Explaining Differences in U.S. Adolescents' Health," *American Journal of Public Health, 89,* 1522–1528; Lowry, R., Kann, L., Collins, J. L., & Kolbe, L. J. (1996) "The Effect of Socioeconomic Status on Chronic Disease Risk Behaviors Among Adolescents," *Journal of the American Medical Association, 276,* 792–797; Alderman, E. M. & Friedman, S. B. (1995) "Behavioral Problems of Affluent Youth," *Pediatric Annals, 24,* 186–191; Neumark-Sztainer, D., Story, M., Falkner, N. H., Beuhring, T., & Resnick, M. D. (1999) "Sociodemographic and Personal Characteristics of Adolescents Engaged in Weight Loss and Weight/Muscle Gain Behaviors: Who Is Doing What?" *Preventive Medicine, 28,* 40–50.

6. Pipher, M. (1997) *Reviving Ophelia.* New York: Ballantine.

7. See Goode, E. (2000) "Thinner: The Male Battle with Anorexia," *New York Times,* Sunday June 25, 2000, Men & Health Desk and Crister, G. (2000) "Let Them Eat Fat: the Heavy Truths about American Obesity," *Harper's Magazine, 300,* 41–47 (March, 2000). Also in an article by Jerome, R. (2000) "A Body to Die for," *People Weekly,* October 30, 2000 108–118, the statistic from the American Society of Plastic Surgeons that in 1999, 30,000 liposuction operations were performed on men, a 350% increase; Pope, H., Jr. et al., *The Adonis Complex.*

8. For information on Andro and creatine see *www.mayohealth.org* "Do Andro, Creatine Work?" 11/9/98 Mayo Clinic Health Oasis.

9. Table of survey results regarding body image satisfaction and weight-loss behavior.

	BOYS N = 298	GIRLS N = 352
Trying to lose weight	63 (21%)	215 (61%)
Trying to gain weight	97 (33%)	9 (2.6%)
Past month use of nonprescription diet pills, powders or liquids	10 (3.7%)	40 (11.4%)
During past month has vomited or taken laxatives to lose weight	4 (1.3%)	28 (7.9%)
Has fasted for 24 hours or more in effort to lose weight (past month)	8 (2.7%)	59 (16.7%)
Past month use of creatine or creatinelike substance	49 (16.4%)	3 (< 1%)
Past year use of steroids	14 (4.7%)	0 (0%)

CHAPTER 9

1. According to CDC reports "Leading causes of mortality and morbidity in all age groups in the United States are related to the following six categories of health behavior: behaviors that contribute to unintentional and intentional injuries; tobacco use, alcohol and other drug use; sexual behavior that contributes to unintended pregnancy and STDs, including human immunodeficiency virus (HIV) infection; unhealthy dietary behaviors; and physical inactivity. These behaviors are frequently interrelated **and often are established during youth and extended into adulthood**" (emphasis mine). This quote can be found on page 3 of U.S. Department of Health and Human Services, Centers for Disease Control and Prevention, *Youth Risk Behavior Surveillance—United States, 1999*. Washington, D.C.: Available: *www.cdc.gov/epo/mmwr/preview/mmwrhtml/ ss4905a1.htm*

2. The statistics on trends in smoking come from Centers for Disease Control and Prevention, National Center for Chronic Disease Prevention and Health Promotion, *Adolescent and School Health*, Available: *www.cdc.gov/*ccdphp/dash/yrbs/trends.htm. Also note: Reporting on findings presented in the January 28, 2000 edition of *Morbidity and Mortality Weekly,* the March, 2000 edition of *The Nation's Health*. One-third of white HS students smoked some form of tobacco in the past month. What is particularly troubling about this is that youth is the time when almost all tobacco initiation occurs; there is virtually no one who starts smoking after age 29. More worrisome is the fact that while the number of heavy users of alcohol and illicit drugs decreases over time, this is not the case for cigarettes. Cigarettes are the most persistent of any drug used. See: Chen, K. & Kandel, D. B. (1995) "The Natural History of Drug Use from Adolescence to the Mid-Thirties in a General Population Sample," *American Journal of Public Health, 85*, 41–47.

3. Mischel, W., Shoda, Y. & Rodriguez, M. L. (1989) "Delay of Gratification in Young Children." *Science, 244*, 933–938. For another discussion of Mischel's research see pages 80–83: "Impulse Control: The Marshmallow Test" in Goleman, D. (1995) *Emotional Intelligence,* New York: Bantam. For a discussion of infant precursors of delay of gratification ability see: Sethi, A., Mischel, W., Aber, L., Shoda, Y., & Rodriguez, M. L. (2000) "The Role of Strategic Attention Deployment in Development of Self-Regulation: Predicting Preschoolers' Delay of Gratification from Mother-Toddler Interaction," *Developmental Psychology, 36*, 767–777. In Mischel's research the linear regression slope predicting SAT verbal scores from seconds of preschool delay was .10 (SE = .04); for predicting quantitative scores the slope was .13 (SE = .03).

4. See for example some of the classic research on predisposition to impulsivness and related characteristics such as behavioral disinhibition, in: Kagan, J. (1991) Etiologies of adolescents at risk, *Journal of Adolescent Health 12* 591–596; Koschanska, G. (1991) "Socialization and Temperament in the Development of Guilt and Conscience." Buss, A. & Plomin, R. (1984). *Temperament: Early developing personality traits*. Hillsdale, NJ: Erlbaum., Plomin, R., McClearn, G. E., & Friberg, L. (1988). "Neuroticism, Extraversion and Related Traits in Adult Twins Reared Apart and Reared Together."

Journal of Personality and Social Psychology, 55, 950–957. Thomas, A., Chess, S. and Birch, H. G. (1968) *Temperament and Behavior Disorder in Children,* New York: New York University Press.

5. For information on neural plasticity and self-control see: Davidson, R. J., Jackson, D. C., & Kalin, N. H., (2000) "Emotion, Plasticity, Context, and Regulation: Perspectives from Affective Neuroscience," *Psychological Bulletin, 126,* 890–909.

6. A classic study of parents as models of self-control is found in: Bandura, A. & Mischel, W. (1965) "Modification of Self-Imposed Delay of Gratification Through Exposure to Live and Symbolic Models," *Journal of Personality and Social Psychology, 2,* 698–705. For a more general discussion see: Kail, R. V. (1998) *Children and Their Development* (pages 302–307), Upper Saddle River, NJ: Prentice Hall.

7. Diener, M. (2000) "Gift from the Gods: A Balinese Guide to Early Child Rearing," J. DeLoache & A. Gottlieb (Eds.) *A World of Babies: Imagined Childcare Guides for Seven Societies* (pages 91–116), Cambridge UK: Cambridge University Press. The quote is from page 115.

8. For a discussion of the Project on Human Development in Chicago Neighborhoods, especially its Community Survey component from which these data are taken, see Sampson, R. J., Raudenbush, S. W. & Earls, F. (1997), "Neighborhoods and Violent Crime: A Multilevel Study of Collective Efficacy," *Science, 277,* 918–924. For readers interested in the details of the research conducted for this book, the actual percentages are as follows:

	NUMBER IN GROUP	%COMPLETED COLLEGE	% ATTENDING CHURCH/SYNAGOGUE	% WHITE
Lower Income	2967	9	52	18
Middle Income	2606	31	61	38
Upper Income	173	76	56	68

Percent believing that it is extremely wrong or very wrong for a 13-year-old to . . .

	SMOKE CIGARETTES	DRINK ALCOHOL	SMOKE MARIJUANA
Lower Income	87.20	90.79	92.24
Middle Income	84.98	90.96	91.42
Upper Income	79.07	85.38	82.94

Percent believing that it is extremely wrong or very wrong for a 19-year-old to . . .

	SMOKE CIGARETTES	DRINK ALCOHOL	SMOKE MARIJUANA
Lower Income	48.57	62.28	71.39
Middle Income	44.28	58.81	72.07
Upper Income	42.35	40.59	57.56

9. In the PPM survey, the association between level of affluence and attitudes toward drug use was seen only for the question regarding 19-year-olds. These data are presented in the table below:

Percent indicating that it is "extremely wrong" or "very wrong" for a 19-year-old to use . . .

	LESS THAN $50,000 (N = 98)	50–$100,00 (N = 263)	MORE THAN $100,000 (N = 646)
Marijuana	67.45%	71.1%	65.3%
Alcohol*	58.2%	55.9%	39.8%
Cigarettes	74.5%	78.3%	73.4%

Note: This difference is statistically significant, p < .01.

10. Garis, D. (1998) "Poverty, Single Parent Households, and Youth At-Risk Behavior: An Empirical Study," *Journal of Economic Issues*, *32*, 1079–1105.

11. See Weber, M. (1999) *Sociological Writings*, New York: Continuum Publishing. Pages 180–181 and Pope, L. (1948) "Religion and Class Structure," *The Annals of the American Academy of Political and Social Science*, *256*, 84–91.

12. On the heroin epidemic see: Hamid, A., Curtis, R., McCoy, K. et al. (1997) "The Heroin Epidemic in New York City: Current Status and Prognosis," *Journal of Psychoactive Drugs*, *29*, 375–391. Comments on growing use among certain segments including young people lured by heroin chic whose spiritual mentors are Kurt Cobain, John Coltrane, and Andy Warhol. Example: See also an older study: Frank, B., Marel, R., Schmeidler, J. & Lipton, D.S. (1984) "An Overview of Substance Use Among New York State's Upper-Income Householders," *Alcohol and Drug Abuse in the Affluent*, New York: Haworth Press. Pages 11–36. From the abstract: "A 1981 survey of substance abuse among household residents in New York State found rates of use consistently higher among the upper income group . . . than among groups with lower incomes . . . the availability of disposable income in the upper-income group and some situational factors may facilitate that group's substance-using behavior."

13. PPM adolescent survey results for drug use are:

REPORTED USED DURING THE PAST 30 DAYS	ALL TEENAGERS (N = 653)
Alcohol only	172 (26.3%)
Alcohol and marijuana only	47 (7.2%)
Cigarettes only	19 (2.9%)
Cigarettes and alcohol only	46 (7.0%)
Marijuana only	5 (.8%)
Marijuana and cigarettes only	6 (.9%)
Cigarettes, alcohol, and marijuana	54 (8.3%)
Cigarettes, alcohol, marijuana, and other illicit drugs	17 (2.6%)
Other drug use combinations	12 (1.8%)
No reported drug use	275 (42.1%)

14. See for example, Wise, R.A. (1996) "Neurobiology of Addiction," *Current Opinion in Neurobiology*, *6*, 243–251. Wise, R.A. (1996) "Addictive Drugs and Brain Stimulation Reward," *American Review of Neuroscience*, *19*, 319–340.

15. Centers for Disease Control and Prevention Fact Sheet: Youth Risk Behavior Trends. Available at *www.cdc.gov/nccdphp/dash/yrbs/trend.htm*. See for example, Franks, L. (2000) "The Sex Lives of Your Children," *Talk*, February, 2000 102–107, 157 and Jarrell, A. (2000) "The Face of Teenage Sex Grows Younger," *The New York Times*, Sunday Styles, Section 9. 1,8. Sunday April 2, 2000.

CHAPTER 10

1. See Max Weber (1930) *The Protestant Ethic and the Spirit of Capitalism.* (Translated by Talcott Parsons) London: Routledge, especially pages 171–172 where the *irrational* acquisition of wealth is seen as idolatry of the flesh, p. 104. See Matthew 19:24. The eye of the needle referred to was actually a city gate that was too narrow for a fully loaded camel to squeeze through. Weber, M. (1999) *Sociological Writings*, New York: Continuum Publishing. Pages 180–181; Pope, L. (1948) "Religion and class structure," *The Annals of the American Academy of Political and Social Science*, *256*, 84–91.

2. See the poll conducted for the AARP by the Employee Benefit Research Institute as reported in the *Boston Globe*, May 17, 2000, page 1 showing that 73% of men and 60% of women say that they would like to be wealthy. Data are taken from a nationally representative sample of more than 2,300 people 18 and older, which appears in the July–August 2000 issue of *Modern Maturity* magazine.

CHAPTER 11

1. PPM survey on parents' rating of satisfaction with their own parenting are as follows:

Parents of Teenagers

PARENT IS	PARENTS OF BOYS	PARENTS OF GIRLS
Completely satisfied with his/her parenting ability	13.0%	15.1%
Not very satisfied with his/her parenting ability	1.0%	3.4%

Parents of Elementary Schoolchildren

PARENT IS	PARENTS OF BOYS	PARENTS OF GIRLS
Completely satisfied with his/her parenting ability	10.2%	15.8%
Not very satisfied with his/her parenting ability	.8%	2.9%

2. See Renkel, M. (2001) "Afraid to Discipline?" *Parenting*, December/January 2001, pages 132–136. Henner, M. & Sharon, R.V. (1999) "I Refuse to Raise a Brat: Straightforward Advice on Parenting in an Age of Overindulgence"; Condrell, K.N. & Small, L.L. (1999) "Wimpy Parents: From Toddler to Teen: How Not to Raise a Brat"; Ezzo, G. & Bucknam, R. *On Becoming Babywise: Book Two: Parenting Your Pretoddler, Five to Fifteen Months,* Sisters, Oregon: Multnomah Books; Ehrensaft, D. (1997) *Spoiling Childhood: How Well-Meaning Parents Are Giving Their Children Too Much— But Not What They Need,* New York: Guilford.

CHAPTER 12

1. These findings are very similar to those of the National Longitudinal Study on Adolescent Health (Add Health), which is a nationally representative sample of youth in grades 7 through 12. Web site address: *http://www.cpc.unc.edu/addhealth/.* See also Resnick, M. et al. (1997) "Protecting Adolescents from Harm: Findings from the National Longitudinal Study on Adolescent Health," *Journal of the American Medical Association.*

2. For information on T.L.C. and other needs of adolescents see: Roth, J., Brooks-

Gunn, J. (2000) "What Do Adolescents Need for Healthy Development? Implications for Youth Policy," *Social Policy Report, 14,* Society for Research in Child Development.

3. I have been very impressed with the parent training materials using behavior modification techniques developed by Carolyn Webster-Stratton. These are available at: *http://www.incredibleyears.com/programs/parent-basic.htm.* For other web-based advice on parenting see: *http://www.parentingresources.ncjrs.org; http://www.mediacampaign.org/, http://www.mayohealth.org/home,* and *http://www.usda.gov/cnpp/.*

4. See for example page 14 in Hitti, M. (2000) "Teach Your Children Well," *Fidelity Focus,* August, 2000.

5. See the National Campaign to Prevent Teen Pregnancy web site: *http://www. teenpregnancy.org/tips.html* (Facts and STAT). Citation given for abstinence wish is: EDK Associates for *Seventeen* magazine and the MS. Foundation for Women (1996). *Teenagers Under Pressure.*

EPILOGUE

1. See Abbott, J. (1871) *Gentle Measures in the Training of the Young,* New York: Harper and Brothers. See also Cable, M. (1972). *The Little Darlings: A History of Child Rearing in America,* New York: Charles Scribner's Sons.

2. Some of the sources consulted regarding Gilded Age children grown up were: Vaill, A. (1998) *Everybody Was So Young,* New York: Broadway Books.; Wohl, R. (1979) *The Generation of 1914,* Cambridge, MA: Harvard University Press; Burlingham, M.J. (1989) *The Last Tiffany: A Biography of Dorothy Tiffany Burlingham,* New York: Atheneum. Also, Randall Knoper, Ph.D. English professor and expert on America during the Gilded Age writes regarding fictional portrayals of Gilded Age children grown up: *One of the most poignant portrayals of such a person is Edith Wharton's portrayal of Lily Bart. Wharton's best-known novels, aptly, have returned to us in our own Gilded Age, in the form of star-studded Hollywood movies:* The Age of Innocence *(1993, directed by Martin Scorsese) and most recently* The House of Mirth *(2001, directed by Terence Davies). Pertinent to our Gilded Age, too, are Wharton's concerns about wealth and values. In* The House of Mirth, *for example, the heroine Lily Bart is raised among the wealthy. Though her dimly remembered, usually absent father failed in his business shortly after her debut party, dictating that she marry "well," her childhood was one of luxury—governesses, maids, footmen, cooks, butlers, summers in Newport or Southampton or Europe, fashion shopping in Paris. Her exquisiteness causes the ineffectual "hero" of the novel to note that "she must have cost a great deal to make." As Wharton writes, "Her whole being dilated in an atmosphere of luxury; it was the background she required, the only climate she could breathe in." But Lily's story is a tragedy, driven by a conflict between money value and values that transcend the cash*

nexus—those of love, family, morality, a rich inner life, the life of art. Wharton's world is one in which such older values of the nineteenth century as hard work, character, and standards of conduct are gone. In its place are human relationships based on exchange, in which people are treated, and used and consumed, as commodities. Lily's mother raises her daughter for success in this world pervaded by market exchange. As a woman, her exquisite beauty is her capital, to be exchanged through marriage for financial security. Lily vaguely recoils from her mother's "crude passion for money," but on the other hand "there had been nothing in her training to develop any continuity of moral strength." Without the ambition to participate in the crass world of exchange, and without counterbalancing values to resist it, she is crushed. No wonder that Wharton's work has newfound popularity. Her pessimistic view resonates with our turn-of-the-21st-century culture, in which parents, over concerned about the material and social success of their children, raise kids who lack the inner, ethical gyroscopes that might give them the means to navigate with balance the fluctuations and forces of crass exchange. (R. Knoper, personal communication [1/7/01]).

3. See Garrett, L. (1995) *The Coming Plague: Newly Emerging Diseases in a World Out of Balance*, New York: Penguin and Garrett, L. (2000) *Betrayal of Trust: The Collapse of Global Public Health*, New York: Hyperion.

4. See for example page 62 in Collins, C., Yeskel, F. & United for a Fair Economy (2000) *Economic Apartheid in America: A Primer on Economic Equality and Insecurity.* New York: The New Press: *A 4 percent levy on the world's 225 most well-to-do people would suffice to provide the following essentials for all those in developing countries: adequate food, safe water and sanitation, basic education, basic health care, and reproductive health care.*

5. History is full of examples of how people have been unable to effectively cope with adversity. One example that strikes me as particularly poignant is that of many mid-19th-century prospectors in the California gold fields who had a pervasive naïveté and magical strike-it-rich solution to the unaccustomed hardship with which many of them struggled. Their inability to better adapt to their hardship led many of them to their demise. As Ulysses S. Grant writes of these men: *Many were young men of good family, good education, and gentlemanly instincts. Their parents had been able to support them during their minority, and to give them good educations but not to maintain them afterwards. . . . All thought that fortunes were to be picked up without effort, in the gold fields on the Pacific. Some realized more than their most sanguine expectations, but for one such there were a hundred disappointed, many of whom now fill unknown graves; others died wrecks of their former selves, and many, without a vicious instinct, became criminals and outcasts.* Grant, U.S. (1885) *Personal Memoirs of U.S. Grant, Volume 1* (From Ulysses S. Grant: *Memoirs and Selected Letters*) New York: The Library of America (1990). A classic study on adaptation to financial hardship may be found in:

Elder, G.H. (1974), *Children of the Great Depression: Social Change in Life Experience*, Chicago: University of Chicago Press.

6. Populations Projections Program, Population Division, U.S. Census Bureau, Washington, D.C., Projections of the total resident population by 5-year age groups, and sex with special age categories: Middle series, 2025 to 2045 (NP-T3-F) and Populations Projections Program, Population Division, U.S. Census Bureau, Washington, D.C.: Projections of the total resident population by 5-year age groups, and sex with special age categories: Middle series, 1999–2000 (NP-T3-A)

7. See Schneider, B. & Stevenson, D. (1999), *The Ambitious Generation: America's Teenagers Motivated But Directionless*, New Haven: Yale University Press.